*Metamorphic Verse*

Clark Hulse

---

# *Metamorphic Verse*

---

## *The Elizabethan Minor Epic*

*Princeton University Press*
*Princeton, New Jersey*

Copyright © 1981 by Princeton University Press

Published by Princeton University Press, Princeton, New Jersey
In the United Kingdom: Princeton University Press, Guildford, Surrey

All Rights Reserved

Library of Congress Cataloging in Publication Data will be
found on the last printed page of this book

This book has been composed in Linotron Bembo

Clothbound editions of Princeton University Press books
are printed on acid-free paper, and binding materials are
chosen for strength and durability

Printed in the United States of America by Princeton
University Press, Princeton, New Jersey

*for Carolyn*

# Contents

Illustrations    *ix*

Acknowledgments    *xi*

A Note on Texts    *xiii*

Introduction
Metamorphic Verse    *3*

Chapter 1
Minor Epic as Genre    *16*

Chapter 2
Petrarchan Rhetoric    *35*

Chapter 3
Marlowe, The Primeval Poet    *93*

Chapter 4
Shakespeare, Poet and Painter    *141*

Chapter 5
Chronicle, History, Legend    *195*

Chapter 6
Spenser's Ovidian Epics    *242*

Conclusion
Metamorphosis as Literary System    *279*

Index    *285*

# Illustrations

1. The Monogrammist HE. *Queen Elizabeth and the Three Goddesses.*    73
2. *Homer and Chapman.* Title page, Homer, *Batrachomyomachia*, trans. George Chapman.    139
3. Titian. *Venus and Adonis.*    144
4. Giulio Sanuto after Titian. *Venus and Adonis.*    145
5. Sebastiano del Piombo. *The Death of Adonis.*    149
6. Follower of Verrocchio. *Tobias and the Angel.*    150
7. *Animal-headed Gods.* Vincenzo Cartari, *Le imagini de i dei de gli antichi.*    160
8. *Three Venuses.* Vincenzo Cartari, *Le imagini de i dei de gli antichi.*    161
9. *The Death of Adonis.* Ovid, *Metamorphoses,* ed. Johannes Sprengius.    162
10. Baldassare Peruzzi. *The Death of Adonis.*    163
11. *The Death of Lucan.* Title page, Lucan, *Pharsalia,* trans. Thomas May.    203
12. *Ovid.* Ovid, *Metamorphoses,* trans. William Caxton.    246
13. *The Creation.* Ovid, *Metamorphoses,* ed. Raphael Regius.    251
14. *The Creation.* Lodovico Dolce, *Le trasformationi.*    252

# Acknowledgments

For permission to reprint the material in Chapters 1 and 4, which appeared earlier in article form, I am grateful to the editors of *Studies in Philology, PMLA,* and *Shakespeare Survey.*

A special debt of gratitude is due to the staff of the Newberry Library, who over the last eight years have aided and encouraged this project and provided on several occasions a sympathetic audience. This debt was materially deepened when the Newberry Library and the National Endowment for the Humanities jointly provided fellowship support in 1979 for the completion of the manuscript. The University of Illinois Research Board generously assisted at several points.

For their attentive reading of the manuscript and many helpful suggestions, I am grateful to Judith Kegan Gardiner, Michael Lieb, Martin Wine, Stephen Orgel, John Wallace, Judith Anderson, and Walter R. Davis. David Rosand offered valuable guidance for Chapter 4. Thanks are due to Marjorie Sherwood and Marilyn Campbell of Princeton University Press, who have skillfully guided the manuscript into print. Robert Mahony and John Huntington endured endless lectures over coffee. Chapter 6 is humbly submitted to French Fogle in place of the term paper he never received for English 264.

# A Note on Texts

Citations of frequently mentioned authors are to the editions listed below. Citations of other authors are to first editions unless otherwise noted. Manuscript abbreviations have been silently expanded; "i" and "j," "u" and "v" have been modernized throughout.

Francis Beaumont: *Salmacis and Hermaphroditus*, in *Elizabethan Minor Epics*, ed. Elizabeth Story Donno (New York: Columbia University Press, 1963).

Samuel Daniel: The first, unauthorized, printing of Daniel's sonnets was in *Syr P. S. His Astrophel and Stella* (London: Thomas Newman, 1591), cited as *Newman*. For the 1592 authorized version, entitled *Delia* (hereafter cited as *1592*), and for *The Complaint of Rosamond*, I have followed the text of *Poems and A Defence of Ryme*, ed. Arthur Colby Sprague (Cambridge: Harvard University Press, 1930). Citations of Daniel's other works are to the following editions: *The Civil Wars*, ed. Laurence Michel (New Haven: Yale University Press, 1958); *The Tragedy of Philotas*, ed. Laurence Michel (New Haven: Yale University Press, 1949); *The Collection of the History of England*, in *The Complete Works of Samuel Daniel*, ed. Alexander B. Grosart (London, 1885).

Michael Drayton: *The Works*, ed. J. William Hebel et al., 5 vols. (Oxford: Shakespeare Head Press, 1931-1941).

Phineas Fletcher: *Venus and Anchises*, in *Elizabethan Minor Epics*, ed. Elizabeth Story Donno (New York: Columbia University Press, 1963).

George Gascoigne: *Complete Works*, ed. John W. Cunliffe, 2 vols. (Cambridge: Cambridge University Press, 1907).

Thomas Lodge: *Complete Works*, ed. Edmund Gosse, 4 vols. (1883; reprint ed., New York: Russell & Russell, 1963).

Christopher Marlowe: *The Poems*, ed. Millar MacLure (London: Methuen, 1968).

Shakerley Marmion: *Cupid and Psyche* (London, 1637). *The Short Title Catalogue* (STC #17444) notes differences due to press corrections among the extant copies. My citations are to the Newberry Library copy. The editions of Singer (1820) and Saintsbury (1906) are not reliable.

John Marston: *The Poems*, ed. Arnold Davenport (Liverpool: Liverpool University Press, 1961).

William Shakespeare: *The Poems*, ed. F. T. Prince (London: Methuen, 1960). Citations of the sonnets and plays are to *The Pelican Shakespeare*, ed. Alfred Harbage, rev. ed. (Baltimore: Penguin, 1969).

Sir Philip Sidney: *The Poems*, ed. William A. Ringler, Jr. (Oxford: Clarendon Press, 1962).

Edmund Spenser: *The Works*, ed. Edwin Greenlaw et al., 9 vols. (Baltimore: Johns Hopkins University Press, 1932-1949).

*Metamorphic Verse*

# Metamorphic Verse

In the decade of the 1590s, Elizabethan poets took two great bodies of traditional materials, the classical myths and the English chronicles, and worked them into a rich and elaborate body of verse. The result was the minor epic, a genre consisting of about two dozen short narrative poems telling of amorous seductions and violent rapes and even occasionally of virtue triumphant. Marlowe's *Hero and Leander* (1593) is the best of them. Shakespeare's *Venus and Adonis* (1593) and *Lucrece* (1594) and Spenser's *Muiopotmos* (1591) are familiar to enough readers, while Thomas Lodge's *Scillaes Metamorphosis* (1589), Samuel Daniel's *Complaint of Rosamond* (1592), and Michael Drayton's *Peirs Gaveston* (1593) all were popular in their time.

If today the minor epic is the least read and least understood of the major types of Elizabethan verse, it was in its time a form of obvious importance. Except for Sidney, every major Elizabethan poet, and most of the minor ones, wrote minor epics. Our failure of understanding lies in separating the minor epic (as we do so much old art) from the culture that bore it, in order to search for its timeless values. By and large the poems of the minor epic genre have no great ethical import and little redeeming social value. They are by turns artificial, frivolous, arcane, even subversive, and so it is often hard for an age that has liked its poetry plain and confessional to see what all the fuss was about. But, restored to its place in the network of Elizabethan theory and practice, the genre of minor epic takes on a significance that its individual members lose in isolation.

This book is a study of the form of the minor epic. Inevitably, though, its foremost concern must be transformation.

Metamorphosis underlies the subject matter of the genre, its narrative principles, its mode of symbolism, its ability to combine and to remake other genres, and its power to transform the poet. Indeed, the study of metamorphosis within the poems leads one beyond them, so that Elizabethan literature as a whole can be seen, not just as an assortment of interesting texts, but as a literary system, dominated by the interplay of forms, changes of style, and the search for growth of the individual poet. The metamorphic qualities of the minor epic place it paradoxically at the center of this literary system, and, by corollary, may refashion our image of that system into something less static, more fluid, than such phrases as the "Elizabethan world picture" would lead us to believe. Like the world of Ovid's *Metamorphoses*, it is a system where recurring instances of flux build toward a view of a world in process, a view that always threatens to break down into the chaos of its parts.

A theory of the minor epic must account for this transformation in the genre and in the culture that bore it, the transformation in their meaning that takes place if we change our way of reading. Such a theory must describe the conditions by which the minor epic is understood to have meaning beyond (or even in) its surface triviality. Propounding such a theory is a prerequisite to understanding the minor epic, but there is no Renaissance critical discussion of the genre, and the general principles of Renaissance critical theory can be made to apply only loosely and indirectly. Any modern theory must finally be empirical, derived from an analysis of specific poems in the genre. In the studies that follow, I shall unashamedly combine close reading with Renaissance and modern theory to construct a poetics for the minor epic. Such a poetics may itself suggest new ways of reading the poems, ways of reading that on one hand reveal their formal artifice, and on the other define the meaning of that artifice in the Elizabethan literary system.

To begin at the beginning: the metamorphic qualities of the minor epic derive largely from Ovid's *Metamorphoses*.

The Elizabethans pillaged Ovid's poem for its erotic tales of Adonis, Narcissus, Ganymede, and the rest, and regarded him as the master rhetorician, the model for elegant artifice. Ovid was also to them a philosopher of change whose poem was thought of as a historical epic which described a world of flux from the creation down to the present, and which set forth its system of beliefs in the Pythagorean sermon of Book 15. Yet the metamorphic qualities of the minor epic are not solely due to the influence of Ovid. Indeed, its sources range from Musaeus, Vergil, and Apuleius to the English chronicles, with exotic and domestic materials frequently mingled, so that Shakespeare's Adonis shares the fields with Wat the hare and Greek Ganymede is ancestor to English Gaveston.

Nor is metamorphosis simply a matter of subject. In its remorseless alteration of the old stories, Elizabethan minor epic comes closest among the literary types of its day to revealing the pure play of form. A poem like Marlowe's *Hero and Leander* might be called, in Arthur Golding's phrase, a "philosophy of changed shapes," a series of transformations in narrative form, undertaken, it seems, for the sheer delight of transformation itself. Again Ovid is the master. His *Metamorphoses* is something of a catalogue of narrative techniques, and in its own transformation (and at times trivialization) of the form of Vergilian epic it defines the experimentation with form as the central task of the sophisticated poet.

One reason for the high formalism of the Elizabethan minor epic is its content, which is fictive much more than, say, the sonnet. Its mythical or chronicle tales are *istoria*, story or imagining, not history. The rise of a clear distinction between history and story was occurring at just this time in England, and its gradual impact on literature is a significant part of the subject. Tales of the pagan gods are about unreal things, and tales of people who may have existed in a dim past are unreal or invented in their details. The literal is dissolved nearly away, so that the importance of a tale is in its other senses, its allegory, that is, in the transformations of

meaning through which the poet puts it.[1] So while the minor
epic can be thought of as a form of imaginative play, it none-
theless can make significant statements. *Serio ludens* was a
proverb on the lips of more than one humanist. Above all,
the common subject of the poems is mutability itself, and
the poems' approach is often inquisitive and philosophic.
The minor epic is particularly able to compare the erotic val-
ues of sonnet and pastoral with the heroic values of epic in
a continuous interplay of the mutable and eternal qualities of
life. Shakespeare's Tarquin must choose between royalty and
rape; his Adonis must mount either Venus or his horse.
These moral crises are sometimes nearly drowned in the flow
of a poem's artifice and conceit, so that the philosophic con-
tent of a poem emerges not by direct statement but by im-
plication. The ethical issues in Marlowe's *Hero and Leander*,
for instance, are so persistently undercut and sidetracked that
the final significance of the poem may lie in the very inability
of poet or reader to fix any pat moral to the events. The flux
of poetry imitates the flux of the universe.

The action of minor epic, then, is too easily thought of as
casual coupling and late lamenting, and its form too often
passed off as trivial decoration. If, as Aristotle would have
it, a work of art is an imitation of an action, action may be
understood not just as what happened, but as mental event—
a series of mind-states that make up a unified sequence. The
form itself may be a significant mental action, a way of
thinking about physical experience. While, loosely speaking,
any metaphor is metamorphic, it is useful to define the met-
amorphic image more narrowly, as that which describes the
transformation of one substance into another. The more fa-
miliar metaphysical image as defined by Dr. Johnson finds
an unexpected likeness in two things that have no superficial

---

[1] My use of the term "allegory" is based on the derivation, common in
the Renaissance, from "alla agoreuein," "to speak other (than you mean)."
For a discussion of allegory in its etymologically correct derivation from
"agora" as a "closed or hidden meaning," see Michael Murrin, *The Veil of
Allegory* (Chicago: University of Chicago Press, 1969).

resemblance. Donne's flea is like a marriage temple or a marriage bed. The metamorphic image, in contrast, sees their resemblance and gradually extinguishes all points of unlikeness: a woman is like a tree and becomes identical to that tree; her fingers grow into branches, her feet to roots. Even as the metamorphosis occurs in the story, it may take a symbolic or allegorical form. The tree-maiden with her rough-bark skin suggests the fear and loathing of the body and becomes, indeed, chastity itself. Flesh and tree are inseparable from their abstract concept. The metaphysical image emphasizes the unique qualities of each object; it is finally differential, while the metamorphic is integral, minimizing differences. It may suggest the ecstasy or terror of the flesh made free to move across the categories of substance, and of the mind to move across the categories of thought. Indeed, it may call into question our ability to categorize experience at all.

Literary scholars (especially Spenserians) have in the last several decades amply demonstrated that Elizabethan poets were as rational and intellectual as the Metaphysicals. Yet there is an irreducible core of truth to the old impression that they created a golden world of "ocean-dewy limbs and naked childlike souls."[2] It is, I suggest, the pervasive metamorphic image that reconciles this paradox, for it is at once allegorical and sensual. One might offer as an illustration Spenser's description in Book 3 of the *Faerie Queene* of the wounded Timias at the moment Belphoebe discovers him:

> Shortly she came, whereas that woefull Squire
> With bloud deformed, lay in deadly swownd:
> In whose faire eyes, like lamps of quenched fire,
> The Christall humour stood congealed rownd;
> His locks, like faded leaves fallen to grownd,
> Knotted with bloud, in bounches rudely ran,

[2] C. F. Tucker Brooke, *Essays on Shakespeare and Other Elizabethans,* ed. Leicester Bradner (New Haven: Yale University Press, 1948), p. 196.

And his sweete lips, on which before that stownd
The bud of youth to blossome faire began,
Spoild of their rosie red, were woxen pale and wan.
[3.5.29]

The transformation of Timias begins in a rhetorical trope:
blood would merely cover him, not deform him, so "bloud"
must be metonymy for wounds. There follows a series of
transferences in which objects are defined by their opposites:
lamps of quenched fire, so no longer fiery; fair eyes like
quenched lamps, hence no longer fair; the crystal humor
(hence liquid) congealed, and so no longer liquid. The
phrases contrast past and present states, and continue the liq-
uid/solid play of "with bloud deformed," especially since the
liquid humor that "stood congealed" clots like blood. Lines
5–6 bring together the two major images of the stanza, blood
and leaves, as the squire's hair, clotted with blood, is likened
to faded leaves fallen from a tree (which is thereby de-
formed). Congealed with blood, the locks bunch, and hence,
ironically, are also like the summer's leaves clustered on the
bough. At the same time, the bunches "rudely ran"—as if
they had become the blood (with a play on rudely/ruddy).
Lines 7–9 link the vegetation image to the past/present con-
trast of "fair eyes, like lamps of quenched fire," and then
link both to the blood image with "Spoild of their rosy red."
This phrase inverts the image of his bloody locks, since what
*should* be blood-red no longer is. In another inversion,
"woxen" would be appropriate to the blossoming bud, and
so heightens the pain of "pale" and "wan," with the whole
figure underscored by the play on "wax" and "wane."

The stanza, in sum, has only a few concrete details about
Timias: his eyes are dull, he lies still, his hair is congealed
with blood, his lips are pale. The force of the stanza is di-
rected toward analyzing a series of transferences, inversions,
and identifications. Pale things become bloody and red
things pale; liquids become solids; the past and present define
each other. Timias himself is transformed into withered veg-

etation and then, by recollecting the beauty which has been deformed, into the pristine state of that vegetation. The transformation of Timias is then set into a larger frame, for Spenser is describing what Belphoebe sees, and our reaction is also hers: "Saw never living eye more heavy sight" (3.5.30). The situation is an inversion of a conventional setting in Petrarchan sonnets, where the lover marvels at the lady's beauty and is astonished by her golden hair and ruby lip. Unlike the haughty and disdainful Petrarchan mistress, Belphoebe is moved to charitable solace, and her reaction is itself placed by the structure of the narrative into an even larger frame as an analogue to the Garden of Adonis. In the Garden, forms undergo continual metamorphosis, as Time, like Timias's wounds, cuts them down, and Venus, like Belphoebe, brings new life. The human pathos of the scene is set against the superhuman forces which Spenser sees at work in it, and the reader's involvement with these particular characters is balanced by the intricate conceptual shifts which he must undergo to grasp that all creation is one.

The example of Timias might seem inappropriate, since Spenser is not writing minor epic. However, one could just as well analyze passages from Shakespeare or Marlowe, such as a sentence describing Hero's tears:

> Forth from those two tralucent cisterns brake
> A stream of liquid pearl, which down her face
> Made milk-white paths, whereon the gods might trace
> To Jove's high court.
> [1.296-99]

The image of Hero's eyes weeping liquid pearl treats literally a number of Petrarchan conceits: the mistress's tears are pearls; her eyes are stars; to see her is to glimpse heaven itself; she is just divine. While the passage mildly parodies such verse, Hero herself is elevated, placed on a level of fantasy equal with Jove or the constellations. The Milky Way as a path to heaven (recalling perhaps its association with

terrestrial pilgrimages to Campostello) places Hero in the
position of the supreme deity, or his shrine, and recalls the
poem's opening assertion that young Apollo courted her, as
well as the description of Leander praying to her that has just
preceded these lines. Hero is momentarily the mistress of the
cosmos, subjecting man and god to her rule (as does the
nectar-quaffing country maid in the Mercury digression),
until we think that this may be poetic hyperbole, vain aspi-
ration, and false worship.

The passages from Marlowe and Spenser alike mingle Pe-
trarchan imagery with epic elevation. Spenser amplifies the
heroic proportions of his subject by working parallels to
English chronicle history throughout the book (Timias is,
after all, Arthur's squire, and Belphoebe stands for Eliza-
beth), while Marlowe adds a countermovement of ironic de-
flation that is characteristically Ovidian.[3] The irony of *Hero
and Leander* has been enough to cause several writers to see
Spenser and Marlowe as exemplars of opposed tendencies in
Elizabethan poetry. As Roger Sale puts it, the *Faerie Queene*
is undramatic, suppressing intellectual conflict in the name of
an inherited view of the universe "that was still harmonious
and still able to engender a common culture which gave him
all the materials he needed."[4] *Hero and Leander* (like Donne's
verse) is dramatic, revealing conflicts and ironies, and avoid-
ing dogmatic positions in favor of an awakening skepticism.

[3] For an incisive discussion of Ovidian irony, see William Keach, *Eliza-
bethan Erotic Narratives* (New Brunswick: Rutgers University Press, 1977),
chap. 1.

[4] Roger Sale, *Reading Spenser* (New York: Random House, 1968), p. 27;
his position is endorsed by Keach, *Elizabethan Erotic Narratives*, pp. 219-22.
Paul Alpers attempts to contrast the two poems, but cautiously concludes
that Spenser's poetic language "should be regarded as a specialized devel-
opment of characteristics and potentialities that belong to Elizabethan Eng-
lish and Elizabethan verse" (*The Poetry of the Faerie Queene* [Princeton:
Princeton University Press, 1967], p. 90). Those who feel sure of themselves
in measuring the irony in *Hero and Leander* should be sobered by Rosemond
Tuve's discussion, in *Elizabethan and Metaphysical Imagery* (Chicago: Uni-
versity of Chicago Press, 1947), pp. 216-17, of the passage I have cited.

Sale's portrayal of the intellectual milieu of Spenser—who was, after all, a Protestant and imperial apologist in a Europe torn by Reformation—is too patently inaccurate to require comment. More importantly, his thesis overlooks the fact that Spenser can be ironic, and Marlowe harmonious, *when their subjects require it*. A particular poetic form does not intrinsically express a particular ideology; a metamorphic image may, in different context, evoke either the underlying stability or the instability of the universe. The violent, ironic metaphors that make metaphysical poetry seem so "skeptical" and "dramatic," and hence so modern, are examples of the figure catachresis (which "expresses one matter 'by the name of another which is incompatible with it, and sometimes clean contrary' ").[5] It is a figure that deprecates its subject and is appropriate to satire and epigram, while Spenser's metaphors are more persistently elevating, in accordance with the primary goal of epic: to praise the good. Marlowe, writing minor epic, inevitably both praises and blames, elevates and deprecates. The different uses of irony among our poets, then, seem to have more to do with what genre they are writing than with their *Weltanschauung*. The epic of Spenser and the minor epic of Marlowe are different kinds of poems, but written from the same poetic. The relationship of minor epic to epic will be explored further in Chapter 6, which examines in detail the connection between Spenser's *Muiopotmos* and Book 3 of the *Faerie Queene*; suffice it now to say that Book 3 is something like a minor epic writ large. The passages examined above suggest that the central qualities of the Elizabethan minor epic are indeed qualities of the epic, and of Elizabethan poetry generally.

The metamorphic character of subject matter, narrative technique, and imagery in the minor epic presages the metamorphic character of Elizabethan poetic forms, and of the poet himself. The lyric poet of the 1590s felt the whole weight of his great predecessors, from Petrarch to Sidney,

[5] Tuve, pp. 130-33.

while the epic poet bore the added burden of an elaborate
critical theory hammered out in the long debate between the
partisans of Ariosto and Tasso. No critical theory at all ex-
isted for the minor epic, and its precursors, especially Ovid
and Chaucer, were varied and flexible poets. The poet of
minor epic, then, had a relative freedom to try out new
forms, to recombine the elements of lyric and epic in new
ways. The minor epic's lack of a great didactic burden left
the poet free to make formal experiment his primary pur-
pose, to make minor epic into the true avant-garde poetry of
the Elizabethan period. The minor epic was, in effect, the
proving ground for lyric and epic, the experimental labora-
tory from which new ideas of both emerged.

Marking the time between the publication of Books 1-3 of
the *Faerie Queene* and the completion of Books 4-6, Spenser
addressed to a series of noble patrons his 1591 volume of
*Complaints*, including *Muiopotmos*, his slender Ovidian fable.
After Samuel Daniel caught the public eye in 1591 (when his
sonnets were printed with Sidney's), Spenser himself urged
Daniel to "rouze thy feathers quickly" to "tragick plaints
and passionate mischance."[6] Daniel's next poem, *Rosamond*,
was both an appendage to his sonnet sequence *Delia* and a
prelude to his Senecan tragedies and historical epic. When
Shakespeare turned from the stage in 1593 and set his hand
to polite poetry, he called *Venus and Adonis* the "first heir"
of his invention and followed it with the "graver labour" of
*Lucrece*. The two poems stand at the watershed between his
apprenticeship and early maturity as a dramatic writer. By
the very fact of its identity as a "mixed" genre (combining
the features of high and low genres), the minor epic was the
medium by which the poet could transform himself from
ephebe to high priest. It was a genre for young poets ceasing
to be young, a form somewhere above the pastoral or sonnet
and below the epic, the transition between the two in the
*gradus Vergilianus*.

---

[6] Edmund Spenser, *Colin Clouts Come Home Again*, ll. 424-27.

This sense of order among the forms of literature and the varieties of poetic behavior can itself be seen as the fundamental constituent of the Elizabethan—or indeed of any— literary system. The emergence of a literary system, however fluid, is a defining characteristic of the Elizabethan Renaissance. English literature in the sixteenth century becomes an autonomous realm of intellectual endeavor, endowed with a past and a future, with virtuoso practitioners and a trained audience, and with a body of general principles and standards of performance. Such a network of people and ideas existed in the courts, universities, monasteries, and guildhalls of Henrician England, only to disintegrate in the violent last years of Henry's reign. The rapid expansion of court, university, and Inns of Court and the establishment of permanent theaters in London provided the settings and personnel for a new literary culture in Elizabeth's reign. Simultaneously, a wave of intellectual novelties from the Continent in the last three decades of the century provided its ideas: the third-generation Petrarchism of the Pléiade; the interest in emblems, *imprese,* and other symbolic devices; the systematic poetic theory of the "Age of Criticism" in France and Italy; humanist art theory; the new historiography of Patrizi and Bodin—the list could as well go on to logic, law, philosophy, and theology. All shared a common linguistic base and all testified to the power of language to order the world.

The role of the minor epic as a vehicle for the assimilation of the new learning into England gave it a particular importance to the practitioners of the new culture. In Petrarchism the minor epic poets found a suitable diction and imagery and, what is more, a profound speculation on the place of the poet's private experience in the social order. From the emblematists they learned intricate modes of symbolism; from the theorists of art came ideas about representation of the passions and audience response; from the historians came new arguments about the origins of mythological and chronicle materials and speculation about their appropriate forms of narration. Above all, the French and Italian literary theorists provided justifications for experimentation and the mixing of genres. Nowhere is this more visible than in the theory and commentary surrounding Ovid, who provided a particular challenge to Aristotelian ideas of epic in the Renaissance. The new learning accounts for many odd details in the minor epic; more importantly, it provides a set of structural principles by which the Elizabethans made their startling transformations in traditional materials. Above all, it is the basis for the unique place of the minor epic in the Elizabethan system of literary forms.

Talking about a historical system of forms poses some delicate problems for scholarship. Merely by considering any work as part of a group one risks violating the unique identity of that work in the search for characteristics that it shares with others. But to see a work in isolation is to see it as mere words. It is the fit between the work and its culture that makes the choice of each word a critical decision for the poet. The study of genre is the level of investigation midway between the individual work and its culture. It gives us access to that fitness between the minor epic and the environments of Elizabethan society, of Elizabethan literature as a whole, and of the developing mind of the individual writer.

Such fitness points up a second danger of genre history—that in tracing the historical changes of a literary form, it ignores the conditions of literature at each moment in history, its manifold connections to other genres and to other works by the same authors. The minor epic presents the literary historian with peculiar opportunities to overcome these dangers and to write a full literary history that reveals both the literary moment and the direction of change. Its identity as a mixed genre makes it a *summa* of the literary forms of its day, while its function as the transitional form by which a minor poet becomes a major one thrusts both poet and poem back into the world of flux.

The chapters that follow are approaches to minor epic poetry through a series of aspects, each of which has already given

form to the material before the individual artist sets his hand
to it. Hence each is a part of both the mixture that makes up
the genre and the larger system of Elizabethan literature. My
aim in each case is to read a major work or works in a way
that will simultaneously illuminate the wider dimensions of
the genre and the system. The first of these aspects is the
idea of genre itself, which is explored in Chapter 1. Subse-
quent chapters examine particular genres that formed the
minor epic and were re-formed by it. Chapter 2 deals with
sonnet and satire in relation to poems by Lodge, Daniel, and
others. Chapter 3 looks at Marlowe's and Chapman's *Hero
and Leander* as primeval poetry. Chapter 6 examines Spenser's
*Muiopotmos* and Book 3 of the *Faerie Queene* as Ovidian epics.
The intervening chapters take up the neighboring disciplines
of painting and historiography: Chapter 4 deals with picto-
rial elements in Shakespeare's poems and Chapter 5 traces
the role of the minor epic in forming the historical vision of
Daniel and Drayton. Together the two chapters illustrate
how the sister arts used the same narrative materials in dif-
ferent ways and to different ends. If there is a defect in this
organization, it is in the omission of pastoral as a separate
concern. Something of a mixed genre itself, the pastoral is
discussed in Chapters 2 and 3 amid satiric, Petrarchan, and
primeval poetry. This is the unavoidable result of the second
principle of organization, whereby the chapters constitute an
informal poetics for the minor epic. In addition to the dis-
cussion of genre in Chapter 1, Chapter 2 analyzes the rela-
tionship between the work and its audience; Chapter 3 ex-
amines the figure of the poet and the nature of inspiration;
Chapter 4 looks at imagery; Chapter 5 examines the idea of
fictionality; and Chapter 6 is intended as a synthesis of them
all, by way of looking at the overarching problem of system-
building itself. Each may be read independently, but loosely
they move, like the minor epic itself, between context and
text, from the rhetorical to the iconic, and from small forms
to large ones.

# Chapter 1

## Minor Epic as Genre

The formalism of minor epic is not simply a matter of line lengths and rhyme schemes. As Sidney said in his *Defence*, verse alone does not make a poet, and an orator in arms is no soldier. The definition of any single literary form must involve an understanding of the general notions of form by which a work was written and by which it was and is read. Such a definition requires as well an understanding of the critical choices available to a poet when he opted for one form over another. What specifically was at stake in the choice between minor epic and some other form such as sonnet or epic?

This question is especially important in defining the genre of minor epic, for in its close relations with sonnet and epic it has seemed at times to be not a distinct type at all but a poor mixture of these other kinds of poetry. The poems of minor epic have, indeed, traveled under far too many names. Some have been labeled "romance," "verse romance," "Ovidian verse," "erotic narrative," "mirror," or just "narrative verse." Most often, they have been divided into two major categories on the basis of subject matter: the epyllion or minor epic, dealing with classical mythology; and the historical complaint, drawing on the English chronicles. Hallett Smith arranges them this way in his chapter "Ovidian Poetry" in *Elizabethan Poetry*, without, regrettably, explaining at any length why he put them together.[1] C. S. Lewis has used the

---

[1] "Because of the special nature of the new complaint poems, their concern with love and chastity, the Ovidian tradition had an opportunity to influence and color the complaint. . . . So eclectic was the Elizabethan mind that it could find satisfaction in a piece which combined the stern and sober

category of epyllion, or minor epic, for poems like *Hero and Leander* and *Venus and Adonis*, and Elizabeth Story Donno has endorsed the term, though with reservations.[2] The fruit of their work, especially that of Smith, is a description of each kind as a cluster of motifs.[3] Epyllion, characteristically following Ovid's *Metamorphoses* as a model, relates a sexual consummation by young lovers in a witty narrative enforcing the lessons of *carpe diem*. The historical complaint, modeled on the *Mirror for Magistrates*, uses dramatic monologue to tell of a female protagonist who confronts seduction (or rape) and death, as a solemn and moral warning against lust.

As clear and useful as this distinction is, one might ask if it reflects the poets' own sense of their materials and accounts for the full range of their practice. Donno and Smith both recognize such genre divisions as uneasy compromises between utility and accuracy, and that uneasiness suggests that new grounds might be sought. The generic distinction based on subject matter must be questioned unless Renaissance po-

---

warnings of the old wheel of Fortune and the titillating, decorative, luscious matter from the Italianate Ovidian tradition" (Hallett Smith, *Elizabethan Poetry* [Cambridge: Harvard University Press, 1952], pp. 103-4).

[2] C. S. Lewis, *English Literature in the Sixteenth Century, Excluding Drama* (Oxford: Oxford University Press, 1954), pp. 486-89; Elizabeth Story Donno, ed., *Elizabethan Minor Epics* (New York: Columbia University Press, 1963), p. 6; see also Louis R. Zocca, *Elizabethan Narrative Poetry* (New Brunswick: Rutgers University Press, 1950); M. C. Bradbrook, *Shakespeare and Elizabethan Poetry* (London: Chatto, 1951), pp. 51-74; Paul W. Miller, "The Elizabethan Minor Epic," *Studies in Philology* 55 (1958):31-38; Elizabeth Story Donno, "The Epyllion," in *English Poetry and Prose, 1540-1674*, ed. Christopher Ricks (London: Longmans, 1971), pp. 82-100; and William Keach, *Elizabethan Erotic Narratives*, (New Brunswick: Rutgers University Press, 1977), pp. xvi-xvii.

[3] "Perhaps I should explain my attitude about genres. The book does not use the word much, or emphasize it. Instead it talks about Conventions, . . . commonplaces, ideals, values. Even though my chapters could be called essays on Pastoral, Ovidian, Sonnets, Satire, The Lyric and The Epic, and these could certainly be called literary genres, I was clearly shying away from this classification" (Hallett Smith, "An Apologie for *Elizabethan Poetry*," *New Literary History* 1 [1969]:36).

etic theory clearly differentiated between historical and mythological materials, or unless modern criticism can uncover a difference in their treatments. History and poetry are indeed distinct disciplines in humanist thought, but Renaissance historical poetry generally was regarded as belonging to the discipline of *poetry*, and subject to its rules. Tasso, for instance, urged that the epic poet select his material from history but alter events which were improbable, however factual.[4] Daniel and Drayton, the leading English historical poets, came into contact in the 1590s with the new historiography of Bodin in France and Camden and Stow in England, but the full impact of these new attitudes and techniques did not come until their later historical works of the 1600s. More often, poetic techniques were seen creeping into pure history; Daniel remarked in the preface to his *Civil Wars* that even Livy and Sallust might properly be called poets for their practice of inventing speeches for historical characters.

Within poetry, theorists sometimes distinguished between true and false material, but the designations were often whimsical, and in any event had little effect on treatment, which was guided by Aristotle's dictum of verisimilitude. George Puttenham in 1589 contrasted Musaeus's "true treatise of the life & loves of Leander and Hero" with Homer's "fabulous or mixt report of the siege of Troy," and spoke of his own efforts in writing what he called "a litle brief *Romance* or historicall ditty" in the manner of the tales of King Arthur.[5] Spenser, in his preface to the *Faerie Queene*, listed "the antique Poets historicall": Homer, Vergil, Ariosto, and Tasso. And as late as 1619, Michael Drayton defined the genre of his chronicle poems *Peirs Gaveston* and *Matilda* as "legend":

---

[4] Bernard Weinberg, *A History of Literary Criticism in the Italian Renaissance*, 2 vols. (Chicago: University of Chicago Press, 1961), 2:649.

[5] George Puttenham, *The Arte of English Poesie*, in *Elizabethan Critical Essays*, ed. G. Gregory Smith, 2 vols. (Oxford: Oxford University Press, 1904), 2:42-44.

The word *Legend*, so called of the Latine Gerund, *Legendum*, and signifying . . . things specially worthy to be read, was anciently used in an Ecclesiasticall sense, and restrained therein to things written in Prose, touching the Lives of Saints. Master *Edmund Spenser* was the very first among us, who transferred the use of the word, *Legend*, from Prose to Verse, . . . the Argument of his Bookes being of a kind of sacred Nature. . . . To particularize the Lawes of this Poeme, were to teach the making of a Poeme. . . . But the principall is, that Being a *Species* of an *Epick* or Heroick Poeme, it eminently describeth the act or acts of some one or other eminent Person; not with too much labour, compasse, or extension, but roundly rather, and by way of Brief, or *Compendium*.

[*Works* 2:382]

To each, the difference between "history" and "story" in poetry is just not crucial; all see epic, romance, and historical poetry as subcategories within a single class of the heroic poem, subject to a common set of rhetorical resources and a common purpose (in Puttenham's words) of "honest recreation and good example."

The other criteria for differentiating epyllion from historical complaint are no more substantial under scrutiny. The principal model for the epyllion, the *Metamorphoses*, was also a major source for the chronicle poems *Rosamond* and *Peirs Gaveston*, while the *Mirror for Magistrates* influenced Lodge's *Scillaes Metamorphosis*, the progenitor of the epyllion. Shakespeare's *Lucrece* draws principally on Ovid's *Fasti* and secondarily on Chaucer and Livy. Is it then minor epic or historical complaint? The literary model alone will not tell us. The dramatic manner of complaint, with its heavy use of apostrophe, is common to Lodge's Ovidian poem *Scillaes Metamorphosis*, to both *Venus and Adonis* and *Lucrece*, to Heywood's *Oenone and Paris*, and to the chronicle poems. And

while many epyllia are indeed lascivious, and many com-
plaints serious, Drayton's *Endimion and Phoebe* and Chap-
man's *Hero and Leander* spurn physical lust on behalf of a
Neoplatonist transcendence, while Daniel's *Rosamond* carried
so little in the way of "stern and sober warnings" (Smith's
words) that one contemporary complained that it actually
excused sexual indulgence.[6]

In short, the similarities between the epyllion and the his-
torical complaint are so great, the exceptions to any rule so
numerous, that it is hard to think of them as separate types.
Since it would be difficult to proceed with a definition of
their common type without a word for it, I shall apply at
this point the term "minor epic" for both groups of poems,
although the full justification of it must wait until later in the
argument. Already we can regard them all as subcategories
of a common type, just as epic, romance, and historical po-
etry are subcategories of the heroic. Drayton's definition of
*Peirs Gaveston* as a "legend" establishes a prima facie connec-
tion between the short chronicle poems and the epic proper;
and it is superficially apparent that "minor epic" is at least as
appropriate to many of the chronicle poems in a strictly de-
scriptive sense as it is to mythological poems like Lodge's
*Scilla* or Marston's *Pigmalion*.

To find some general rules by which to define genre, we
must inevitably begin with Aristotle's *Poetics*. As Northrop
Frye reminds us, "we discover that the critical theory of gen-
res is stuck precisely where Aristotle left it"[7]—or was when
Frye wrote—not perhaps because of any failure of genera-
tions of theorists, but because Aristotle himself considers so
many alternatives at one point or other. He divides works
according to their manner of presentation—narrative, dra-
matic, and lyric. He traces the historical growth of poetry to
show the successive development of a series of genres: first
the celebrations of the gods in hymns; then celebrations of

⁶ Drayton, *Works*, 1:214.

⁷ Northrop Frye, *Anatomy of Criticism: Four Essays* (1957; reprint ed., New
York: Atheneum, 1970), p. 13.

the deeds of heroes in epic and tragedy; and finally satiric and comic forms which arise from different parts of ancient ritual. On psychological grounds he distinguishes tragedy (and hence epic) from comedy on the basis of the action unfolded, tragedy showing a progress through suffering to recognition, comedy presumably (for its treatment is incomplete) showing triumph. To these he adds further distinctions according to the objects imitated (men better or worse than in real life), and secondary points of technique concerning diction and verse form.

So far we have a set of familiar criteria for distinguishing genres: a poem's origin, its relations to an audience, the object imitated (action, character, and thought), the manner of imitation (narrative, dramatic, or lyric), and the material (diction and verse form). After this initial clarity, though, come some important ambiguities. First, Aristotle does not make utterly clear whether he means his genres to be prescriptive or descriptive. Frequently he reminds us of his empirical stance, simply observing what has been done by poets and analyzing the best works to discover their essential characteristics. But he then offers his findings to others to guide their own compositions, suggesting that rules could be codified for each genre. Secondly, Aristotle is sketchy about how genres change—whether genres are static or progressive, and, if progressive, whether they move toward a single, finite, perfect form from which they then degenerate, or whether they advance in pursuit of an infinite perfectibility. He speaks once of tragedy "perfecting its proper types," which would seem to put him with the school of the finite perfectibles—but he seems more to open the question than to resolve it.

If Aristotle yields no final answers, he at least lays out alternatives both for assessing past definitions of minor epic and for attempting a new one. First we must examine what preconceptions Elizabethan poets held about the nature of genre and how those theoretical conceptions guided the compositions of the poems. Then we can move to a descrip-

tion of the models and origins of the genre and its relation
to other genres; to the nature of its content, manner, and
materials; and, last, to a history of its development and end.

The first point that must be grasped very firmly is that the
term "minor epic" simply does not exist in the Renaissance.
It is used occasionally in antiquity, but not in its modern
sense.[8] I can locate only one occurrence of "epyllion" in the
Renaissance, in an index reference to Callimachus in the Re-
gius-Micyllus commentary to Ovid's *Metamorphoses* (1543),
but the term is not defined there and has no direct bearing
on the poems in question. The modern use of the term orig-
inated in the nineteenth century, and has now been repu-
diated as a prescriptive or theoretical term among classicists,
though it retains some descriptive use.[9]

The relevant Renaissance critical discussions are those con-
cerning the nature of epic. The controversies which swirled
around the works of Ariosto and Tasso demonstrate that
there was no single conception of the proper form of epic.[10]
But a central idea of epic can be defined: it is a narrative
celebrating a hero and his deeds in a marvelous style so as to
incite men to emulation. In this simple sentence we have
specified the object to be imitated (a hero), the manner (nar-
rative), the materials of imitation (the marvelous), the audi-
ence (men), and the intended effect (wonder and emulation).

But these are in practice not strict rules. The hero might
be a single figure, or there might be multiple heroes, each
embodying a separate virtue; Spenser used both schemata in

---

[8] J. F. Reilly, "Origins of the Word 'Epyllion,' " *Classical Journal* 49
(1953): 111; however, L. P. Wilkinson asserts that the word "epyllion" does
occur once in its modern sense in a classical writer (Athenaeus 65A), in *Ovid
Recalled* (Cambridge: Cambridge University Press, 1955), p. 144n.

[9] Walter Allen, Jr., "The Non-Existent Classical Epyllion," *Studies in Phi-
lology* 55 (1958):515-18; D.W.T.C. Vessey, "Thoughts on the Epyllion,"
*Classical Journal* 66 (1970):38-43; Brooks Otis, *Ovid as an Epic Poet*, 2nd ed.
(Cambridge: Cambridge University Press, 1970), pp. 5-7.

[10] See John Steadman, *Milton and the Renaissance Hero* (Oxford: Oxford
University Press, 1967), pp. 2-20; and Weinberg, *Italian Renaissance*, 2:954-
1073.

the *Faerie Queene*, with imperfect knights as protagonists of the several books and Prince Arthur as a perfect composite of all virtue. The partisans of Ariosto loosened the strict narrative unity of epic to allow more variety of incident and character in the manner of romance. The heroic virtues would traditionally be military valor and prowess, but here the controversy was thickest, as critics put forth alternative values of reason, justice, piety, and wisdom. To these must then be added amorous values, which find a major place in the verse epics of Ariosto and Spenser, and in Sidney's prose *Arcadia*, regardless of their precise justification in theory. This broadening of theme in turn brings the epic into contact with other genres, particularly the pastoral in the *Arcadia* and in Book 6 of the *Faerie Queene*; it brings a widening of the intended audience to include females as well as males; and it seeks to move that audience to revulsion and horror at the misdeeds of heroes as well as to wonder and emulation at their virtues. If in its narrowest sense the epic is an easily prescribable genre, it is in its widest sense an encyclopaedic genre which mixes all characters, actions, and themes in a varied style which draws on the full range of poetic resources, from high to low.

Minor epic is linked most closely to epic in its materials; its characteristic diction, verse forms, and mythological imagery all seek out the marvelous and often the extravagant. Its amorous action is quite literally the minor action of epic, set in counterpoint to the major themes of public and military virtue. Its characters are divine or royal, though again not heroic themselves, but gods of love or royal mistresses. And, like so many epics, it is a mixed genre, presenting its objects with motifs from drama and lyric, especially the sonnet and pastoral.

Among the varieties of epic, the one most crucial for the understanding of the minor epic is, of course, Ovid's *Metamorphoses*, although its generic identity was often forgotten until Brooks Otis's masterly study, *Ovid as an Epic Poet* (1967). Superficially Ovid organizes his work as a linear his-

tory, moving from the creation of the world to the death of
Caesar. The poem as a whole, though, proceeds through
juxtapositions, recollections, and parallels among episodes,
rather than through sequential narration. Renaissance com-
mentaries unanimously recognized it as an epic and a history
of the world, but nonetheless chopped it up into its separate
episodes—232 in the widely used gloss of Lactantius Placi-
dus—and treated each piece as a more or less self-contained
narrative. Ovid's story of Adonis, for instance, coming after
the tale of Myrrha's incestuous passion for her father Ciny-
ras, is interrupted by the story of Atalanta and Hippomenes,
and is followed by the story of Orpheus and Eurydice, so
that the whole sequence mingles two themes, the fragile
beauty of youthful passion and the violence of full-blown
desire. In Renaissance commentaries the autonomy of each
is asserted so that even the life of Adonis becomes two sep-
arate stories, one of his miraculous birth, the other of his
death.

Renaissance Ovidian narratives commonly take for their
plot a single episode detached from the *Metamorphoses* in the
manner of the commentaries. But they also characteristically
use digression and inset narrative, working toward meaning
through analogy, recollection, and juxtaposition—the kind
of nonlinear narrative structure on which the *Metamorphoses*
as a whole is built, so that the single spinoff episode tends to
reproduce in miniature the structural principle of the whole
work. Shakespeare's *Venus and Adonis*, for instance, intro-
duces the narrative of the stallion and the jennet in place of
Atalanta and Hippomenes, and weaves its debate on the
value of passion into the poem by means of naturalistic
digressions and apostrophes which cluster around the main
narrative.

A similar development can be traced for poems in the *de
casibus* form of the *Mirror for Magistrates*. Each of the "trage-
dies" in Chaucer's "Monk's Tale," for instance, is told as
briefly as possible, with the narration boiled down to the
bare pattern of rise and fall. The omnipotence of Fortune is

demonstrated by the multiplication of these tales into an infinite series, and the Monk indicates that he could go on indefinitely before he is stopped by the anguished cry of the Knight. In the *Mirror for Magistrates* Baldwin orders his tales on a plan nearly as simple, adding only a vague historical sequence to them. But he added no narrative connections to unify the action, and so it was easy to detach single tales from the group. Sackville's "Induction" and Churchyard's "Shore's Wife" stand forward of their own accord, and are elaborated and extended into self-contained narratives by the development of their complaint frames, by ekphrastic digression, and especially by the amplification of character through apostrophe.

The poetic form for the minor epic that evolved from these models mingled the brief action of a short narrative with expansive and digressive materials more often found in a long narrative. This mixing of materials and manners, blending lyric and drama with narrative, has been the principal target of criticism of these poems. For instance, Douglas Bush, tracing the origins of Lodge's *Scilla*, complains:

> Lodge's pattern in the main resulted from a combination of the stock theme and style of Italian pastoral with the stock conventions of love poetry. The marriage could not be regarded as altogether eugenic. . . . Incongruities of costume and allusion have been partly indicated; not the least remarkable is the combination of an Ovidian metamorphosis with figures from medieval allegory.[11]

F. T. Prince in turn complains of Shakespeare's *Lucrece* that "it should be related in the true narrative manner of Ovid or Chaucer, not in the semi-dramatic, semi-rhetorical manner of Shakespeare's poem."[12]

---

[11] Douglas Bush, *Mythology and the Renaissance Tradition in English Poetry*, rev. ed. (New York: Norton, 1963), p. 87.

[12] F. T. Prince, ed., *Poems of Shakespeare* (London: Methuen, 1960), p. xxxvi.

The mixing of different manners and of materials of disparate origins are not separate issues, and respond to a single solution. The issue is whether or not that mixing destroys the unity of the poem in question. Though no one would maintain that every poem of the genre is a masterpiece, the answer in general is no; for it is precisely the combination of "medieval" and "Italianate" materials, precisely the mixing of narrative, dramatic, and lyric movements, that creates the distinctive effect of the poems of this genre. The poems attain their unity by subordinating their different materials and manners to a unified *cause*, the desired rhetorical address to the audience around which the poem is built.

Thomas Wilson, in his *Arte of Rhetorike*, describes three kinds of causes: to praise or dispraise (the demonstrative); whether a thing be profitable or unprofitable (the deliberative); and whether a thing be right or wrong (the judicial). Wilson then adds: "And yet this one thyng is to be learned, that in every one of these three causes, these three severall endes, may every one of them be conteined in any one of them."[13] So the cause of a poem may be not a simple, but a complex unity. The two poems generally recognized as the first in the new forms, Lodge's *Scillaes Metamorphosis* and Daniel's *Rosamond*, yield unexpected riches when regarded in this light.

The cause of Lodge's *Scillaes Metamorphosis* is the deliberative type, but exactly what is found profitable is not at first clear. In the opening complaint frame, the poet encounters the god Glaucus on the banks of the Isis, where both bemoan the pangs of love and the transience of earthly pleasures, to which the god applies the lessons of mutability. So the opening of the poem establishes a cause of the worthlessness of love and of the virtue of stoic resignation. But as the narrative slides into a more erotic vein, Glaucus finds himself

---

[13] Thomas Wilson, *The Arte of Rhetorike* (London, 1580), p. 11; cf. Rosemond Tuve, *Elizabethan and Metaphysical Imagery* (Chicago: University of Chicago Press, 1947), p. 12.

cured of lovesickness and the scornful nymph Scilla is tormented instead, which is pointedly directed as a moral that "Nimphs must yeeld, when faithfull lovers straie not." The final cause refutes the initial cause, and is itself a double one directed at a double audience, as defined by the poem's subtitle: "the detestable tyrannie of Disdaine, and Comicall triumph of Constancie: Very fit for young Courtiers to peruse and coy Dames to remember." The inversion of the cause from a "moral" to an "immoral" one midway through the poem may seem ungainly if one has pasted a label of "medieval allegory" on the opening and "Ovidian" on the middle. But it is exactly the kind of witty inversion which sonneteers like Philip Sidney loved.

Daniel, on the other hand, may seem to have disrupted the sober morality of *Rosamond* with trivial mythological decorations. But again the poem's cause will show us otherwise. The poet is again a frustrated lover, to whom the ghost of Rosamond appears and chronicles her fall from chastity to sin. But the poem is less a moral exhortation than an assessment of the process of the fall. Elaborate digressions and mythological imagery bring to the story of Rosamond a series of illuminating parallels with Eve and the pagan Danae, who were both seduced through pride and material desire. Simultaneously they contrast Rosamond with her namesake, the Virgin Mary, emblem of female perfection; and the complaint frame develops a final contrast between Rosamond and the poet-narrator's own mistress, Delia, who alone among modern women has resisted the corruptions of pride. So the demonstrative poem lamenting the destruction of virtue becomes secondarily a poem in praise of the poet's mistress (the poem is published as an appendage to the sonnet sequence *Delia*), and both ends are accomplished through the poem's Ovidian additions.

I. A. Richards once remarked that the different aspects of a poem create "psychological relations, correspondences between different systems of activity in the mind," a "rhythm

of the mental activity through which we apprehend not only
the sound of the words but their sense and feeling."[14] In the
blending of their disparate manners, these poems describe
such a rhythm of apprehension, which might finally be de-
fined as the *mode* of minor epic—a characteristic movement
between involvement and detachment, between incident and
analysis. As the poem progresses through its narration, re-
current digressive materials such as *ekphrasis*, in which the
poet describes a painting or tapestry, move the reader
through analogy away from the main narrative toward re-
flection, and back again.

In *Lucrece*, Shakespeare describes a painting of the fall of
Troy in which he emphasizes the power of the painter to
create illusions, to make his audience mistake his images for
reality, and at the same time to embody in those images a
clearly stated abstract significance:

> At last she calls to mind where hangs a piece
> Of skilful painting, made for Priam's Troy,
> Before the which is drawn the power of Greece,
> For Helen's rape the city to destroy,
> Threat'ning cloud-kissing Ilion with annoy;
>     Which the conceited painter drew so proud,
>     As heaven, it seem'd, to kiss the turrets bow'd.
> . . . . . . . . . . . . . . . . . . . . . . . . . . . . . . .
> To this well-painted piece is Lucrece come,
> To find a face where all distress is stell'd.
> Many she sees where cares have carved some,
> But none where all distress and dolour dwell'd,
> Till she despairing Hecuba beheld,
>     Staring on Priam's wounds with her old eyes,
>     Which bleeding under Pyrrhus' proud foot lies.
>
> In her the painter had anatomiz'd
> Time's ruin, beauty's wrack, and grim care's reign.
>                           [ll. 1366-72, 1443-51]

[14] I. A. Richards, *Practical Criticism* (London: Kegan Paul, 1929), pp. 229,
361.

Through Lucrece's sympathetic reaction to the painting, the fall of Troy becomes, of course, analogous to her own rape, which is explained as part of the inevitable decay of all earthly splendor, regardless of its guilt or innocence. This passage and a series of flower metaphors in turn link *Lucrece* in theme and imagery with *Venus and Adonis*, whose original version in Ovid's *Metamorphoses* is the classic story of youth and beauty as fragile flower.

In *Hero and Leander* Marlowe uses *ekphrasis* more indirectly to establish a central metaphor in his description of the mosaic floor in the temple of Venus at Sestos:

> Of crystal shining fair the pavement was;
> The town of Sestos call'd it Venus' glass.
> There might you see the gods in sundry shapes
> Committing heady riots, incest, rapes:
> For know, that underneath this radiant floor
> Was Danae's statue in a brazen tower,
> Jove slyly stealing from his sister's bed,
> To dally with Idalian Ganymede,
> Or for his love Europa bellowing loud,
> Or tumbling with the Rainbow in a cloud;
> Blood-quaffing Mars, heaving the iron net
> Which limping Vulcan and his Cyclops set;
> Love kindling fire, to burn such towns as Troy.
>                                        [1. 141-53]

The passage, indeed the whole temple, reveals the violent side of passion which the naive Hero and Leander do not yet know, and which is learned only in Neptune's embraces and in the poem's final consummation. Love for them is at first all bliss and joy and heavenly fire, just as it is for the blithe Mercury when he deposes the wicked and bloody Jove and Mars, the main actors in the mosaic, in Marlowe's little digression at the end of the first sestiad. But Jove and Mars regain their seats, and the violence of desire mingles with the bliss as Leander at last embraces Hero:

Love is not full of pity (as men say)
But deaf and cruel where he means to prey.
Even as a bird, which in our hands we wring,
Forth plungeth, and oft flutters with her wing,
She trembling strove: this strife of hers (like that
Which made the world) another world begat
Of unknown joy.
            [2. 287-93]

In both poems the sensuous descriptive image is func-
tional, but they differ in the activity required of the reader
to move from sensation to function. In *Lucrece* we submit to
the analysis of the image's significance delivered by the nar-
rator (Hecuba as time's ruin), and the application of it to the
main narrative made by Lucrece herself (Lucrece as time's
ruin). In *Hero and Leander* the significance of the image and
its relation to the main narrative are never explicitly stated,
and depend upon the willingness of the reader to explore.
The distinction is not just between two ways of constructing
images, but between two narrative structures, which we
might call the emblematic and the allusive. The emblematic
narrative is more linear and progressive, moving from be-
ginning to end, and using its digressive elements to move in
explicit steps from incident to reflection and analysis. It em-
ploys the emblematic image; the complaint frame, in which
a repentant ghost comments upon its youthful sins; and the
apostrophe, in which a character breaks away from the ac-
tion to analyze himself and his situation.[15] The allusive struc-
ture moves back and forth by analogy among semi-inde-
pendent portions of the narrative, depending upon the reader
to respond to the conventional significance of images, espe-
cially the codified allegorical significance of mythological
images. The narration is discontinuous, and progresses to

---

[15] Although some writers use "emblematic" for any image that refers to,
or is drawn from, emblem books, I here restrict it to images in which the
full emblematic structure of image and explication appears in the text.

meaning only through suggestion, leaving ample room for wit and irony.

Most minor epics combine the emblematic and the allusive modes. *Venus and Adonis* and *Lucrece* both use emblematic imagery, but leave suspended among contrary arguments such central questions as the right course of action for Lucrece after her rape or the value of Venus's erotic passion. The emblematic structure is most consistently embodied in Drayton's *Endimion and Phoebe* and Giles Fletcher's *Richard III*, while the allusive structure finds its masterpiece in the Mercury digression of *Hero and Leander*. This passage is a kind of grand mockery of the explanatory digression so common in the genre. Marlowe's narrator introduces the episode to describe why the Fates hate Cupid and lovers, and thus why the story of Hero and Leander must end badly. But after a long ramble with Mercury through heaven and earth, the narrator at last arrives at his moral:

> And but that Learning, in despite of Fate,
> Will mount aloft, and enter heaven gate,
> And to the seat of Jove itself advance,
> Hermes had slept in hell with Ignorance.
> Yet as a punishment they added this,
> That he and Poverty should always kiss.
> And to this day is every scholar poor.
> [1. 465-71]

However much we may sympathize with the sentiment, we must admit that it has next to nothing to do with the rest of the poem, and pointedly ignores the obvious parallel between the fates of Mercury and Leander, which is presumably the point of the story. It is, in short, a distraction, another witty inversion, a shaggy god story.

Neither the allusive nor the emblematic mode can be labeled unequivocally "Continental" or "native," or "medieval" or "Renaissance." The allusive structure finds its great

model in the *Metamorphoses*, but also in such Ovidian poems
as Chaucer's *Book of the Duchess*, or in the interlace structures
of medieval romance. The emblematic is firmly rooted in the
long tradition of Ovidian iconography which received new
impetus from Boccaccio; filled the sixteenth-century hand-
books and commentaries of Natali Conti, Vincenzo Car-
tari, Regius, Micyllus, and Sabinus; and inspired the dense
imagery of George Chapman's *Ovid's Banquet of Sense* and
continuation of *Hero and Leander*. The major development in
the use of mythological imagery in the sixteenth century was
not a move away from "medieval allegory," but a shift
within the allegorical image from moral to philosophical sig-
nificance.[16]

The shift in the nature of allegorical imagery and the in-
creasing use of the allusive structure account for much of the
difference between the minor epics of the 1590s and earlier
English Renaissance narratives. Often that development is
described in terms of a period of brief freedom from allegory
in the 1590s under Continental influence, and a lapse back
into the allegorical straitjacket with the seventeenth-century
Ovid of George Sandys. But poems like those of Drayton
and Chapman, with their Neoplatonism, are, if anything,
more intricately allegorical than anything produced earlier or
later. In terms of the internal organization of the poems, the
new development is not a freedom from allegory, but a turn-
ing of old allegorical structures to new purposes. Lodge's
*Scillaes Metamorphosis* is a *carpe diem* allegory; Daniel uses the
complaint frame of *Rosamond* to deepen sympathy for his
sinning heroine; and Spenser in his *Muiopotmos, or the Fate of
the Butterflie*, spins an ornate narrative in the manner of alle-
gorical romance, complete with mythological digressions,
ending in mock-heroic, and even in mock-allegory. The his-
tory of the genre becomes a series of experiments with tech-
nique, using its resources to find different solutions to a re-

[16] Rosemond Tuve, *Allegorical Imagery* (Princeton: Princeton University
Press, 1966), pp. 54-55.

markably constant problem—the evocation of its characteristic double-edged tone, bittersweet, erotic and reflective, meditating on the central proposition of the decay of physical beauty and the transience of earthly pleasure. Under the Stuarts, the genre changes—not a degeneration really, but a turning to new effects—when the multiple cause and the double tone are simplified. Erotic narrative changes to the simply lascivious or the simply passionate, as in Phineas Fletcher's *Venus and Anchises* (c. 1605-1615) or Abraham Cowley's *Pyramus and Thisbe* (1628). Chronicle poems, like Drayton's *Peirs Gaveston* in its last major revision of 1605, revert to the simpler pattern of the mirror, stripped of mythological imagery and reduced to sober, detached narration.

The genre of minor epic, like any uncanonical genre, must remain loosely defined, embracing a number of subgroupings with different bases. We can distinguish between the matter of Britain and the matter of Greece and Rome, though that division does not provide a very illuminating comparison between two poems as different as *Hero and Leander* and *Lucrece*. We can distinguish between poems written on serious causes and those written on light or trivial causes, though the judgment is a moral one and particularly difficult to make with poems containing complex causes. Or we can make the distinction, also interpretive, between poems written in the emblematic or in the allusive variants on the minor epic mode. But the value of the broad category of minor epic lies in its ability to reach across this network of overlapping families to include poems like Spenser's *Muiopotmos* and Fletcher's *Richard III*, neither of which deals with love, in the same group as the epyllion and mirror poems which they so closely resemble in technique.

As an uncanonical genre with a variety of bases, the Elizabethan minor epic amounts not to a set of rules for the poet, but to a set of critical choices among literary models, narrative modes, and contrasting realms of experience. When we turn to specific poems in the genre, we shall find that this set of choices amounted to a constant demand for experimentation which is revealed whenever a mirror poem becomes luxuriant and witty or an epyllion mingles some pith with its sensuousness. Unanointed by theory, the genre of minor epic may be thought of as "a set of interpretations," in Rosalie Colie's words, "of 'frames' or 'fixes' on the world" which may be used "to understand how literary works were thought to come into being."[17] In the next five chapters we shall use a series of such "frames" or "fixes," looking out on different vistas of the Elizabethan literary landscape, to suggest both how minor epics came to be written and how they may be read.

[17] Rosalie Colie, *The Resources of Kind: Genre-Theory in the Renaissance*, ed. Barbara K. Lewalski (Berkeley: University of California Press, 1973), p. 8. The idea of genre, in the sense of "a preconception as to the type and nature of the text or Whole which conditions [and is in turn conditioned by] our apprehension of the various parts" (in Fredric Jameson's words), has had a revival in critical theory in recent years ("Metacommentary," *PMLA* 86 [1971]: 18n.1). One thinks, for instance of E. D. Hirsch, Jr.'s *Validity in Interpretation* (New Haven: Yale University Press, 1967); Jonathan Culler's *Structuralist Poetics* (Ithaca: Cornell University Press, 1975); and Tzvetan Todorov's *The Fantastic: A Structural Approach to a Literary Genre* (Ithaca: Cornell University Press, 1975).

# Chapter 2

# Petrarchan Rhetoric

The modern reader of an Elizabethan sonnet sequence is apt to find it bound with others of its kind, so that the development of the lyric from Sidney to Donne is visible in a single volume. The Elizabethan reader, however, might have found the latest adaptations of Petrarch in the company of a minor epic. This was in part a matter of commercial convenience, since a sequence of fifty-odd lyrics and a narrative of a thousand or so lines make up a neat volume of eight or ten signatures in octavo. From this joint publication and from the shared erotic concerns of the two genres came a natural exchange of vocabularies. While Petrarch had for the most part limited his mythological allusions to the story of Apollo and Daphne, the English sonneteers increasingly drew on the body of mythology available in the Ovidian narratives; more than one minor epic, in turn, is a tissue of Petrarchan conceits.[1] Nor is this mutual indebtedness limited to tropes and figures of speech, for the techniques of the Petrarchan sonneteers affected the construction of the minor epic as well.[2]

[1] Petrarchan influence on the minor epic is mentioned by Yvor Winters, "The Sixteenth-Century Lyric in England: A Critical and Historical Reinterpretation" (1939), in *Elizabethan Poetry*, ed. Paul J. Alpers (London: Oxford University Press, 1967), p. 107; Louis R. Zocca, *Elizabethan Narrative Poetry* (New Brunswick: Rutgers University Press, 1950), p. 192; Hallett Smith, *Elizabethan Poetry* (1952; reprint ed., Ann Arbor: University of Michigan Press, 1968), p. 103; Douglas Bush, *Mythology and the Renaissance Tradition in English Poetry*, rev. ed. (New York: Norton, 1963), pp. 79, 86; and William Keach, *Elizabethan Erotic Narratives* (New Brunswick: Rutgers University Press, 1977), p. 37.

[2] In his article, "Petrarchism in Short Narrative Poetry of the Renaissance," *Comparative Literature* 26 (1974):318-33, William J. Kennedy explores the use of two Petrarchan strategies, multiple address and contrarieties, in

A minor epic such as Lodge's *Scillaes Metamorphosis* may resemble a string of lyrics or, as Daniel's *Complaint of Rosamond*, share the architecture of a sonnet sequence. This reciprocal relationship between minor epic and sonnet is a crucial factor in the development of both forms in the Renaissance. In 1589 Thomas Lodge was, under the influence of the lyric, able to transform the moral and satiric complaint into a vehicle of erotic delight appropriate to the new literary coterie shaped by Sidney and Spenser. In the decade of the 1590s, a succession of poets—Daniel, Shakespeare, Marston, and Francis Beaumont—explored the ambivalences of the Petrarchan experience in order to reexamine the tensions between the sensual and moral uses of poetry. The resolution of these tensions was in turn the goal of Stuart poets such as Phineas Fletcher and Shakerley Marmion who used the minor epic to place the private, erotic, and low subject matter of the sonnets in a public, philosophical, and morally defensible context.

This struggle by poets to turn the Petrarchan sonnet into narrative was both stylistic and ethical. It required that the poet define the moral norms by which he evaluated his erotic experience and, as a consequence, that he define the audience that would assent to those norms and approve his verse. While the shaping of an audience is often a slow process, determined by the pace of social change within a society, the relationship of a poet to his audience may be the most rapidly changing of all aspects of literature, varying with every inflection of his voice. Such at least is the case with the minor epic. The late sixteenth and early seventeenth centuries saw the slow emergence and consolidation of a coterie humanist literary class in England as the consumers of its new literature. At the same time, the genres of sonnet and minor epic underwent rapid transfigurations in style to reflect the shifting moral relationship between the poet and that audience.

Boscan's *Leandro y hero*, Shakespeare's *Venus and Adonis*, and Marino's *La sampogna*.

The poet's role in defining that relationship may be thought of as essentially rhetorical, that is, as a dimension of his address to an auditor. It is by examining the role of Petrarchism in shaping that rhetorical relationship that we may best define the place of the minor epic and its audience within Elizabethan society. In the process, we may also recover the logic that underlies the changes in both lyric and narrative form in the last years of Elizabeth's reign and the first years of the Stuarts.

## SWEET CONSPIRING HARMONY

Thomas Lodge is best known today as a University Wit whose *Rosalynde* (1590) and *Phyllis* (1593) are typical of the Golden style of the early 1590s. Yet Lodge began his career in the early 1580s as a satirist working in a style that C. S. Lewis would have called the purest Drab, and only with *Scillaes Metamorphosis* (1589) did he seek out a newer, erotic, and decorated style. While that style can be explained in part by the importation of Continental fashions in poetry, one must remember that Petrarch and Petrarchism had been around for a long time, long enough for Chaucer to include a lyric based on Petrarch in *Troilus and Criseyde*. To understand the revolution in late Elizabethan poetry of which *Scilla* was a part, one must ask what advantage Petrarchism conferred on the poet in the years around 1590 that suddenly made it so compelling an idiom.

An answer to this question requires a glance at the aesthetic principles of Lodge's early verse in the old manner. From his first poetic venture, the unsigned *Reply to Gosson in Defense of Poetry* (in prose, 1580?), Lodge conceives of poetry in humanist terms: rhetorical in method, allegorical in meaning, and didactic in purpose.[3] In his first published poem, *Truth's Complaint over England* (in *An Alarum Against*

---

[3] For instance, Lodge, a product of the Merchant Taylors' School and Oxford, accuses Gosson, another Oxford boy, of forgetting his lessons:

*Usurers*, 1584), he applies this humanist poetic to the post-Chaucerian dream-vision. In thirty rhyme-royal stanzas, Truth presents a satiric anatomy of the corrupt state of English society, following the basic rhetorical scheme that Renaissance schoolboys learned from Cicero: *exordium, narratio, confirmatio*, and *peroratio*.[4] The complaint framework in which the poet sees the apparition of Truth performs the function that Cicero suggested for the *exordium*, of establishing the credibility of the speaker with his audience. Though the poet-figure is seized by an appropriate fit of melancholy, he is established not as a fictional character but as a mere reflector of Truth's warning, and her complaint is in no way colored by passing through his consciousness. Truth and the poet of the complaint frame are poetic veils for the author of the kind that the *Reply to Gosson* suggested he draw over his didactic burden; but they are the thinnest veils, for *Truth's Complaint* is appropriately naked, cast in the vocabulary of *vanitas* prophecy, and consequently disavowing its poetic or fictional qualities.

In the *Reply to Gosson* and *Truth's Complaint*, we can see the paradox of Lodge's poetic thinking: poetry is a fiction only that it may speak the truth. The volume issued in 1589

---

You have dronke perhaps of *Lethe*, your gramer learning is out of your head, you forget your Accidence, you remember not, that under the person of *Aeneas* in *Virgil* the practice of a dilligent captaine is discribed [;] under yᵉ shadow of byrds, beastes and trees, the follies of the world were disiphered, you know not, that the creation is signified in the Image of *Prometheus*, the fall of pryde in the person of *Narcissus*.

[*Reply to Gosson*, sig. A2ʳ⁻ᵛ]

The allegorical commentaries on Vergil and Ovid that Lodge recalls here are, like his "Accidence" (Lyly's grammar), the purest humanism. Lodge appears never to have abandoned his allegorical conception of poetry; cf. his translation of Simon Goulart's *Learned Summary Upon the famous Poeme of William of Saluste Lord of Bartas* (London, 1621), p. 61.

[4] Cicero, *De Partitione Oratoria*, secs. 27-60; cf. Quintilian, "Proemium," *Institutio Oratoria*, 4; *Rhetorica ad Herennium*, 1. 4, which adds *divisio* and *refutatio*; and Thomas Wilson, *The Arte of Rhetorique* (London, 1553), Book 2, where *propositio* and *divisio* (parts of Cicero's *confirmatio*) are given independent status.

with the title *Scillaes Metamorphosis: Enterlaced with the unfortunate love of Glaucus. Whereunto is annexed the delectable discourse of the discontented Satyre: with sundrie other most absolute Poems and Sonnets* immediately presents itself as a new departure. Though it remains rhetorical and even in a sense allegorical, the volume is thoroughly ornate and fictional, subordinating the didactic ends of the dream-vision to the conscious construction of a unified voice, which Lodge first espouses as his own, and then veils under his mythic gods and satyrs. The unifying tone of the volume is Discontent, which indeed was the subject of the *Alarum Against Userers* volume. There, however, the discontent was public and impersonal, inspired by social corruption, while here it is amorous and private.[5]

The voice is established in his prefactory epistle to a friend at the Inns of Court. This preface has commonly been read for evidence of pirated editions, lost poems, and Lodge's relations with the Elizabethan stage,[6] but it is more useful to see it as an extension of the text itself by which the poet establishes his attitudes toward his various audiences. In his first sentences, Lodge declares that he has not earlier published these "passions" or "discontented thoughts so long inured to obscuritie," because he had no thirst for "vaine glories inordinate follie." He claims to have been forced to publish only by the threat of a pirate, who, basely driven by the need to eat, is about to issue an unauthorized version. The truth or falsehood of this claim is incidental, for it gives our "discontented" author a pretext to rail at the folly of the

---

[5] G. K. Hunter traces a similar shift in the sixteenth century from an ethical to a courtly humanism in *John Lyly* (London: Routledge, 1962), pp. 1-35. In "Drab and Golden Lyrics of the Renaissance," in *Forms of Lyric*, ed. Reuben Brower (New York: Columbia University Press, 1970), pp. 1-18, Hunter compares the "formulaic abstractions" of the Drab lyric with the "aesthetic autonomy" of the Golden lyric.

[6] See N. Burton Paradise, *Thomas Lodge: The History of an Elizabethan* (New Haven: Yale University Press, 1931), pp. 79-81; E. A. Tenney, *Thomas Lodge* (Ithaca: Cornell University Press, 1935), pp. 100-101; and Keach, *Elizabethan Erotic Narratives*, pp. 36, 50.

times, especially the hunger for public attention that the booksellers feed:

> Our wits now a daies are waxt verie fruitefull, and our Pamphleters more than prodigall; So that the postes [of the book stalls] which stoode naked a tedious *non terminus*, doo vaunt their double apparrell as soone as ever the Exchequer openeth; and everie corner is tooke up with some or other penilesse companion that will imitate any estate for a twopennie almes.

[sig. ★ᵛ]

The "penilesse companion" has been identified as a player, and the "twopennie almes" as the admission charge to the theater, but surely the setting is the Great Hall at Westminster, cluttered with bookstalls, adjacent to which stood the Court of Exchequer.[7] Lodge, the gentleman of the Inns of Court, is thumbing his nose at his indigent "mates" from Grub Street whose unbound sheets, dealing with subjects beyond their social reach, are hawked by the booksellers' prentices for tuppence.

In the same vein, Lodge describes his own trials with the printer in a cryptic passage that is most likely a further sneer at the vulgar book trade:

---

[7] In his article, "Westminster Hall and Its Booksellers," *The Library*, series 2, 6 (1905):380-90, Henry R. Plomer concludes that almost from the time of its opening in 1397, "stalls and booths for the sale of all kinds of wares appear to have been set up within Westminster Hall, and it seems probable that stationers were amongst the first to avail themselves of this privilege. . . . The stationers, as we know, soon began to trade in books, and so in course of time stalls for the sale of new and second-hand books became a feature of Westminster Hall. . . . It will be found that the leading men in the bookselling trade made a practice of renting a stall there during the term time in addition to their other places of business." Plomer is able to cite no documentary evidence of book trade before 1640, although he is certain it began much earlier. Lodge's reference would thus constitute the earliest piece of direct evidence about the Westminster Hall book trade by some fifty years.

I pittie to particularize simple fellowes imperfections, and am altogether loath to adventure my paines in so ungratefull a Province. For transformed *Scilla* how ever she hapned now to bee disjoyned from disdainfull *Charybdis*; thinke not, but if they have good shipping they wil meete ere long both in one shop: and landed they had at this instant, in one and the selfe same bay, if *Scilla* (the unfortunater of the two) had not met with a needie pirate by the way. Arived shee is, though in a contrary coast, but so wrackt, and weatherbeaten, through the unskilfulnes of rough writers, that made their poast haste passage by night, as *Glaucus* would scarce know her, if he met her: yet my hope is Gentlemen, that you wil not so much imagine what she is, as what shee was; insomuch as from the shop of the Painter, shee is falne into the hands of the stainer.

[sigs. ★$^v$-Ai$^r$]

Charybdis is invoked as the logical subject of a companion piece to *Scilla* that some author in his vanity will inevitably undertake; Lodge is indeed surprised that such a poem has not appeared. The rest is an elaboration of a formula for describing the mutilation of a poem by drunken typesetters and clumsy engravers—hence his closing metaphor describing the parallel fate of the painter whose works are crudely reproduced by the makers of stained cloths.[8]

[8] The *Oxford English Dictionary* cites Lodge as an example of this sense of the word, s.v. "stainer." Lodge's complaints about the printer may be compared to those of Abraham Fraunce:

Amintas [i.e., the poem *The Lamentations of Amyntas*] is one, which being first prepared for one or two, was afterward by the meanes of a few, made common to manie, and so pitifully disfigured by the boistrous handling of unskilfull pen men [transcribers], that he was like to have come abroad so unlike himselfe, as that his own Phillis would never have taken him for Amintas. Which utter undoing of our poore shepeheard, I knew not well otherwise how to prevent, but by repairing his ragged attire.

[*Amyntas & The Lamentations of Amyntas*, ed. Walter F. Staton, Jr., and Franklin M. Dickey (Chicago: University of Chicago Press, 1967), p. 8.]

In what may be an interpolation made as he prepared the poem for print, Lodge concludes *Scillaes Metamorphosis* with yet another expression of the horror felt by the polite author at the treatment given by printer and public to a manuscript originally designed for a coterie. He vows:

> To write no more, of that whence shame dooth grow:
>   Or tie my pen to *Pennie-knaves* delight,
>   But live with fame, and so for fame to wright.
>                                                [sig. C4ᵛ]

The irony of Lodge's epistle is that, even as he addresses his poem to the public, he rejects them as his audience. The actual readership of Lodge's poem is probably impossible to determine, and it would in any event require an excursion into the sociology of literature that is beyond our scope. With its rhetorical bias, Renaissance literary theory recognized that the poet posits a fictional audience to hear his fictional discourse. The fictional audience of Lodge's printed poem is the coterie he would normally reach by manuscript. While we invariably assume that one must reach a mass audience to win renown, Lodge seems to be assuring us that, in 1589 at least, fame dwells only within the confines of Temple and Court.

The voice of Lodge's preface is that of the discontented gentleman, his stomach turned by the nauseating spectacle around him. The poem that follows is an investigation of the rival ways available to the private gentleman for curing his melancholy—philosophy and sexual indulgence. *Scilla* opens with the expected figure of the poet wandering about the landscape suffering from despair until he encounters the sea-god Glaucus moaning for the love of Scilla. It is commonly though not quite accurately assumed that this frame is based on Sackville's Induction to the *Mirror for Magistrates*, in which the poet encounters a supernatural figure who undertakes his instruction. Perhaps more similar to Lodge's poem would be the *complaint d'amour*, in which a poet-lover overhears the

complaint of another whose amorous feeling is deeper than
his own, and departs wiser in the school of love. The role of
teacher occasionally falls not to a human, but to a bird or
other creature endowed with speech—obviously a divine
messenger of sorts. The poet and the Black Knight in Chau-
cer's *Book of the Duchess* are the best example, and the form
remained current throughout the sixteenth century in such
poems as Thomas Feyld's *Contraversye Bytwene a Lover and
a Jaye* (1522) and George Gascoigne's *Complaint of Philomene*
(1576). Since the *Mirror* is itself a melding of the amorous
complaint frame with historical material, Lodge's opening
could announce either an erotic or a didactic poem. We may
speculate that it suggested both to his original audience, for
only as the poem progresses does eros triumph over moral
illumination.

The first result of the encounter between god and man is
an intense identification between the two melancholics.
Glaucus immediately chides the poet for his failure to take to
heart the lessons of his schoolbooks:

> In searching then the schoolemens cunning noates,
> Of heaven, of earth, of flowers, of springing trees,
> Of hearbs, of mettall, and of *Thetis* floates,
> Of lawes and nurture kept among the Bees:
>> Conclude and knowe times change by course of fate,
>> Then mourne no more, but moane my haples state.
>>                                        [sig. A2ᵛ]

One may wonder why Glaucus doesn't take his own advice,
and in a later poem in the volume, "In praise of the Countrey
life," the poet will find just such philosophic relief from
"publique plagues" (sig. D3ᵛ). The point in *Scilla* seems to
be the failure of self-consolation for erotic discontent. What
Glaucus does offer the poet is what the interlocutor of the
*complaint d'amour* traditionally offers, subsuming the poet's
grief into the greater woe of the character.

"But (loe) a wonder;" upon the river appears a flotilla of

nymphs, led by Themis, the goddess of law and justice. They dance around the males like the stars of Ariadne's crown (recalling how the Cretan maid, abandoned by Theseus, received solace at the hands of Dionysus). One of them, Nais, sings of love; Themis herself listens to the nightingale; and Clore and Chelis exchange bawdy puns. The overt burden of the episode is still didactic:

> . . . all the whole consort
> In publique this sweete sentence did assigne;
>    That while some smile, some sigh through change of
>      time;
>    Some smart, some sport amidst their youthlie prime.
>
> > > > [sig. A3$^r$]

The contrast between their joyful view of life's variety and Glaucus's dour moralization on mutability underscores that the nymphs embody the "consorts" of sexual fulfillment. As they enjoy the emotion that the males are seeking, so they are bodily the means by which the males might attain it (the daughters of Themis being especially appropriate companions for the lawyers of the Inns of Court). Even Cupid, normally prepubescent, is so stirred by Nais that he is seen "searching out his powerful shaft to prove her," as later he "smiled upon the Nimphes for pleasure" and desires to touch Scilla's thigh. The poet is confronted, in effect, with two rival forms of consolation (resignation and fulfillment), both embodied in mythological figures (Glaucus and Themis), and both conveyed by lyric (the complaint and the erotic song).

The rest of the poem is structured as a kind of singing match between the two voices, the "whole consort" of nymphs and the two males "consorted in our gronings." Glaucus delivers a long complaint in two parts, which itself invokes or contains numerous lyrics: the complaints of Venus, Angelica, and Aurora, a blazon of Scilla, and a stanza

set off in hexameters and heptameters whose fidgetting line
has the nervous quality of Petrarchan paradox:

> Wretched Love let me die, end my love by my death;
> Dead alas still I live, flie my life, fade my love.
> Out alas love abides, still I joy vitall breath:
> Death in love, love is death, woe is me that doo prove.
> Paine and woe, care & griefe every day about me
>     hovers:
> Then but death what can quel all the plages of haples
>     lovers?

[sig. B2<sup>v</sup>]

The nymphs, in turn, offer medicinal herbs and "cheerefull
laies." When Glaucus's mother Thetis arrives,[9] she proposes
"good exercise" as her nostrum, but quickly tries instead a
hymn to Venus. The practical solutions, then, offered by
Glaucus, Themis, and Thetis—of philosophy, medicine and
exercise—all fail, and each turns to the lyric intensification of
passion as the necessary prelude to its cure.

For the internal audience of these lyrics, that is, for the
nymphs and the narrator, the immediate effect is a height-
ening, not a calming of woe, as each is absorbed in the la-
ments of Glaucus. It is this intensification of feeling that al-
lows Glaucus and the poet to see what philosophy could not

---

[9] Lodge deviates from classical precedent in giving Glaucus a divine par-
entage. Usually he is said to have been a fisherman transformed after eating
a magical herb, giving Ovid occasion to portray him as a comically gro-
tesque monster. William Keach surely errs in suggesting that Lodge has
followed Ovid here in presenting Glaucus as a "hairy, moss-covered sea-
god" (*Elizabethan Erotic Narratives*, p. 39). Lodge places no particular stress
on Glaucus's haircut, and moss is apparently correct attire among marine
deities, for the nymphs "trick up mossie garlands . . . For lovely Venus and
her conquering Sonne" (sig. C4<sup>v</sup>). For an alternative iconography, depicting
a more presentable Glaucus, see the frontispiece by Giacomo Franco to
Book 14 of Giovanni dell' Anguillara's translation of the *Metamorphoses*
(Venice, 1578).

show them: that the ultimate cause of their sorrow is not universal mutability, but the individual power of Fancy:

> Leave me that loose my selfe through fancies power,
>     Through fancies power which had I leave to loose it,
>     No fancie then should see me for to choose it.
> [sig. A4ʳ]

It is Fancy which has led Glaucus, at the end of his blazon of Scilla, to a maddening speculation on the mount, the vale, and the font "Whose lovely *Nectar* dooth all sweetes surmount." This fancy is the defining element of desire and poetry alike. "Confounded with descriptions [of her beauty], I must leave them," Glaucus summarizes, "Lovers must thinke, and Poets must report them."

In a series of asides, the poet affirms this identification of his quest for sexual fulfillment with his quest for verse. "Yeeld me such feeling words," he begs his Muse, "that whilst I wright, / My working lines may fill mine eyes with languish." While these asides show a witty toying with the poet's power to create fictions, they are more than just play. They show the poet consciously establishing the fiction of the poem as a subjective realm which embodies the arousal and fulfillment of his erotic desires. This is made explicit when Scilla is punished by Cupid and the whole company of divinities crosses the seas to witness the final triumph of the male lovers over the objects of their desire:

> What neede I talke the order of my way,
> Discourse was steersman while my barke did saile,
> My ship conceit, and fancie was my bay:
> (If these faile me, then faint my Muse and faile).
> [sig. C3ᵛ]

The wandering bark is itself a Petrarchan conceit for the lover lost on a sea of passion, one which Lodge will use again in *Phyllis* (nos. 2, 11). The landscape of the minor epic becomes in Lodge's hand a collection of reified figures of speech in which Petrarchan metaphors for psychological states are unexpectedly treated as if they were physical realities. Fancy propels the poet-lover toward the objects of desire and the topics of invention, equating the fictional journey toward sexual release with the act of writing poetry.

The relationship between the poet and his invention can perhaps be made most clear by comparison with an earlier Renaissance poem in the form of a mythological *complaint d'amour*, Gascoigne's *Complaint of Philomene*. In that poem, the poet walks abroad one evening, hears the song of the nightingale, and wonders at its strange cry before falling asleep. Nemesis appears in his dream to tell him the story of Philomele (drawn from Book 6 of the *Metamorphoses*) as an example of the evil passions of lust and vengeance that can disturb man's calm of mind. Nemesis explicates the moral at some length, and the poet takes the warning to heart, resolving in the *peroratio* to sin no more:

> Beare with me (Lord) my lusting dayes are done,
> Fayre *Phylomene* forbad me fayre and flat
> To like such love, as is with lust begonne,
> The lawful love is best, and I like that,
> Then if you see, that (Lapwinglike) I chaunce,
> To leap againe, beyond my lawful reache,
> (I take hard taske) or but to give a glaunce,
> At bewties blase, for such a wilful breache,
> Of promise made, my Lord shal do no wrong,
> To say (*George*) think on *Phylomelâes* song.
> [*Complete Works*, 2:206]

The sequence of Gascoigne's poem is, like *Truth's Complaint*, that of the Ciceronian oration.[10] The frame constitutes the

[10] Douglas Peterson has demonstrated Gascoigne's use of a Ciceronian rhetorical structure in "Gascoigne's Woodsmanship," *The English Lyric from Wyatt to Donne* (Princeton: Princeton University Press, 1967), pp. 155-62. Nonetheless, he perversely concludes that "the poem, then, is medieval in style, structure, and convention."

*exordium*, after which Nemesis appears as orator to argue in dispraise of lust; the myth of Philomele constitutes her *narratio*, with her moral interpretation of it in the place of a *confirmatio*. As audience, Gascoigne confesses himself to be convinced. Hence the psychological focus of the poem is on the contrite George, as it is in other poems, such as "Gascoigne's Lullaby" or "Gascoigne's Woodsmanship." The myth of Philomele and the dream-vision act as simple veils of the sort Lodge advocates in his *Reply to Gosson*;[11] the poem progresses by removing those veils to reveal its core of universal moral truth.

Gascoigne's poem depends upon an internalizing of social experience. Closely allied to his satire, *The Steel Glas*, it takes a common moral pattern and casts it as the specific experience of the poet. Lodge's *Scilla* is concerned with externalizing personal experience; it is the vehicle by which the melancholy gentleman of the preface blots out the degraded world around him. He substitutes the emotional vocabulary of desire and consolation for Gascoigne's moral vocabulary of sin and conversion, and passes this emotional burden through his series of veils. The poet-narrator, Glaucus, and the nymphs each partake of grief and consolation, but each does so through conversing with others: the narrator drowns his lament in the greater woe of Glaucus; Glaucus is nursed by the nymphs; and they in turn withstand the "pricks" of love through the sweet balm offered by the songs of Nais and the nightingale. We are presented with interlocking consolations, like a nest of Chinese boxes. While Gascoigne's character "George" is fully released from melancholy at the end of his poem, Lodge refuses to give us a resolution within the limits of his fiction. His nymphs at the end alternate between sympathy for Scilla and rejoicing with Glaucus. His

---

[11] In his *Certayne Notes of Instruction*, Gascoigne advocates the use of the allegorical veil even for the love poet: "If I should disclose my pretence in love, I would eyther make a straunge discourse of some intollerable passion, or finde occasion to pleade by the example of some historie, or discover my disquiet in shadowes *per Allegoriam*" (*Complete Works*, 1:466).

poet, deeply moved by the torments of Scilla, is left out of the final celebration and must turn to his own audience for solace:

> Alonely I apart did write this storie
> With many a sigh and heart full sad and sorie.
> . . . . . . . . . . . . . . . . . . . . . . . . . . . . . . .
> Ladies he left me, trust me I missay not,
> But so he left me as he wild me tell you:
> That Nimphs must yeeld, when faithfull lovers straie
>     not,
> Least through contempt, almightie love compell you
>     With *Scilla* in the rockes to make your biding
>     A cursed plague, for womens proud back-sliding.
>
> [sig. C4ᵛ]

As such, Lodge's poem is not centered in the consciousness of a particular character or narrator; each is a particle in the system of grief and consolation which makes up the poem, and which can only be assembled by the audience. The poem, in turn, is the single biggest part in the longer assemblage of the volume, which continues on with pastoral, satire, and sonnet, all alike celebrating discontent and its cures.

This method bears no small resemblance to the rhetorical method of Spenser's *Faerie Queene*, which Paul Alpers has described as "a continual address to the reader."[12] While the poem presents us with a fiction, it is in the end neither self-contained nor internally consistent. We cannot ask what Glaucus, Themis, and the rest are doing in England; how Glaucus knows the syllabus at Oxford; or where he has picked up a copy of *Orlando Furioso*. For the audience as well as the characters, sexual release is offered in the "sweet consort" of one or the other form of song. It is not surprising, then, that when Venus appears she is invoked in song and

---

[12] Paul Alpers, *The Poetry of the Faerie Queene* (Princeton: Princeton University Press, 1967), p. 21.

called "Mistris of sweet conspiring harmonie," "conspiring" having here not our modern sense of "plotting" but its etymological sense of "breathing together," appropriate to music or passion. Since the mode of solace among the characters is language itself—conceit and dialogue—the central erotic act is the poet's fictionalizing. Gascoigne's poem claims to be a morally truthful record of a fictional consoling experience. Lodge's poem is itself the experience of consolation. For the young males of the Inns of Court, Lodge has built a soft pornography into the poem's design; the act of reading is the act of arousal and release. For the nymphs and ladies of his acquaintance, he offers a masochistic pleasure in the torments that await their refusal to accept the tyranny of male desire. Hence Lodge has come as close as possible to the experience of the self-contained artifact while remaining within the social terms of the rhetorical process.

The advantage that the Golden style offered to Lodge in 1589 seems to be the possibility of subjecting his narrative to the discipline of lyric. Lodge has adopted the technical innovations of Gascoigne's Ciceronian style (in fact, had done so as early as *Truth's Complaint*), but here has turned them to contrary effects, rejecting the philosophical consolation and social satire of the old poetry. The lyricism that he offers in their place still carried as late as the 1590s associations to music as the expression of just proportion and universal order, and, by extension, social harmony and balance within the individual. The lyric dimension of *Scillaes Metamorphosis*, advanced as it is by the goddesses Themis, Thetis, and Venus, is explicitly a metaphor for the curing of individual melancholy and the establishment of a new social order composed of those who have a shared erotic and literary experience:

> He that hath knowne the passionate mishappes
> That nere *Olimpus* faire *Lucina* felt
> When as her *Latium* love her fancie trappes,
> How with suspect her inward soule dooth melt:

> Or markt the Morne her *Cephalus* complaining,
> May then recount the course of all our paining.
>
> [sig. A4ʳ]

By his fundamental alteration of the relationship between poet and audience, Lodge has changed the function of the artifact itself. Without being in any way autobiographical or personal, Lodge's poem asserts the primacy of the individual voice, with private emotion as its burden, and as its audience the community of desire. But even as it claims immediacy, Lodge's poem betrays the instability of its achievement, for to the degree that its sexual delights are allegorical, they are voyeuristic. Indeed, the poem becomes doubly so at the moment of its printing, for it exposes the diversions of Lodge's amorous coterie to the novelty-seeking mob who hang around bookshops. Gascoigne's pursuit of a proverbial voice (like Lodge's own earlier works) allowed him a poetic mastery of mutability at the cost of a moral rejection of erotic experience. Leaving behind Gascoigne's poetic aim with his morals, Lodge achieves arousal, at the cost of admitting that poetry may be as transient and unsatisfying as desire.

## "Il Vario Stile"

Samuel Daniel, the second innovator of the minor epic, followed a course in his *Delia* and *Rosamond* that on the surface is almost point-for-point the reverse of Lodge's. While Lodge claimed that he never meant to display his passions in public, Daniel genuinely was the victim of a pirate, his sonnets in early form being appended to Thomas Newman's 1591 unauthorized edition of *Syr P. S. His Astrophel and Stella*. The changes from this state to the revised poems published in 1592 as *Delia* are in large part corrections of misprints, or improvements of meter or phrasing. In a few significant cases, we may also see a shifting of poetic intention, specifically, an altering of the poet-lover's relation to his mistress and hence to the poems themselves. In those shifts, pursued further in his treatment of the Petrarchan elements of *Rosamond*, we may see him struggling to find new answers to the problems posed by Lodge: the value of erotic experience, and the position of the erotic poet in society. For no sooner did the Golden poetry of 1590 gain supremacy as the mark of the new literary coterie than some poets—such as Daniel and Shakespeare—found its exaltation of the private realm of delight inadequate to their situation.

While Lodge drew on a Petrarchan vocabulary, his commitment in *Scilla* is to a generalized idea of the lyric, leaving Daniel to probe more deeply into the Petrarchan experience and to confront more directly the problem of immediacy. He starts in *Newman* where Lodge left off; the poet-lover wallows in his passion, and writing heightens his torment:

> I figured on the table of my hart
> The goodliest shape that the worlds eye admires,
> And so did perish by my proper arte.
>                                [*Newman*, 7]

By equating love and inspiration, Daniel connects poetry with experience in much the way Dante does when he declares:

> . . . I'mi son un che, quando
> Amor mi spira, noto, e a quel modo
> ch'e' ditta dentro vo significando.

> (I am one who, when love breathes in me,
> take note, and in that manner which he
> dictates within go on to set it forth.)[13]

Dante's "dolce stile" serves him both on earth and in heaven, for the erotic power that generates it is reconcilable to the

---

[13] *Purgatorio* 24. 52-54; trans. John D. Sinclair (New York: Oxford University Press, 1961).

erotic longing for the lost God. In the opening sonnet of the *Canzoniere*, Petrarch speaks of the "vario stile in ch'io piango e ragiono," the "varying style" in which he weeps and talks, under the direction of the "wandering fury characteristic of lovers." Like Dante, Petrarch identifies the lover's voice as his own, while seeing it in the second perspective of Christian morality. But Petrarch's "vario stile" expresses the more humble quest of the idolatrous earthly lover who celebrates "il mio primo giovenile errore," his youthful error, so that, in age and wisdom, "di me medesmo meco mi vergogno," he is overwhelmed with shame.

The debate between the "dolce stile" and the "vario stile" continues in Elizabethan Petrarchist poetry, as poets sought a medium that was aesthetically and morally correct, and yet true to private experience. Sidney concedes that his love is a foolish error, diverting him from more important tasks, but boasts that his plain, terse speech of passion is superior to the sugared style of feigned lovers. Only when imitating others does his verse "halt" or limp (*Astrophel and Stella*, 1). Thomas Watson, the first Elizabethan Petrarchist, likewise espoused the decorum of the "vario stile," but sees in it a necessary imperfection.[14] Inverting Sidney's metaphor, he asks the reader to "survey the faultes herein escaped, as eyther to winke at them, as oversightes of a blinde Lover; or to excuse them, as idle toyes proceedinge from a youngling frenzie; or lastlie, to defend them, by saying, it is nothing *Praeter decorum* for a maiemed man to halt in his pase, where his wound enforceth him, or for a Poete to falter in his Poeme, when his matter requireth it" (sig. A4ʳ). Daniel is less trustful that the appropriateness of the "vario stile" will redeem him; it is wandering, or errant, as surely as is the passion it expresses. Hence he contrasts the stumbling manner of the poet-lover with a more correct and controlled poetic style, and wants only other lovers for his audience, since they are equally blind, and will let his faults escape (*Newman*, 1).

[14] Thomas Watson, Preface to *The Hekatompathia, or Passionate Centurie of Love* (London, 1582).

While one expects love poetry to praise its object, Daniel calls his verse "A monument that whosoever reedes, / May justly praise and blame my loveles *Faire*" (*Newman*, n.s.). To show the erratic mind of the lover, Sidney keeps his praise and blame of Stella in an ironic counterpoint, for while the love she inspires is degrading, the poetry she inspires is commendable. Characteristically he develops this paradoxic state through his exploitation of sonnet structure. He will unravel an intricate logical argument for twelve or even thirteen lines, and swiftly reverse himself in an epigrammatic last line. *Astrophel and Stella*, 18, for instance, uses bookkeeping imagery for three quatrains in which the poet finds that love has left him morally bankrupt. The couplet that concludes it, though, is a lover's sigh:

> I see and yet no greater sorow take,
> Then that I lose no more for *Stella's* sake.

The more consistently bitter state of Delia's lover is reflected in Daniel's habitual use of a simpler rhetorical scheme. The opening poem in *Newman* is typical:

> Go wayling verse the infant of my love,
> *Minerva* like, brought foorth without a mother:
> That beares the image of the cares I prove;
> Witnesse your fathers griefe exceeds all other.
>
> Sigh out a Storie of her cruell deedes
> With interrupted accents of dispaire,
> A monument that whosoever reedes,
> May justly praise and blame my loveles *Faire*.
>
> Say her disdaine hath dried up my blood,
> And sterved you in succours still denying,
> Presse to her eyes, importune me some good,
> Waken her sleeping crueltie with crying,
>     Knock at her hard hart: say, I perish for her,
>     And feare this deed will make the world abhor her.

The proposition of the first stanza, couched in the imagery of paternity, is amplified by images of oratory in the second and physical torture in the third. While we are confronted with new figures in each quatrain, they lead without any shifts in logical direction toward the general and summary couplet in a crescendo of self-pity and abuse.

While the poems in *Newman* are uniform in lamenting the poet's rejection and doubting their own poetic enterprise, it is possible to detect the rudiments of a movement from infatuation and anger to resignation. Several poems at the end of the sequence speak of the poet's impending death and the next to last, a translation of Desportes, introduces a new theme:

> I Once may I see when yeares may wrecke my wrong,
> And golden haires may change to silver wyer,
> And those bright rayes (that kindle all this fier)
> Shall faile in force, their power not so strong.
> . . . . . . . . . . . . . . . . . . . . . . . . . . . . . .
> Goe you my verse, goe tell her what she was:
> For what she was, the best may finde in you.
> Your fierie heate lets not her glorie passe,
> But *Phoenix* like to make her live anew.
> [*Newman*, 26]

Daniel develops this conceit into a major motif of *1592* by inserting five linked sonnets on the same theme after "I Once may I see." To augment this new emphasis, he alters the opening of the sequence. The first poem of *Newman* is placed second, with a significantly altered conclusion:

> Waken her sleeping *pittie* with your crying.
> Knock at that hard hart, *beg till you have moov'd her*;
> And *tell th'unkind, how deerely I have lov'd her.*
> [*1592*, 2; revisions italicized]

This more hopeful note is anticipated by the new introductory sonnet that Daniel placed before it in *1592*:

Unto the boundles Ocean of thy beautie
Runs this poore river, charg'd with streames of zeale:
Returning thee the tribute of my dutie,
Which heere my love, my youth, my playnts reveale.
Heere I unclaspe the booke of my charg'd soule,
Where I have cast th'accounts of all my care:
Heere have I summ'd my sighes, heere I enroule
Howe they were spent for thee; Looke what they are.
[*1592*, 1]

The burden of the verse is heavily shifted to praise, with doubt remaining only as an allusive undercurrent. He invokes the usual metaphors of the lady as divinity and sovereign, but as he descends from heavenly and earthly courts to the counting house, he may suggest that only the lover's error gives the lady any divine or secular authority, and in the final casting of accounts, his zeal is idolatry.

The effect of the new sonnets and the calmer, more ironic opening is to make the poet-lover significantly more detached from erotic experience, more in control of the verse and the situation. Again we might cite Watson. His motto on the title page of *Amyntas* (1585) declares, "Nemini datur amare simùl et sapere"; one cannot be both wise and a lover. While it has been observed that Daniel's revisions consistently transform a dramatic and immediate record of passionate experience into something more graceful and sober,[15] one must not miss the importance of this transformation to the poet's act of self-definition. Not in sexual conquest, but in his power to memorialize the beloved, can he win fame; the poet must subdue the lover.

It is the act of publication that both requires and threatens this poetic harnessing of amorous experience, for it subjects the poet to the ignorant misconstructions of the public.[16] "I

---

[15] E. H. Miller, "Samuel Daniel's Revisions in *Delia*," *Journal of English and Germanic Philology* 53 (1954):58-68; Joan Rees, *Samuel Daniel* (Liverpool: Liverpool University Press, 1964), p. 21.

[16] See J. W. Saunders, "The Stigma of Print: A Note on the Social Bases

rather desired to keep in the private passions of my youth, from the multitude, as things utterd to my selfe, and consecrated to silence," he says in reference to Newman's exposure of him (*1592*, p. 9). Dante, Sidney, and Lodge had used their unusual styles to define a coterie audience. Dante addressed the first poem in his new style to "Donne ch'avete intelletto d'amore." Sidney scorns those court ladies who are familiar only with amorous posturings, by implication defining his audience as those who have truly known love's force (*Astrophel and Stella*, 54). Each in his way is seeking to limit his audience to those who understand his passion, and so can understand the difficulties presented by his unusual verse. Daniel readily concedes that Sidney's cultural and poetic superiority make him immune to the debasement of print and the judgment of the multitude: "*Astrophel*, flying with the wings of his own fame, a higher pitch then the gross-sighted can discerne, hath registred his owne name in the Annals of eternitie, and cannot be disgraced, howsoever disguised" (*1592*, p. 9). Daniel's own verse, however, celebrates no transcendent mysteries and contains only a single reference to the chasteness of his love (*1592*, 15). His situation is closer to that of Petrarch, who addresses his *Canzoniere* to Italians generally, while his *Africa* is for the literary elite. Hence it is Petrarch, of Daniel's predecessors, who confesses to the shame both of an errant passion and of its public exposure. Daniel's verse has been private simply because it is not on a publicly and morally defensible subject.

Among middle-class Elizabethan love poets, the *gradus Vergilianus* seems to undergo a shift into a moral key. In critical theory, the poet progresses from low to high style, but the Elizabethans constantly talk of a move from "light" to "grave" subject matter.[17] This moral complication creates a special dilemma for the poet seeking to live by his pen. He

---

of Tudor Poetry," *Essays in Criticism* 1 (1951):139-59. The "critical corollaries" with which Saunders concludes are highly suspect.

[17] For an excellent discussion of the dilemma of the Elizabethan poet who is trapped between conflicting moral and aesthetic conceptions of poetry,

must publish to eat, but publication of "trifles" or "weeds" (Gascoigne's term) bring shame. Thus the printer of Barnabe Barnes's *Parthenophil* (1593) explains that the work is anonymous because the author is "unwilling (as it seemeth) to acknowledge them, for their levity, till he have redeemed them with some more excellent worke hereafter."[18] Shakespeare similarly pledges to redeem his *Venus and Adonis* with the "graver labour" of *Lucrece*. The earlier poem can be seen as a struggle over the moral value of passion, resolved in the second poem, where Lucrece and the poet rise above its taint. To defend his *Amyntas*, Watson was forced to point out that Homer, Vergil, and Petrarch all wrote on trivial subjects before writing epic (this despite our present knowledge that much of the *Canzoniere* was finished after the *Trionfi* and *Africa*). Watson concedes that it is far more difficult "to publish anything that had not been done before on a striking and universally respected subject: for it is easier to write about base and contemptible subjects" (*Amyntas*, p. 3).

For Daniel, then, the way to true fame is not by exalting his beloved, but by abandoning her. In *Colin Clouts Come Home Again*, the dedicatory epistle of which is dated "from my house of Kilcolman, the 27. of December. 1591,"[19] Spenser addressed Daniel's concern:

And there is a new shepheard late up sprong,
The which doth all afore him far surpasse:
Appearing well in that well tuned song,
Which late he sung unto a scornfull lasse.
Yet doth his trembling *Muse* but lowly flie,

see Richard Helgerson, "The New Poet Presents Himself: Spenser and the Idea of a Literary Career," *PMLA* 93 (1978):893-911.

[18] Barnabe Barnes, *Parthenophil and Parthenophe*, ed. Victor A. Doyno (Carbondale: Southern Illinois University Press, 1971), p. 1.

[19] Since the dedication to *Daphnaida* is dated from London on 1 January 1591 (1592 new style?), either the place or the date of the dedication to *Colin Clout* may be a fiction. See the Variorum edition of Spenser's *Minor Poems*, ed. C. G. Osgood and H. G. Lotspeich (Baltimore: Johns Hopkins University Press, 1943), 1:450-51.

As daring not too rashly mount on hight,
And doth her tender plumes as yet but trie,
In loves soft laies and looser thoughts delight.
Then rouze thy feathers quickly *Daniell*,
And to what course thou please thy selfe advance:
But most me seemes, thy accent will excell,
In Tragick plaints and passionate mischance.
                                                              [ll. 416-27]

The dating of this passage is problematic, since it was not published until 1596, and Spenser may have revised the poem and updated his allusions at any time in the four years since writing the epistle. If we may take the epistle at face value, as being written after the poem, Spenser would certainly know the *Newman* sonnets (an assumption affirmed by his reference to a "scornfull lasse"), and judging from the last line, at least knows of the plans for *Rosamond. Delia* and *Rosamond* were entered in the Stationers Register on 4 February 1592, so Spenser may even have seen Daniel's poem in manuscript. Daniel, in turn, may have seen Spenser's poem and have responded to it in the makeup of his volume. The similarity of Spenser's call to "rouze thy feathers" to Daniel's description of Sidney "flying with the wings of his own fame," though commonplace enough, could be Daniel's modest response to the great poet's praise.

Whoever is echoing whom, Daniel's thought lay in the same direction as Spenser's, for he chose on his title page the literary motto he would keep throughout his life: "Aetas prima canat veneres / postrema tumultus": the first age sings of love, the later ones of war. Besides describing his own intention of moving from sonnet to epic, it declares for the poet a new public theme, the decline of society from the age of gold to the age of iron—the very decline which has transformed innocent desire to raging lust and forced a division between public and private standards of conduct. The revisions of the sonnets can be seen as part of this new intent. He exposes the corruption of genuine religious and social values by the force of desire, and he begins to examine the universal force of mutability that threatens to obliterate all private happiness. One should not be surprised, then, that *Delia* is followed in the 1592 volume by an ode based on Tasso, celebrating that golden age in which "each creature joyes the other," condemning by contrast the chastity of his mistress, and ending with the Petrarchan adage that "well he'ends for love who dies."[20]

In *Rosamond*, which comes after this pastoral interlude in the *1592* volume, Daniel uses the characters in the complaint as veils, as Lodge did, so that he may continue to explore the ambivalences of Petrarchism. The double-edged voice of Petrarch is divided between the repentant ghost of Rosamond, who tells how passion has destroyed her, and the infatuated poet-lover who writes down what she says. The Petrarchan mistress is likewise divided between the youthful Rosamond, proud and disdainful like the lady of the *Newman* sonnets, and Delia, now even more chaste and mild than in the sonnets of *1592*. In her perfection, Delia represents a release from erotic suffering toward which both Daniel and the ghostly Rosamond aspire, he through reciprocation, and she through redemption. Initially, the ghost has approached Daniel because of his skill as an amorous poet whose "just lamenting Muse" has "Toylde in th'affliction of thine owne distresse" (l. 37). Rosamond subtly identifies her religious prayer with his sexual entreaty as she complains that her soul has been denied passage to Elysium, "Till Lovers sighes on earth shall it deliver" (l. 14). She has failed to attain these sighs because her fame has waned, yet fame, based on poetic celebration, can in itself bring moral justification:

> *Shores* wife is grac'd, and passes for a Saint;
> Her Legend justifies her foule attaint;
>     Her well-told tale did such compassion finde,
>     That she is pass'd, and I am left behinde.
>                                     [ll. 25-28]

---

[20] *1592*, p. 36. Cf. Petrarch, *Canzoniere*, 140 and translations by Wyatt and Surrey.

The poet's task, then, is to win redemption for Rosamond and affection for himself. He can accomplish both at once by moving Delia herself to sigh, "Whereby thou might'st be grac'd, and I be blest" (l. 46).

As Rosamond recites to the poet her tale, her voice takes on the detached wisdom normally reserved to a sententious narrator, and between her two persons, the proud courtesan and the repentant ghost, she enacts the inner debate of the Petrarchan lover. As the mistress of Henry II, though, she commands a wider sphere of reference than just the morality of private acts. While the opening of the poem has glanced ironically at the mild blasphemies of erotic verse, the story of her triumph at court moves Daniel's new subject, the decline of religious zeal—and indeed, the fragility of all cultural values—to the center of focus. Pressing Petrarchan tropes into the service of a general social critique, Rosamond tells how she has subdued her secular lord so that his failure to govern his own lust is a symbol of misrule in the political sphere:

> Who would have thought, a Monarch would have ever
> Obayed his handmaide, of so meane a state;
> Vultur ambition feeding on his lyver.
> [ll. 176-78]

The king's amorous entreaties, furthermore, are a form of false worship, echoing the charge of idolatry that the poet leveled against himself in *Delia*:

> Idol unto thy selfe, shame to the wise,
> And all that honors thee idolatrise.
> [ll. 146-47]

By the end of the poem, Rosamond foresees the inevitable overthrow of all religious devotion and spiritual authority as well as the destruction of the arts. Daniel thus gives a double significance to the love situation of the sonnets by seeing in the passion women inspire and the disdainful pride with which they answer it the sources of all social corruption, even as he exalts Delia in *Rosamond* as the image of passive female perfection and the embodiment of the private life.

As the ghost of Rosamond recounts her sexual errors, she uses the rhyme-royal stanza much as Daniel uses the sonnet in *Delia*:

> Now did I find my selfe unparadis'd,
> From those pure fieldes of my so cleane beginning:
> Now I perceiv'd how ill I was advis'd,
> My flesh gan loathe the new-felt touch of sinning:
> Shame leaves us by degrees, not at first winning.
> For nature checks a new offence with lothing:
> But use of sinne doth make it seeme as nothing.
>                                                  [ll. 449-55]

From the reiterated "Now . . . Now" to the image of her flesh dreading the old king's touch in l. 452, the stanza immerses itself in the experience of the bedchamber. But the perspective of the whole is that of the ghost, not the maiden, as the bed becomes a fallen Eden, and Henry's fingers the serpent; l. 453 is spoken in the impersonal voice of proverbial wisdom, and the concluding couplet is detached and sententious. The movement of detachment is in fact double, for the latter half of the stanza describes the moral sloth that besets Rosamond after her initial revulsion, and blocks any true understanding as long as she carries the burden of the flesh. Like that of Petrarch, the scope of her recollection includes both her fallen state and the struggle to conversion.

As the stanza enacts Rosemond's renunciation of eros, so the poem as a whole moves from an anatomy of desire to a preoccupation with remorse and death. When Eleanor of Aquitaine discovers Rosamond and poisons her, she comes not as a human revenger, but as the embodiment of hatred and jealousy, the children of lust that Rosamond has borne to herself. As in *Delia*, the poet again finds that fame is the only defense against the antierotic consequences of eros. Weeping over Rosamond's corpse, Henry vows:

> Yet ere I die, thus much my soule doth vow,
> Revenge shall sweeten death with ease of minde:
> And I will cause posterity shall know,
> How faire thou wert above all women kind.
> And after ages monuments shall find,
>     Shewing thy beauties title not thy name,
>     Rose of the world that sweetned so the same.
>                                         [ll. 687-93]

The poem ends, then, as it began, with a meditation on the contradictory nature of fame. It was the desire for renown that first led Rosamond from country to Court, and the fame (or rather infamy) of her conduct that led to her death at the hands of Queen Eleanor. It is the coin of fame with which Henry tries to pay Rosamond for her services, yet the rich tomb that he builds for her at Godstow Abbey is inevitably to no avail. Rosamond must turn to Daniel the poet, having learned what Shakespeare is shortly to discover:

> Not marble, nor the gilded monuments
> Of princes shall outlive this pow'rful rime,
> But you shall shine more bright in these contents
> Than unswept stone, besmeared with sluttish time.
>                                         [Sonnet 55]

Henry the tomb-builder yields to the poet, who for the first time in the poem acknowledges the voice of wisdom as his own. Internalizing Rosamond's perspective, Daniel confronts their joint desire for fame:

> So vanisht shee, and left me to returne,
> To prosecute the tenor of my woes:
> Eternall matter for my Muse to mourne,
> But ah the worlde hath heard too much of those,
> My youth such errors must no more disclose.
>     Ile hide the rest, and greeve for what hath beene,
>     Who made me knowne, must make me live unseene.
>                                         [ll. 736-42]

Daniel's poetic success is in the end balanced by his amorous failure, so that he resigns himself to eternal frustration, and announces that he shall no longer deal publicly with the theme.

The dilemma posed by Daniel's paradoxical last line is that of both the professional poet and the professional courtesan. In the rakish and genteel circles of the Inns of Court, Lodge can safely defy prudery, while Sidney, secure in his coterie audience and his identity as a gentleman and statesman, can finally be indifferent to poetic fame. Fellow poet Fulke Greville's biography of Sidney scarcely mentions his literary activities. For a middle-class poet like Daniel or Shakespeare, not just fame but public identity itself rests upon the publication of his poetry, but that very publication leaves him forever suspect by the moralists. If this paradox seems a likely truth for Shakespeare's sonnets, it is acknowledged overtly in the twinning of *Venus and Adonis* (for "the younger sort") with *Lucrece* (for "the wiser sort"). We usually assume that the poet's boast that he will immortalize his beloved issues from the serene self-confidence of the Renaissance artist, but in the Elizabethan England of the 1590s, the opposite seems to be the case. Shakespeare fears the rival poet as one more fashionable than himself and forever apologizes for his low social and moral station as one who can only bring disgrace to his friend if their relationship is known:

> I may not evermore acknowledge thee,
> Lest my bewailèd guilt should do thee shame;
> Nor thou with public kindness honor me
> Unless thou take that honor from thy name.
>                                              [Sonnet 36]

The broadening of theme in the lyric and narrative alike in the early 1590s, then, seems determined at least in part by a reaction to the subjective aestheticism of a poem like Lodge's *Scilla*. The earlier style of Gascoigne's *Philomene* gave to the poets of the 1590s a manner both autobiographical and objective, which took all of society for its audience. From the lyrics of Petrarch, the English poets learned the opposite lesson that style must be true to the personality in the midst of feeling and so can be communicated only to the few able to share that feeling. Lodge's emotive lyricism represents one way of combining the two strands, a way that uncovers an immoral potential to literature that threatens to move its coterie audience to the periphery of society. The logical outgrowth of Lodge's subjectivism is the Elizabethan pastoral, where the lords of the earth mask their power in rustic garb, or in the obsessive and antisocial eroticism of Marlowe's *Hero and Leander* (discussed in Chapter 3). In the verse of Daniel and Shakespeare we may see an alternative solution that synthesizes the new private rhetoric with the old public rhetoric. In their verse we hear the self-reflexive voice of the wise man or woman who admits the intensity of passion while struggling to rise above it. The result is a poetry that maintains an "objective" or public moral stance while not abandoning a decorum between its style and the experience it relates. Only such a poetry can speak, however haltingly, both to the initiates of the new poetry and to the society around them.

## "JERKING SHARP-FANG'D POESIE"

It is evident that so long as the social basis of Elizabethan poetry remained stable, so long as high literature was primarily produced by the aristocracy and their retainers (among whom Shakespeare, Marlowe, and Spenser must be numbered), literary style might undergo shifts without its underlying manner changing in a fundamental way. The opposition between Lodge and Daniel, wherein one values subjectivity while the other recoils from its extreme form, is more accurately thought of as a stylistic polarity that defines the range of English Petrarchism until the smashup of the Civil War. To be sure, in any given season one pole or the other might exert attraction, but the other was never deeply submerged or far from sight.

As a result, English Petrarchism is a very unsettling phe-

nomenon for those who like literary history to evolve stead-
ily in one direction at a time. It alternates rather than pro-
gresses—something visible a full decade before Lodge and
Daniel when Sidney explored both poles of the Petrarchan
style. The sonnet craze of the 1590s, supposedly inspired by
Newman's publication of Sidney's *Astrophel*, in turn consists
to a great extent of the kind of poetry that Sidney had at-
tacked:

> You that poore *Petrarch's* long deceased woes,
> With new-borne sighes and denisend wit do sing;
> You take wrong waies, those far-fet helpes be such,
> As do bewray a want of inward tuch:
> And sure at length stolne goods do come to light.
>                                    [*Astrophel and Stella*, 15]

The stilted poetry that Sidney is decrying could not be the
English sonnets, since they are not yet written. We may as-
sume it is the verse of the Pléiade, to which he may have
been introduced as early as 1572 when he was in Paris. It is
they, more than he, from whom Lodge and the rest took
their models. The increasingly ironic treatment of Petrarch-
ism toward the end of the decade with which we associate
the name of Donne can be seen as a reunderstanding of the
true heritage of Sidney.

With Donne we associate the rebirth not only of irony but
of satire. The relationship of minor epic to lyric in the late
1590s is in large part determined by the increasingly ironic
view of both Petrarchism and Ovidianism that is one of the
tools of the satirist in cataloguing the sexual corruption of
his society. John Marston's *Metamorphosis of Pigmalion's Image*
(1598) is published in a volume filled out not with sonnets
but with "Certaine Satyres." On the surface, this satiric style
is an attack on poetry like Lodge's, a development of the
uneasiness expressed by Daniel. In a deeper sense, however,
it represents an extreme form of Lodge's immoral subjectiv-
ism, for Marston is convinced that the English are sexually

depraved and scoffs at the idealism of the Petrarchists. Literary fashion has quite simply taken another step, and nothing is more "out" than what was "in" last year. But Marston's eagerness to be in step has an important consequence. In his attack on erotic idealism, he questions the lyric style of love poetry itself and so, ironically, turns the minor epic back toward its lost origins in the social criticism of the Drab age complaint. His challenge is whether or not social satire can itself become a private form.

The relation of minor epic to satire—and the special place of Marston—has been splendidly analyzed by William Keach in *Elizabethan Erotic Narratives*. Even as I refer the reader to Keach's study, it will be apparent that we disagree about the nature of satire in the minor epic *before* Marston, specifically in Lodge's *Scilla*. Keach sees the irony of the poem directed at the Petrarchist love-posturings of Glaucus, and in that irony he finds the seeds of *fin de siècle* satire. While one cannot deny the irony inherent in the complexly layered structure of Lodge's *Scilla* and its treatment of Fancy, I hesitate to see the poem as satiric or even an anticipation of satire, for the butt of that irony is late medieval satire as much as it is Petrarchism. Indeed, as we have seen, the double-edged quality of Petrarch's voice is inherently ironic, but one would hesitate to call it satiric. A better definition of satire, I think, would emphasize the social object of its raillery. If there is satire in *Scilla*, it comes from the poet's lyric response to social degeneration; hence the "Discontented Satyre" that immediately follows "Glaucus Complaint" in Lodge's volume is an analysis of the role of discontent in all social achievement, couched in a style that mixes Lydgate with Ronsard. It is hard to imagine Lodge writing an anti-Petrarchan satire and four years later producing his sonnet sequence *Phyllis*. The continuity between Lodge and Marston lies not in any particular content or attitude toward erotic experience. It lies in the relationship of poet to audience, where in each case the poet's ironic voice is the result of a shared secret.

Whatever the case of Lodge, in *Pigmalion* the target of
Marston's satire is unmistakable:

> I oft have smil'd to see the foolery
> Of some sweet Youths, who seriously protest
> That Love respects not actuall Luxury,
> But onely joy's to dally, sport, and jest:
>     Love is a child, contented with a toy,
>     A busk-point, or some favour still's the boy.
>
>                                        [stanza 19]

Keach, following the lead of Philip Finkelpearl, sees in Pig-
malion the embodiment of this ingenuous Petrarchan lover. [21]
The sculptor worships a statue of his own making, as the
poet loves a woman who lives only in his fancy and his lines.
Keach differs from Finkelpearl, I think rightly, in seeing the
further satiric dimension opened when Marston elevates Pig-
malion as a model lover:

> Marke my *Pigmalion*, whose affections ardor
> May be a mirror to posteritie.
> Yet viewing, touching, kissing, (common favour,)
> Could never satiat his loves ardencie:
>     And therefore Ladies, thinke that they nere love you,
>     Who doe not unto more then kissing move you.
> . . . . . . . . . . . . . . . . . . . . . . . .
> O wonder not to heare me thus relate,
> And say to flesh transformed was a stone.
> Had I my Love in such a wished state
> As was afforded to *Pigmalion*,
>     Though flinty hard, of her you soone should see
>     As strange a transformation wrought by mee.
>
>                                        [st. 20, 32]

[21] Keach, *Elizabethan Erotic Narratives*, pp. 138-43; Philip J. Finkelpearl,
*John Marston of the Middle Temple* (Cambridge: Harvard University Press,
1969), pp. 95-104.

Up to this moment, the narrator has played the jaded roué who snickers at the fumbling naiveté of Pigmalion. Now he ironically reverses their positions as he sees that Pigmalion's lithophilic perversion is the ultimate refinement in lovemaking.

A skillful debater, Marston has succeeded in telling half-truths about his opponent. The Platonizing element in Petrarchism is inevitably the result of the poet's retrospection; when in the grip of passion, Petrarch freely admits that he wants consummation, not philosophy. Sidney, of course, knew this best:

> So while thy beautie drawes the heart to love,
>   As fast thy Vertue bends that love to good:
> 'But ah,' Desire still cries, 'give me some food.'
>       [*Astrophel and Stella*, 71]

Marston's desire to set his artistic hand to the stony breast of his mistress is a hope to succeed where Daniel confessed to have failed with Delia:

> Behold what happe *Pigmaleon* had to frame,
> And carve his proper griefe upon a stone:
> . . . . . . . . . . . . . . . . . . . . . . .
> [While] still I toile, to chaunge the marble brest
> Of her, whose sweetest grace I doe adore.
> . . . . . . . . . . . . . . . . . . . . . . .
>   O happie he that joy'd his stone and arte.
>               [*1592*, 13]

The relationship of sonnet to minor epic is inevitably that of reality to wish fulfillment. The poet-lover, faced with refusal, acts out his desires in mythological dress, and often, as Keach has noted, discovers the inevitable truth about desire: "Elizabethan epyllia almost never take as their theme the fulfillment of 'healthy, sensual, propagative love' " (p. 144). This is, of course, what Laura, Stella, Delia, Phyllis, and the rest have been telling the poets right along. Marston's satiric diatribe against erotic poetry inevitably hits at the foolish "sweet Youths" and jaded old roués alike, for, as the character of Pigmalion shows, they are the same person. In characteristic fashion, Marston follows *Pigmalion* with a poem of self-praise for the ripeness of his titillations, and then with satires denouncing such filth. He has created a two-handed engine that smites both ways, a fictional artifact that "nothing affirmeth" because it espouses and then denounces every possible position. Lodge and Daniel had each in his way found the essence of a Petrarchan style in its divided world—Lodge's split between social degeneration and private well-being, Daniel's between private sexual error and correct public form. Lodge has championed one term of his division, while Daniel has tried to reconcile them, but in neither case is either half of the division really apprehensible without the other. In Marston's *Pigmalion*, the two parts of the poet's voice are again developed by the positing of two separate audiences, "lewd Priapians" and moral backbiters. But Marston compartmentalizes the two voices and two audiences, juxtaposing two mutually exclusive views of the same experience without admitting intercourse between them. This has led one critic to suggest that Marston is in fact schizophrenic,[22] and while he may well be, Marston's poem is not a unique case, for a similar principle of incoherence shows up a few years later in Francis Beaumont's *Salmacis*, which maintains a tense balance between satire and sensuality by appealing to two *levels* of readers.

On its surface, *Salmacis* hearkens back to the erotic style of the mid-1590s as the author's "wanton Muse" echoes Marlowe on every page. One element—a long description of the Court of Astraea—overtly disturbs this simplicity. Seeking to woo Salmacis, Jove promises to place her among the stars, and the nymph cagily demands that Astraea ratify the god's

[22] Samuel Schoenbaum, "The Precarious Balance of John Marston," *PMLA* 6 (1952):1069-78.

oath before she will yield. When he reaches the court of Astraea, Jove is beset by corrupt officers demanding bribes, so that he is flat broke by the time he is admitted to the presence of the goddess of Justice. Astraea was one of the most common devices for praising Elizabeth, and the passage appears at first glance to be a bit of topical satire which intrudes into the narrative.[23] But it is in fact the key to a thoroughgoing satire that integrates the poem on two levels. For the tale of Jove visiting the Court of Astraea is but one of three digressions that take up nearly half of the poem—a high proportion even for a minor epic. Jove's attempt on Salmacis is followed in kind by Bacchus:

> At Naxos stands my Temple and my Shrine,
> Where I do presse the lusty swelling Vine,
> There with greene Ivie shall thy head be bound,
> And with the red Grape be incircled round;
> There shall Silenus sing unto thy praise,
> His drunken reeling songs and tickling layes.
> Come hither, gentle Nymph.
>                     [ll. 449-55]

When Apollo's turn comes, he offers "the most beauteous boy that ever was," who turns out to be Hermaphroditus, which brings us at last to the main action of the poem. It should be clear at this point that there are not actually three digressions but one, for the appeals to Salmacis by Jove, Bacchus, and Apollo neatly reenact the paradigm of the Judgment of Paris, in which Juno, Minerva, and Venus tempt Paris with fame, wisdom, and love in their strife to be named the most beautiful.

Like any such image, the Judgment of Paris carries a certain literary freight. It could be used by the sonneteer as a compliment to his own mistress, who inevitably excells all the goddesses (as William Smith wrote in *Chloris*, a pastoral-Petrarchan volume dedicated to Edmund Spenser in 1596):

---

[23] Keach, *Elizabethan Erotic Narratives*, pp. 204-5.

No sooner had faire *Phoebus* trimd his car,
Being newly arisen from *Auroraes* bed,
But I in whom dispaire and hope did war,
My unpend flocke unto the mountaines led.
Tripping upon the snowe soft downes I spide
Three nimphs more fairer than those beauties three,
Which did appeere to *Paris* on mount *Ide*,
Comming more neere my goddesse I there see.[24]

In the way that all Petrarchan language was extended as
compliment to Elizabeth, the Judgment became a standard
term for the praise of the Virgin Queen, who epitomized the
virtues of all three goddesses—a Juno in command, a Mi-
nerva in intellect, a Venus in her person. In George Peele's
pastoral drama, *The Araygnement of Paris*, presented by the
Children of the Royal Chapel sometime between 1581 and
1584, Jupiter and Diana still the squabbling deities by deliv-
ering the golden ball "to the Queenes owne hands" as
"Praise of the wisedome, beautie and the state, / That best
becomes thy peereles excellencie."[25] A painting at Hampton
Court dated 1569 shows the three goddesses journeying to
Windsor Castle to present Elizabeth with the ball, here meta-
morphosized into the royal orb [fig. 1],[26] while the prolific
flatterer Richard Barnfield used the conceit in 1595 in his
minor epic poem *Cynthia*.

The Judgment of Paris, like most pastoral imagery, also
has a satiric use, for the shepherd's rejection of Juno and
Minerva can be allegorized as a spurning of the virtues of
both the active and contemplative lives in favor of sloth and
luxury; it is the choice of Paris, after all, that sets in motion

[24] *Chloris*, 8, in *The Poems of William Smith*, ed. Lawrence A. Sasek (Baton
Rouge: Louisiana State University Press, 1970).

[25] *The Life and Works of George Peele*, ed. Charles T. Prouty (New Haven:
Yale University Press, 1970), vol. 3, ed. R. Mark Benbow, p. 114.

[26] The painting has been variously attributed to Hans Eworth, Joris Hoef-
nagel, and Lucas de Heere. See J. A. Van Dorsten, *The Radical Arts: First
Decade of an Elizabethan Renaissance* (Leiden: Leiden University Press, 1970),

1. The Monogrammist HE. *Queen Elizabeth and the Three Goddesses.* 1569.
Panel. Hampton Court Palace.

the destruction of Troy.[27] It is this aspect which seems to be
the immediate point of its use in Beaumont's poem, for Sal-
macis matches and exceeds the shortcomings of Paris. She is
only too willing to yield to all three of her divine suitors,
and only chance keeps her available for the mortal Herma-
phroditus. The worldly fame that Jove offers her is really
infamy, as Venus points out:

> . . . she griev'd to see
> The heaven so full of his iniquity,
> Complayning that eche strumpet now was grac'd,

p. 54; Oliver Millar, *Catalogue of Pictures in the Royal Collection* (London:
Phaidon, 1963), p. 69; Roy C. Strong, *Portraits of Queen Elizabeth I* (Oxford:
Clarendon Press, 1963), p. 79; and Ellis Waterhouse, *Painting in Britain, 1530
to 1790,* 4th ed. (London: Penguin, 1978), p. 32.
[27] For an admirably concise discussion of the Judgment of Paris as a pas-
toral and satiric motif, see Smith, *Elizabethan Poetry,* pp. 3-8.

And with immortall goddesses was plac'd,
Intreating him to place in heaven no more
Eche wanton strumpet and lascivious whore.
[ll. 273-78]

The rapture of wine that Bacchus offers might in the hands
of a skillful Platonist conceal the rapture of philosophy, for
Socrates speaks of Dionysus as the god who inspires the
mystic fury, the second of the four levels of divine madness
(*Phaedrus*, 265b). What Bacchus offers Salmacis, though,
seems less than metaphysical; her acceptance of the three
temptations is a downward path through successive intem-
perances to complete luxury.

The covert satire of the poem would remain at this level
of generality were it not for the digression on the Court of
Astraea. There the attack on the Court of Elizabeth is so
clear that it seems probable that Beaumont's play on the
Judgment of Paris is yet another travesty of the official ico-
nography of Elizabeth, another hint that beneath the thick
paint of Court puritanism, all is not sound. But the attack is
never openly acknowledged; it must be read into the poem
by the audience, and so can be denied by the author, who
has, in addition, published the poem anonymously. Beau-
mont splits his audience between those who read his fable,
and those who read through it. This is not the split between
the public and a coterie, since Beaumont is an Inns-of-Court
gentleman addressing his like. It is a division between two
coteries, the "wanton youth" who look to the minor epic
for titillation, and the deeper wits who can apprehend his
dangerous drift. While Marston with his ever-shifting point
of view denies any stable relationship between poet and au-
dience, Beaumont is the *poeta absconditus*, anonymous, speak-
ing through a featureless mask to a closed audience with a
covert message. Privacy of meaning is elevated to the point
of denying totally to poetry its public role as a source of
either moral or experiential values.

## THE GOLDEN AGE RESTORED

The searching wit and satire of Marston and Beaumont mark the dominant style for a period of roughly five years, from 1598 to 1602, in the history of the genre. Even in that period, nonsatiric verse retained its appeal, as we can see from Hugh Holland's *Pancharis* (1603, written 1601), a lavishly produced volume complete with dedicatory verses by Ben Jonson, containing a mythological-historical-epical poem about the romance between Queen Katharine of England and Owen Tudor. While he attributes to Katharine and Owen Tudor the chastity and heroism appropriate to the progenitors of the ruling dynasty, he does not minimize the extent to which the queen's passion for her Welsh steward violates both social barriers and her private vows of mourning. Still, Holland's poem is essentially celebratory and he was prepared to present the volume to Elizabeth until her death prevented him. In the first years of the reign of James I, there is only a trickle of narrative verse, written by mediocre poets in a style closer to that of the 1560s than that of the 1590s.[28] The evidence of publication dates alone suggests a break in what was a continuous tradition of verse from 1589 to 1603. When sophisticated Stuart poets do take up the form, they employ a decorated and erotic style that constitutes a conscious return to a manner that just predates the revolt of the satirists.

While this style may recall Lodge, Shakespeare, or Marlowe, the Stuart poets seem to have thought of it as neo-Spenserian. Actually, it is an amalgamation of styles on

---

[28] I find nothing published in 1604–1606. William Barksted's *Mirrha, The Mother of Adonis* (1607) is the first of a series of clumsy "continuations" of Shakespeare's *Venus and Adonis*; it was followed by Henry Austin's *Scourge of Venus* (1613) and James Gresham's *The Picture of Incest . . . in the history of Cinyras and Myrrha* (1626). Other works notable for their ineptitude are Richard Brathwait's *Loves Labyrinth* (1615, on Pyramus and Thisbe); Leonard Digges' *The Rape of Proserpine* (1617); and Martin Parker's *Philomela* (1632).

which Spenser held no monopoly, though he practiced them all: the Petrarchism of the *Amoretti*, the pastoralism of the *Shepheards Calendar*, the mythological materials of the *Faerie Queene*. Spenser, then, became a symbol for the Elizabethan manner generally, and the Stuart minor epic is just one form among several that preserves it. In *Cynthia*, Barnfield had used the minor epic as a vehicle for the first imitation of the rhyme scheme of the *Faerie Queene*. By the time of Phineas Fletcher's *Venus and Anchises* (probably written between 1605 and 1615),[29] the poet has become sufficiently skilled in this "Spenserian" manner for a printer to palm off the work as Spenser's own.

The printed version of Fletcher's poem, dating from 1628 and titled *Brittain's Ida*, is divided into cantos and prefaced with arguments in the manner of the *Faerie Queene*. While thus presenting the poem as high matter, the printer, Thomas Walkley, also added dedicatory verses to Mary Villiers, the daughter of the Duke of Buckingham, defending the poem's eroticism as the private recreation necessary to a great mind:

> See here that stately Muse, that erst could raise,
> In lasting numbers great *Elizaes* praise,
> . . . is pleased here,
> To slack her serious flight, and feed your ear
> With *Loves* delightsom toyes; do not refuse
> These harmless sports, 'tis learned *Spencer's* Muse;
> But think his loosest *Poems* worthier then
> The serious follies of unskilful men.[30]

---

[29] Ethel Seaton, ed., *Venus and Anchises* (Oxford: Oxford University Press, 1926), pp. xxiii–iv, xxxix–xl.

[30] Reprinted in *The Works of that Famous English Poet, Mr. Edmond Spenser* (London, 1679), p. 194. For a discussion of the relative merits of the 1628 edition and the Sion College manuscript, see Elizabeth Donno, ed., *Elizabethan Minor Epics* (New York: Columbia University Press, 1963), pp. 305–7; and Seaton, *Venus and Anchises*, pp. xvi–xx. Seaton examines other candidates for "Eliza," none convincing, on pp. xxi–xxii.

An epigram drawn from Martial suggests an analogy to Vergil's *Culex*: "Accipe facundi culicem studiose Maronis, / Ne nugis positis, Arma virumque Canas." In stanzas that appear at the beginning of the Sion College manuscript of the poem (possibly closer to Fletcher's original), the poet identifies himself as Thirsil, not Cuddy—as Spenserian though not Spenser—and maintains the fiction that the poem has been commanded by Elizabeth herself:

> Thirsil . . . ganne to trye his downie Muses wing,
> For soe the fayre Eliza deign'd desire.
> Hir wishes were his lawes, hir will his fire.
>
> [1. 2. 1-5]

Printer and poet are essentially in agreement on the nature of the verse, neither serious enough to warrant a more lofty vein, nor lascivious enough to prevent its address to a great lady.

What follows is a studied re-creation of the poetic manner of 1590. The poet has turned to verse to assuage his own love-torment, though his song only heightens the fire. His dilemma is projected onto the plane of pastoral, where his persona is the shepherd Anchises. By the convention established in *Venus and Adonis* and *Hero and Leander*, Anchises is a pubescent boy, feminine in his beauty, and described with the imagery of the Petrarchan mistress:

> His lilly-cheeke might seeme an Ivory plaine,
> More purely white than frozen Apenine:
> Where lovely bashfulnesse did sweetely raine,
> In blushing scarlet cloth'd, and purple fine.
> A hundred hearts had this delightfull shrine,
>     (Still cold it selfe) inflam'd with hot desire,
>     That well the face might seeme, in divers tire,
> To be a burning snow, or else a freezing fire.
>
> [1. 6]

Like Adonis, Leander, or Narcissus, he is reluctant to woo, and the poem describes his initiation into love's mysteries. As beautiful and reluctant as the lady, and as apt and sophistic as the man, the androgynous adolescent is the perfect embodiment of both sides of the Petrarchan love dialogue.

The poem advances along a rising curve of sensual delight that obliterates the frustrated torment first of the poet and then of his Trojan proxy. When Anchises enters the Bower of Venus, he enjoys a banquet of the senses, as nature delights the eye, the ear, and the nose. The banquet is then repeated on a more intense scale as Anchises encounters Venus herself. Her voice enraptures his ear with singing, her naked beauty astonishes his eye, her breath is sweet perfume. The rest of the narrative moves teasingly toward the satisfaction of taste and touch. To mark the stages in his progress to the couch of Venus, Anchises is repeatedly overcome with sensuous rapture and falls in a swoon. The poet seizes these moments to drop the veil of pastoralism that stands between the reader and the poem's subject and to speak of his audience's own arousal:

Lower two breasts stand all their beauties bearing,
Two breasts as smooth and soft; but ah alas!
Their smoothest softnes farre exceedes comparing:
More smooth and soft; but naught that ever was,
Where they are first, deserves the second place:
  Yet each as soft and each as smooth as other;
  And when thou first tri'st one & then the other,
  Each softer seemes then each, & each then each seemes
    smoother.
                                              [3. 9]

If Fletcher sounds less like a lover than like a greengrocer hawking tomatoes, it is because of the contradictory state he finds himself in when the demand for raw immediacy becomes part of the conventional stance of the poet. To complete the paradox, Fletcher's individual act in this situation is to use the device of the passionate swoon for a moral testing of the erotic involvement of character, poet, and audience. In his rapture, Anchises is like another Trojan prince swept away by divine power—Ganymede raped by Jove in the form of an eagle. Plato's treatment of the myth perfectly illustrates its ambivalence. In the *Laws* (1. 636d) he accuses the Cretans of making up the story to excuse their own unnatural practices; but in the *Phaedrus* (255a), Ganymede is a metaphor of philosophic rapture that transcends sensuality. This second meaning was developed by Xenophon and in the Renaissance by Cristoforo Landino, and disseminated by Andraea Alciati and Natali Conti.[31] But we need not go even so far as Ganymede, for Anchises himself is beloved of a god, and in the end struck by Jove's lightning. Servius accepts the latter as a symbol of the divine afflatus, moved by Vergil's casting of Anchises in the role of prophet in Book VI of the *Aeneid*.[32] Fletcher's Anchises, like Ganymede, experiences a rapture repeatedly compared to the sight of heaven or to death and resurrection:

. . . his flitting soule to heav'n translated
Was there in starry throne, and blisse instated.
                                          [4. 2. 4–5]

Is Fletcher opening a philosophic dimension to his poem, or is the image ironic, pointing up the false heaven of sensuality? The answer comes from Venus, who tells Anchises that "Love is lifes end" (2. 8. 1), meaning it is the goal of physical existence, and playing on the notion of orgasm as the little death. She reveals, though, that it is the great death as well, the limit of the creature who fails to transcend the flesh. Perhaps to cover her self-betrayal, she hastily adds, "an end but never ending." But Fletcher is no narrow moralist

---

[31] Erwin Panofsky, *Studies in Iconology* (1939; reprint ed., New York: Harper, 1962), pp. 213–18. See also Edgar Wind, *Pagan Mysteries in the Renaissance*, rev. ed. (New York: Norton, 1968), p. 154.

[32] Servius, commentary on Vergil, *Eclogues*, 6. 1–28; *Aeneid*, 2. 649.

here; if the rapture of Anchises does not lead him to heaven
and immortality, it does lead him back to the cycle of nature:

> He gladly dies, and death new life applying,
> Gladly againe revives, that oft he may be dying.
> [6. 9. 7-8]

The ultimate ancestry of Fletcher's joking answer to the
moral challenge lies not in Plato's choice between depravity
and transcendence, but in the *Faerie Queene* and the *Aeneid*.
Fletcher's celebration of the flesh is a bawdy and humorous
recollection of the story told by his master Spenser of the
Garden of Adonis, where another mortal beloved of Venus
is forever dying, and forever alive; or of Book 6 of the
*Aeneid*, where it is Anchises himself who tells of the cycle of
regeneration.

Fletcher's search for a realm of natural sensuality again
confronts the check of morality when the poet himself ap-
proaches "love's end," in his blazon of Venus:

> But were thy Verse and Song as finely fram'd,
> As are those parts, yet should it soone be blam'd,
> For now the shameles world of best things is asham'd.
> [3. 11. 6-8]

The inability of the poet to express the beauty of Venus de-
rives not from any immorality of the subject, but from his
own immaturity and the puritanical cant of his society. Like
the Arcadia of Tasso's Golden Age chorus in *Amyntas*,
Mount Ida is a region of the senses, free of the false ideal of
honor that plagues the modern age. Indeed, in their influ-
ential commentaries on Vergil, both Landino and Sebastiano
Regoli regard antebellum Troy as a metaphor for sensual vo-
luptuousness.[33] Perhaps this offers another motive for Fletcher's

---

[33] Don Cameron Allen, *Mysteriously Meant* (Baltimore: Johns Hopkins
University Press, 1970), pp. 150, 158.

portrayal of Anchises as a pubescent androgyne. In the *Homeric Hymns*, the major classical source for his intercourse with Venus, he is a mature and self-assured ox-herder, with none of the youth and innocence which Fletcher needs for his allegorical persona.

In the self-conscious identification of verse-making and lovemaking which Fletcher makes in his blazon of Venus, he prepares for the final lifting of the pastoral veil and revelation of Anchises as his alter ego. When Anchises brags of his luck and is crippled by Jove, the poet turns to his audience and declares the lesson:

> Might I enjoy my love till I unfold it,
> I'de lose all favours when I blabbing told it:
> He is not fit for love, that is not fit to hold it.
>
> > [6. 11. 6–8]

What the gods demand of us is not chastity, but confidentiality. Fletcher's portrayal of an ethical split is exactly that of Lodge's *Scilla*, between a degenerate society and a restorative private realm of the senses, approached through art. His advance on Lodge is to give that realm a double historical identity, in the Golden Age geography of Mount Ida, and the Golden Age poetry of Elizabethan England.

Fletcher's revival of a "Spenserian" style for the minor epic is paralleled by the increased importance of Spenser's subject matter to the Stuart Court masque.[34] Arthurian legends form the basis of the entertainments sponsored by Prince Henry in 1610 and 1611, *Prince Henry's Barriers* and *Oberon*. In Ben Jonson's masque *The Golden Age Restored*, presented at Court in 1615, Jove (James) orders Astraea to

---

[34] My discussion of the Stuart masque is indebted to Stephen Orgel, *The Jonsonian Masque* (Cambridge: Harvard University Press, 1965); Richard S. Peterson, "The Iconography of Jonson's *Pleasure Reconciled to Virtue*," *Journal of Medieval and Renaissance Studies* 5 (1975):123-53; and Leah Sinanoglou Marcus, " 'Present Occasions' and the Shaping of Ben Jonson's Masques," *ELH* 45 (1978):201-25.

descend to earth attended by the "far-famed spirits of this happy isle," the poets Chaucer, Gower, Lydgate, and Spenser, and bring a new golden age of justice.[35] Jonson has cleverly appropriated for the new dynasty the symbols of Elizabethan majesty. In the process, her turbulent reign fades in the memory of the seventeenth century into a vision of Saturnian calm and simplicity toward which the Stuarts aspire, so that the movement to regain the perfection of Elizabethan verse is matched by a political claim to the reform of society as well. The Spenser thus restored is, like Elizabeth herself, remembered with decreasing accuracy, for the poetic synthesis of the early 1590s is unhinged as severely in one direction by Stuart royalists as it had been in the other direction by the Inns-of-Court satirists of the Elizabethan *fin de siècle*.

Thomas Carew bears the clearest witness to this process. In his elegy on the death of John Donne in 1630, he lamented that libertine poets:

> . . . will repeale the goodly exil'd traine
> Of gods and goddesses, which in thy just raigne
> Were banish'd nobler Poems, now, with these
> The silenc'd tales o'th'Metamorphoses
> Shall stuffe their lines, and swell the windy Page,
> Till Verse refin'd by thee, in this last Age,
> Turne ballad rime, Or those old Idolls bee
> Ador'd againe, with new apostasie.[36]

Carew partially fulfilled his own prophesy almost immediately in the opening speech of his masque *Coelum Britannicum*. Presented at Whitehall in 1634, the masque restores the lascivious gods of Ovid, only to reform them. The exemplary life of King Charles and Queen Henrietta Maria has

[35] *The Golden Age Restored*, ll. 111-16, in *Ben Jonson: The Complete Masques*, ed. Stephen Orgel (New Haven: Yale University Press, 1969).

[36] In *The Complete Poetry of John Donne*, ed. John T. Shawcross (Garden City, N.Y.: Doubleday, 1967), p. 4.

moved Jove and Hera to wonder and emulation, to purge themselves of "his wild lusts, her raging jealousies":

> He acted incests, rapes, adulteries
> On earthly beauties, which his raging queen,
> Swol'n with revengeful fury, turned to beasts,
> And in despite he retransformed to stars,
> Till he had filled the crowded firmament
> With his loose strumpets and their spurious race,
> Where the eternal records of his shame
> Shine to the world in flaming characters;
> When in the crystal mirror of your reign
> He viewed himself, he found his loathsome stains;
> And now, to expiate the infectious guilt
> Of those detested luxuries, he'll chase
> Th'infamous lights from their usurped sphere,
> And drown in the Lethean flood their cursed
> Both names and memories.[37]

To the places thus vacated in heaven, the king and queen shall in course of time proceed. A Platonized Petrarchism is asserted as the new ethical norm, dissolving in the process the fundamental conflict in the Petrarchan experience that lay at the heart of the Elizabethan style. While there is no direct evidence that the Stuart minor epic became a vehicle of government policy as the masque did, it shares the stylistic direction of the masque. It remains pastoral, decorated, and erotic, but asserts a loosely Platonist "cleanly wantonness," that amounts to a deliberate suppression of the division between public and private morality in erotic experience.

The poets writing minor epic, such as Abraham Cowley (*Pyramus* and *Thisbe*, 1633), or Shakerley Marmion (*Cupid and Psyche*, 1637), were or would be associated with Stuart

---

[37] *Coelum Britannicum*, ll. 74–88, in *Inigo Jones: The Theatre of the Stuart Court*, ed. Stephen Orgel and Roy Strong, 2 vols. (London: Sotheby Park Bernet, 1973), 2:571.

royalism. Marmion's *Cupid and Psyche* is dedicated to Charles Louis, prince elector of the Palatine (the son of the "Winter King"), and entered in the Stationer's Register on 24 June 1637, two days before Charles Louis set sail for the Continent with the aid of Charles I and the French to wage war against the emperor. While the printing seems timed to exploit a peak of public interest in the prince elector, Marmion claims in his dedication that the poem was intended for Charles Louis from its conception, and not merely dedicated after the fact. Indeed, the title page claims that the poem has been "presented to the Prince" at some unspecified date. If this is not a fabrication, and the evident care with which the volume was prepared argues that it was not, then the presentation could have taken place at any time from Charles Louis's arrival in England in November of 1635 to his departure in 1637. Just eighteen months before the poem was printed, Charles I had sent emissaries to the emperor to negotiate a marriage between Charles Louis and the emperor's daughter, and not until December, 1636 were the negotiations dropped and the ambassadors recalled.[38] The story of Cupid and Psyche would have been a highly appropriate allegorical vehicle for the events of 1636, with Charles Louis figuring as Cupid, Ferdinand's daughter as Psyche, the "Winter Queen" (who inclined toward a French alliance) as the obstructive Venus, and Charles as the Jove who brings peace and harmony at the end. The rapid shift of the wind in late 1636 would then have left Marmion to emphasize other dimensions of his allegory. In any event, the case is only circumstantial.[39]

Whether or not *Cupid and Psyche* is a poem on affairs of

[38] Samuel R. Gardiner, *A History of England from the Ascession of James I to the Outbreak of the Civil War, 1603-1642*, 10 vols. (London: Longmans, 1887), 8:99-102, 159-60.

[39] It may be worth noting that no other English poet considered Charles Louis a likely patron. Other books dedicated to the prince elector between 1635 and 1637 are on religious, political, or military affairs. Anthony van Dyck, resident at the English court from 1635 on, chose Cupid and Psyche as the subject for a painting to be hung in the queen's cabinet at Greenwich.

state, it presents itself to the reader as high matter. After the dedication come four commendatory poems, an "Argument," and "The Mitheology" or allegory, drawn mostly from Fulgentius.[40] This is extraordinary apparatus for a metamorphic poem, especially one based not on Ovid, but on Apuleius's *Metamorphoses, or the Golden Ass*. While keeping to the pastoral and Petrarchan vein, Fletcher had made tentative movements to identify *Venus and Anchises* as the apprentice work of a heroic poet. Marmion's intent is proclaimed by his friends in the commendatory verse: "A Master-piece," declares Francis Tuckyr, that "Runnes in an Epick straine," says Thomas Heywood. While Fletcher had expressed the fruit of his trifle in aside and allusion, Marmion parades his allegory publicly, much as Henry Reynolds does almost simultaneously in his *Narcissus* (appended to *Mythomyestes*) or as Sandys does in his lavish folio edition of Ovid published in 1632.

Though most of Marmion's tale is a close versification and English translation of *The Golden Ass*, he makes additions that consistently push his poem in the direction of a moralized and epic Ovid and of the Platonist interpretations of Apuleius. He begins with a brief cosmogony reminiscent of the lofty opening of Ovid's *Metamorphoses*, adds an *ekphrasis* of Cupid's quiver based on Ovid's description of the tapestry of Arachne, and (with allusions to Pythagoras) invents a metamorphosis of Psyche's wicked sister into a seagull. Cupid, he explains in "The Mitheology," is Desire, which overcomes its allegiance to Lust (Venus), and falls in love with the soul (Psyche). Apuleius never describes how Cupid, sent to punish Psyche for rivalling Venus in her beauty, comes to love her, but Marmion adds an episode showing the intervention of Themis:

> *Themis* a Goddesse, whom great *Jove* had sent
> Into the World, for good, or punishment,

[40] Fulgentius, *Mythologiae*, 3. 6, paraphrased in the influential commentary by Beroaldus on the *Golden Ass* (Bologna, 1500), bk. 4, fol. 95.

*As justice* should require, when she did heare
*Cupid* so proudly boast, againe did sweare,
That *she* his haughty malice would abate,
And turne the edge, both of his *shafts*, and *hate*.
And having thus disarm'd him, ten to one,
Would change his *fury* to *affection*.
                                                              [sig. C3ᵛ]

After a fourteen-line confession of his love, Cupid finds him-
self bereft of his armaments. The episode amounts to a Chas-
tisement of Cupid, in which the god is converted from lust
to constancy. Hence when he embraces Psyche he becomes
her instructor in chaste desire and bequeaths to her his blind-
ness:

So lets sweet *Love's preludiums* begin,
My armes shall be thy *Spheare* to wander in,
Circled about with spells, to charme thy feares.
Instead of *Morpheus* to provoke thy teares,
With horrid dreames, *Venus* shall thee entrance
With thousand shapes of wanton dalliance:
Each of thy senses thou shalt perfect find,
All but thy sight, for *Love* ought to be blind.
                                                              [sig. D3ʳ]

Drawing on Plato and the Orphica, Ficino and Pico inter-
preted Love's blindness as an allegory of that union of intel-
lect and *voluptas* that purifies the senses, otherwise befuddled
by the appetite.[41] The idea was picked up by Philippus Be-
roaldus in his commentary on Apuleius, from which it is a
short step to Marmion's proclamation in his "Mitheology"
that Psyche is prohibited from gazing on Cupid's face, "that
is, not to learn his delights and vanities: for Adam, though
he were naked, yet he saw it not, till he had eaten of the
Tree of Concupiscence."

---

⁴¹ Wind, *Pagan Mysteries*, pp. 58-59.

The trials of Psyche are similarly developed to bring Marmion's "Mitheology" into the text of Apuleius. When Psyche rises in the dark to slay Cupid, thinking he is a dragon, her mental struggle is likened to that of Eve tempted by the serpent:

> Lie still faire maide, thou mayst more honour win,
> And make thy murder glory, not a crime
> If thou wouldst kill those thoughts, that doe beslime
> And knaw upon thy breast, and never cease
> With hishing clamours to disturbe thy peace,
> When thine owne heart with *Serpents* doth abound;
> Seek not without, that may within be found.
>
> [sig. F2ᵛ]

At the sight of Cupid her love wells up, figured by the lamp that boils over and scalds the sleeping god, "for desire," "The Mitheology" tells us, "the more it is kindled, the more it burnes, and makes as it were a blister in the minde. Thus, like *Eve*, being made naked through desire, she is cast out of all happinesse, exhil'd from her house, and tost with many dangers." Her trials and adventures culminate in the descent into hell, by which is meant "the many degrees of despaire," elaborated by Marmion far beyond the account in the *Golden Ass* until it resembles yet another descent based on Apuleius, that of Sir Guyon into the Cave of Mammon in Book 2 of the *Faerie Queene*.

At the same time that Marmion is pushing his poem toward epic, it is a metamorphic, not a Vergilian model of epic that he is following, and so the poem keeps its contact with the lower genres. He makes striking use of the commonplace word or phrase to bring his heroic matter down with a comic bump. Consider Cupid's lovemaking:

> Night and her husband came, and now the sport
> Of *Venus* ended, he began to snort.
>
> [sig. F2ᵛ]

Or the sleeping habits of Venus:

> [The Hours] bring her bathes and ointments for her eyes,
> And provide Cordialls, 'gainst she shall arise.
> These play on Musick, and perfume her bed,
> And snuffe the Candle, while she lyes to read
> Her selfe asleep.
>                                         [sig. G4ᵛ]

The former passage drove Saintsbury to lament the "unnec-
essary ugliness," the "wanton discords [which] are the worst
fault of the 'Metaphysicals'—far worse than their conceits,
their want of central action, and all the other crimes com-
monly charged against them."[42] The trick surely derives
though, not from some spastic reflex of style, but from Mar-
mion's desire to keep the undertone of court satire present in
the background. His gentle mockery of the appetites of
young rakes and the ennui of great ladies is the natural ac-
companiment to the correction of public morals that makes
up the central action of the poem.

If one may venture an argument from negative evidence,
the most striking thing about Marmion's *Cupid and Psyche* is
not the presence of satire but the absence of Petrarchism. To
be sure, there is no Petrarchism in Apuleius, but neither is
there any in Ovid, the English chronicles, or the Homeric
Hymns; yet Lodge, Daniel, Beaumont, Marston, and Fletcher
all managed in their several ways to work it in. And Mar-
mion *has* worked other foreign matter into Apuleius, quite
skillfully; there is nothing tacked-on about his allegory or his
satire. In the way that humanist poets persistently mix up
text and notes, smuggling the commentary into the body,
Marmion has made his epic and moral purpose part of the
conception of the poem, changing the function of the minor
epic irrevocably even in the midst of the Stuart act of resto-

---

[42] George Saintsbury, ed., *Minor Poets of the Caroline Period*, 3 vols. (Ox-
ford: Clarendon Press, 1906), 2:28.

ration. By championing eroticism for the first time as a high and public matter, Marmion simply leaves no place for the introspection and ethical tension of Petrarch. By the same stroke, he transforms his audience from a private coterie into an embodiment of the nation and its social values. If he at times criticizes their behavior, it is to correct them, to warn them against reopening the breach between the individual's amorous longings and the moral condition of his society. He reestablishes the ethically secure relationship between the poet and his audience that was the initial foundation of humanist poetry. Hence Marmion's solution has a formal resemblance to the public voice of Gascoigne, however opposite they may be in the substance of their ethics. This similarity signals the end of the Renaissance experiment with the autonomous artifact as the vehicle of private expression and the reassertion of the social purpose of art which underlies humanist aesthetics.

By reconciling Petrarchism to narrative, the minor epic found for itself a remarkable source of stability that underlies the continual changes of its fifty-year history. While mid-Tudor narrative poets had used Ciceronian rhetoric to establish a moral community with their audience, the poets of the early 1590s discovered in the Petrarchan lyric the means of creating a private aesthetic space and built their narratives across the conflict between public and private uses of rhetoric. Their style remained the touchstone even for the turn-of-the-century satirists who carried aesthetic autonomy to its logical extreme and "made in sonnets pretty rooms," until later Stuart poets at last reopened those rooms to the public.

A guess as to *why* Petrarchism should give to the history of the minor epic such a double pattern of surface change and underlying stability requires that we see in the legacy of Petrarch not just a style, but a way of organizing a poetic audience. The formal analysis of style is finally timeless and ahistorical, and unable to tell us much about why literature develops the way it does. The mechanisms driving literary history must themselves be temporal and contemporary with the events we want to explain. What then are the temporal qualities of literature? As a string of words, a poem exists in time only as an utterance (*parole* in the current vocabulary) spoken by someone to someone else. The temporal element of poetic form is the rhetorical relationship between poet and audience that is mediated by the artifact. The peculiar role of Petrarchism was to provide the vocabulary within which Renaissance poets and their audience discussed that social relationship.

As a rhetorical process, Petrarchism contains two mechanisms of change, one general and one particular, that explain the dual nature of the history of the minor epic. The first mechanism lies in the economic and social organization of Renaissance England, particularly in the process by which an audience arose at Court, the great houses, the Inns, and the universities, that came to think of itself as the arbiter of a high literature that was clearly demarcated from the popular forms of art enjoyed by the public at large. Insofar as this high literature was an ornament to England and a rival to the literature of the Continent, its cultivation added to the claim of that coterie to be the leaders of the nation. Insofar as it dealt with private matter that might not perfectly withstand moral scrutiny, it placed that audience in an apologetic posture such as gave rise to Sidney's *Defence of Poesy*. The shift in style from Gascoigne to Lodge marks the rise of that audience, and the royalist style of the Caroline poets is a last attempt to hold it together and maintain its claim to preeminence. Petrarchism was the badge of that audience, as *fin amour* had been in the Middle Ages, a badge that marked one out for a particular mode of life as well as for a taste in verse. The assimilation of Petrarchism as its vocabulary gave the minor epic its unique position in Elizabethan literature as socially central and morally marginal, and it created a dilemma for the middle-class poet such as Daniel or Shakespeare who found himself more vulnerable morally than he could ever be secure socially.

Between 1580 and 1640, the stability of English class structure determines the underlying permanence of Elizabethan Petrarchism. But the myriad surface shifts in literary style that did occur in those years are simply too rapid to be caused by slow changes in economic and social organization. We must look for a second mechanism of change that operates on a smaller scale. And if we are to have a *literary* history of literature, as opposed to economic or social histories of literature, the factor must lie within poetry itself, on a scale as small as the individual artifact. While social classes and institutions do not have these characteristics, the individual human *consciousness* of those broader patterns can have the requisite particularity. The small-scale historical determinant of form lies in the awareness of both poet and audience of the historical and social dimensions of literature.

The stylistic changes of the minor epic are marked by a pattern wherein each poet crossed the purposes of his predecessor even as he borrowed his technical advances. What distinguishes the art of the Renaissance and earns it that name is its historical self-consciousness, its awareness that style is continually in flux and can, by general agreement, either progress or decline. The immediate consequence of this awareness is a craving for the new at all costs. To delimit for himself a place in such an aesthetic world of cognoscenti, the individual artist must identify norms based on the masters of his genre and his immediate predecessors, and strike a posture toward them. The attitude of the poet striving for innovation is inevitably antinormative, but simultaneously he asserts a new public norm composed of his own private aesthetic preferences, in place of the old "played out" style. This is what Lodge and Daniel do—so successfully that they are sometimes credited with inventing a new genre. And they do it within the vocabulary of Petrarchism because of its insistence that style is finally personal, that it varies to reflect the consciousness of the individual poet. Once such a style acquires the status of a tradition, a poet has alternatives: to see in the shifts of fashion the invalidity of any received manner, and so to proclaim that style can only be private and antinormative, as Beaumont and Marston do; or to strive to restore the previously deposed style, as Fletcher and Marmion do, and only covertly advance a new one. This process of stylistic definition, arising from the historical and social consciousness of the artist as he works within a set of aesthetic assumptions, is what gives to the history of the minor epic its shape. It is a process that may be inevitable in any continuous artistic tradition where there is a value placed on imitation and where there is a "right" and "wrong" to style.

# Chapter 3

# Marlowe, The Primeval Poet

The social dimension of Petrarchism gave poets ways to reconcile themselves to the idea that they came late in a tradition, and gave them ways to define themselves through the social group that valued that tradition. The subjective vein of Petrarchism, however, hinted at the opposite notion as well, the notion of the poet as a profound and unique original. In its characteristic as a mixed genre, the Elizabethan minor epic inevitably gave voice to both dimensions of poetry. The particular vocabulary of poetic originality, however, came not so much from Petrarchism as from the genre of primeval poetry. I say "genre" with some quibbling here, since the very word "primeval" would seem to contradict the notion of genre, and "primeval poetry" is not a familiar item on the list of Renaissance forms. But the phrase "genre of primeval poetry" must stand, for there was in fact a group of poems which Renaissance critical theory recognized as primeval, and poets could indeed imitate them without losing their own claim to originality. And the phrase stands because the notion of the primeval poem gave both poet and audience a unique frame through which to view the acts of writing and reading. In it they found a vehicle for expressing an extreme creative originality which placed both poet and reader on the outer boundary of any socially coherent literary system, and which indeed conceded to them the power to create their own alternative poetic universe.

## MARLOWE'S FURIOUS MUSE

The concept of the primeval poem requires some adjustment to our notion of what, within the terms of Renaissance

aesthetics, a poet like Christopher Marlowe was understood
to be doing. The Horatian dictum that the poet must instruct
and delight surely suits Marlowe less well than it does any
other poet of the English Renaissance, and suits *Hero and
Leander* least of all his works. Its aesthetic is Platonic—that
is, derived from the Plato of *Ion* and *Phaedrus*—for *Hero and
Leander* presents itself as an inspired poem. It is of course a
minor epic, but not so much an Ovidian or Petrarchan one
as a Musaean one. As an imitation of the *Hero and Leander* of
Musaeus, whom the sixteenth century took to be a primeval
poet and the pupil of Orpheus, Marlowe's poem is both a
product of and a commentary on the poetic and amorous
'furor' discussed by Socrates and embodied by Musaeus.
Seen as an inspired poem, *Hero and Leander* is a font of dan-
gerous and erotic paganism that nonetheless contains oracu-
lar revelations of the creative forces that underlie the uni-
verse. The fire of eloquence and the flame of desire are alike
forms of possession or madness. This possession may lift
human beings to the stars or crush them in its grip:

> Even as a bird, which in our hands we wring,
> Forth plungeth, and oft flutters with her wing,
> She trembling strove; this strife of hers (like that
> Which made the world) another world begat
> Of unknown joy.
>
> [Sestiad 2. 289-93]

The purpose of such poetry is hardly to teach, at least not to
teach anything socially constructive; nor does it bring that
moderate delight that Horace admired. Its goal is to astonish,,
to enthrall, and to puzzle.[1]

---

[1] In *Christopher Marlowe, Merlin's Prophet* (Cambridge: Cambridge Uni-
versity Press, 1977), Judith Weil discusses Marlowe's dramatic style as a
provocative and baffling mixture of allegory and nonsense. Her final view
of Marlowe, however, is not as a prophet but as an Erasmian ironist. For
an insightful discussion of enthrallment in the plays, see Michael Goldman,
"Marlowe and the Histrionics of Ravishment," in *Two Renaissance Myth-*

One may resist confessing that *Hero and Leander* is inspired, for to do so forces one to deal with all those elements whose presence makes creation so messy and whose absence makes criticism so neat. Literature as symbolic structure, as a system of signifiers, as a self-contained, self-referential entity, whether its pedigree be New Critical, Neo-Aristotelian, or semiotic, is a literature that writes itself, without conscious human agency and without the complexities and obscurities attendant upon personality and talent.[2] These are concepts of literature that devalue the poet and elevate the critic. Above all, they efface the act of creation from the poem. The Renaissance had its own way of talking about the self-creative poem: it is the voice of the Muse, or of the god. The advantage of the Renaissance vocabulary (aside from the intrinsic value of its historical relevance to such poetry as *Hero and*

---

*makers: Christopher Marlowe and Ben Jonson*, ed. Alvin Kernan (Baltimore: Johns Hopkins University Press, 1977), pp. 22-40.

[2] Cf. René Wellek and Austin Warren, *Theory of Literature* (New York: Harcourt, 1942): "No biographical evidence can change or influence critical evaluation . . . the poem exists; the tears shed or unshed, the personal emotions, are gone and cannot be reconstructed, nor need they be" (p. 74).

R. S. Crane, *Critics and Criticism* (Chicago: University of Chicago Press, 1952): "What is held constant [i.e., nonvariable] in this criticism is the whole complex of accidental causes of variation in poetry that depend on the talents, characters, educations, and intentions of individual authors, the opinions and tastes of the audiences they address, the state of language in their time, and all the other external factors which affect their choice of materials and conventions in particular works. The provisional exclusion of these is necessary if the analysis is to be concentrated upon the internal causes which account for the peculiar construction and effect of the poem qua artistic whole" (p. 20).

Michel Foucault, *The Archeology of Knowledge* (London: Tavistock, 1972), defines an *oeuvre* as "a collection of texts that can be designated by the sign of a proper name" that one imagines is "the expression of the thought, the experience, the imagination, or the unconscious of the author, or, indeed, of the historical determinations that operated upon him. But it is at once apparent that such a unity, far from being given immediately, is the result of an operation; that this operation is interpretative (since it deciphers, in the text, the transcription of something that it both conceals and manifests)" (pp. 23-24).

*Leander*) is that it paradoxically restores to us a figure of the creator as the drunken, irresponsible idiot that critics have long suspected the poet to be.

Hence to recognize *Hero and Leander* as an inspired poem is first of all to recognize Marlowe as an inspired poet. To paraphrase Duke Theseus, he is poet, lover, and madman all at once. Whatever else Marlowe may have been—Catholic convert, Protestant spy, atheist subversive, counterfeiter, scholar—he was to the Elizabethans the image of one gifted and tormented by genius. Contemporary references to Marlowe *as a poet* are unanimous in recognizing his inspiration. To Robert Greene he was one of the band of "mad and scoffing poets, that have propheticall spirits as bred of *Merlins* race."[3] To George Chapman he was the spirit "whose living subject stood / Up to the chin in the Pierian flood" (*Hero and Leander*, 3. 189-90), while Michael Drayton claimed that

> . . . *Marlowe* bathed in the *Thespian* springs
> Had in him those brave translunary things,
> That the first Poets had, his raptures were,
> All ayre, and fire, which made his verses cleere,
> For that fine madnes still he did retaine,
> Which rightly should possesse a Poets braine.
> [*Of Poets and Poesie*, ll. 105-10]

Chapman, Drayton, and even Greene are indulging in what Bernard Weinberg has called "criticism by epithets," a mode already being supplanted in the later sixteenth century, especially in Italy, by critical attitudes rooted in systematic theory.[4] It is easy enough to acknowledge such epithets, especially the claim of inspiration, and then to dismiss them as useless, but they were employed with some precision and

[3] F. S. Boas, *Christopher Marlowe* (Oxford: Clarendon Press, 1940), p. 70. Subsequent allusions to Marlowe by Greene, Thomas Kyd, and Richard Baines are as cited by Boas.

[4] Bernard Weinberg, *A History of Literary Criticism in the Italian Renaissance*, 2 vols. (Chicago: University of Chicago Press, 1961), 1:198.

consistency of meaning in the Renaissance, and cannot be passed off as mere puffery or slander. They can point to quite particular qualities of poetry and establish particular criteria for reading.[5] Not all poets won the epithet "inspired" and not all coveted to be called "mad." The mad poets, starting with the primeval poets Orpheus and Musaeus, were close to nature and to the supernatural, but in turn they lacked rule or art. They are capable of teaching the greatest wisdom, or of propagating the most dangerous lies.

Both terms of this ambivalent tradition of inspiration derive from Plato. In the *Ion*, Socrates argues that the poet is "never able to compose until he has become inspired, and is beside himself, and reason is no longer in him. So long as he has this [reason] in his possession, no man is able to make poetry or to chant in prophecy."[6] As is so often the case with Plato, it is hard to know how seriously to take this, since Socrates is jokingly proving to the self-important rhapsode Ion that neither he nor the poets he recites know what they are talking about. There is far less overt irony in the *Phaedrus*, where Socrates distinguishes between human madness, which is a physical disorder, and divine madness. Of the latter there are four kinds, the prophetic, the mystic, the poetic, and the erotic, sacred to four deities, Apollo, Bacchus, the Muses, and Aphrodite. It is through the infusion of these divine furies that the soul is led from earthly desires to the philosophical life with its reward of true wisdom.

Plato's elevation of the poetic and erotic furies had a profound impact on the place of all the arts in Renaissance society. What justification the pagan poets had in the eyes of the Church depended on its willingness to accept Plato as a

---

[5] My attempt to take seriously the Renaissance vocabulary of poetic epithets is modeled on Michael Baxandall's treatment of the epithetic criticism of painting in *Painting and Experience in Fifteenth Century Italy* (Oxford: Oxford University Press, 1972), pp. 118-51.

[6] *Ion*, 534b, trans. Lane Cooper, in *The Collected Dialogues of Plato*, ed. Edith Hamilton and Huntington Cairnes (Princeton: Princeton University Press, 1961). Subsequent citations of Plato are to this edition.

Christian without Christ, and hence to grasp the analogy between his four furies and the inspiration of the Scriptures. To Ficino the Platonic fury was the source of all knowledge of the divine, and Erasmus, in his famous remark on the *Phaedrus*, "Sancte Socrate, ora pro nobis," could even canonize Socrates. In the Vatican itself, on the ceiling of the Stanza della Segnatura, Raphael placed the figure of Poetry, "Numine Afflatur," presiding over the "Parnassus," the Platonic philosophers of the "School of Athens," and the religious mystics of the "Disputá." The English heirs of this legacy are Spenser, who draws the parallels among Parnassus, Sinai, and the Mount of Contemplation, and Milton, who makes Orpheus the type of the Christian poet in *Lycidas*.

While the inspired poet seeks like the philosopher after truth and beauty, his search is, in Plato's judgment, less controlled and less fruitful than that of the philosopher, and the ironic amusement Socrates felt with the poet in the *Ion* breaks into open hostility in the *Republic*. In Book 2 he denounces the poets for their lies about the gods and advocates the censorship of all tales of divine rebellion, lust, or metamorphosis because of their injurious effect on impressionable youths. In Book 3 he extends his attack to points of style, banning the "imitative" mode—by which he means the dramatic—in favor of the greater dignity of pure narrative. When Socrates returns to the subject in Book 10, Homer is banished along with the tragic and comic poets for employing "imitation" in the ordinary sense of the word, that is, for being bound to the realm of nature. Even the epic poets create copies of copies, and their appeal is to the senses and the baser emotions. "We can admit no poetry into our city save only hymns to the gods and the praises of good men," Socrates concludes. "For if you grant admission to the honeyed Muse in lyric or epic, pleasure and pain will be lords of your city instead of law" (*Republic* 10. 607a).

While the *Ion* won a skeptical allusion from Aristotle in

his *Poetics,*[7] the *Republic* begat two traditions of outright hostility to the *furor poeticus,* one rhetorical and one theological. The rhetorical objection is advanced by Cicero in his *De Oratore,* where he carefully demonstrates the link between eloquence and knowledge. "If we bestow fluency of speech on persons devoid of those virtues [of integrity and supreme wisdom], we shall not have made orators of them but shall have put weapons into the hands of madmen."[8] To Horace, the right poet is the good man, and he laughs in the *Ars Poetica* at those who put on the airs of inspiration. Their unkempt appearance, rudeness, and suicidal behavior are postures to disguise their lack of art. Still, the rules of art alone will not make a poet and Horace concedes that even he has felt rapture. Propounding a formula that becomes a commonplace in the Renaissance, he suggests that the best art arises from a balance between *ingenium* and *ars.*

Of Marlowe's ingenuity, we have seen, there was no doubt. Could he add to it the moderating rule of morality and art? There is a hint of such a Horatian claim in the "Mercury digression" of *Hero and Leander* when Marlowe poses as the man of learning in order to lament over the scholar's poverty. Again, in a letter to Lord Burleigh, Sir Robert Sidney reports Marlowe's arrest for counterfeiting, upon which occasion he seems to have identified himself to the authorities as a "scholar."[9] These postures need not be related to his

---

[7] "Therefore poetic art is the affair of either the gifted man or the madman" (*Poetics,* 1455a22). In *Literary Criticism, Plato to Dryden* (New York: American Book Co., 1940), pp. 117-18, Allan H. Gilbert notes a textual variant derived from Averroes and MS Riccardianus 46: "Therefore poetic art is the affair of the gifted man rather than of the madman." Lodovico Castelvetro follows the latter reading in his commentary on Aristotle, but he does not take it as an attack on Plato, since he thinks the *Ion* is ironic (Gilbert, p. 352).

[8] Cicero, *De Oratore,* 3. 14. 55, trans. E. W. Sutton and H. Rackham, Loeb ed. (London: Heinemann, 1942).

[9] The text of the letter is reprinted by R. B. Wernham in his note on "Christopher Marlowe at Flushing in 1592," *English Historical Review* 91

poetry; they may simply be attempts to secure preferment or to escape the noose. But it is interesting that Robert Greene attacks Marlowe on just these grounds, decrying those "that set the end of scollarisme in an English blank verse." The trouble with Marlowe, he suggests, is that only the show and not the substance of learning has colored his verse.

On the whole, Marlowe's inspiration appears to be of a dark kind; he is one of those whom Cicero feared would be made dangerous by their eloquence. One may wonder, in fact, if Marlowe is not Plato's first kind of madman, whose fury arises not from divinity, but from alcohol, lechery, or mental disturbance. The possibility of natural madness as the source of poetry is suggested by Horace when he calls *ingenium* the gift of both of the Muses and of Nature, and arrays it with *vesania* ("madness") in opposition to *ars*. Often in Renaissance criticism *ingenium* becomes the natural operation of an inspiration that is divine in origin, a distinction that accounted for the genius of classical poets without conceding them a status equal to a Moses or a David.[10] In his *Defence of Poetry*, Sidney distinguishes between the *vates* or divine singer, and the poet or "maker," whose imagination is the handiwork of God, but who in practice "goeth hand in hand with nature . . . freely ranging only within the zodiac of his own wit." In some cases, both the origin and operation of *ingenium* may lie within the realm of nature. J. C. Scaliger

(1976):344–45. The fact that Richard Baines was arrested with Marlowe attests, if not to his objectivity, at least to his firsthand knowledge of Marlowe's character and behavior. Sidney also records that Marlowe and Baines accused each other of intending to go over to the [Spanish Catholic] enemy. It is interesting to note that our poet's name is given as "Marly" both in the Sidney letter and a year later in the Baines note.

    [10] See, for instance, Ronald Witt, "Coluccio Salutati and the Conception of the *Poeta Theologus* in the Fourteenth Century," *Renaissance Quarterly* 30 (1977):538–63; and Baxter Hathaway's discussion of Patrizi in *The Age of Criticism: The Late Renaissance in Italy* (Ithaca: Cornell University Press, 1962), pp. 414–20. G.M.A. Grube points out that the naturalizing of inspiration is as old as Pindar; see *The Greek and Roman Critics* (Toronto: University of Toronto Press, 1965), p. 9.

observed that many poets are "aroused by the fumes of un-
mixed wine, which draws out the instruments of the mind,
the spirits themselves, from the material parts of the body.
Horace said that Ennius was such a poet, and such we con-
sider Horace himself. Tradition says the same of Alcaeus and
Aristophanes. Alcman did not escape such censure, and
Sophocles applies it to Aeschylus: 'Wine,' he said, 'not Aes-
chylus, was the author of his tragedies.' "[11]

These tendencies among humanist literary critics to de-
sanctify inspiration were encouraged by the theological hos-
tility to the *furor poeticus* that arose when the mission of the
Church to the Gentiles brought Christianity into conflict
with Hellenistic philosophy and religion. The opening salvo
comes in Paul's letter to the Romans:

> When they [the pagan Gentiles] counted them selves
> wyse, they became fooles: and turned the glorie of the
> immortall God, unto an image, made not only after the
> similitude of a mortal man, but also of birdes, and foure
> footed beastes, and of crepyng beastes. Wherefore God
> gave them up to uncleaneness, through the lustes of
> their owne heartes, to defyle their owne bodies among
> them selves. Whiche chaunged his trueth for a lye, and
> worshipped and served the creature, more then the cre-
> ator, which is to be praysed for ever. Amen. Wherefore
> God gave them up unto shamefull lustes: For even their
> women dyd chaunge the naturall use, into that which is
> agaynst nature. And likewise also, the men left the na-
> turall use of woman, and brent in their lustes one with
> another, and men with men wrought fylthynesse, and
> receaved to them selves the rewarde of their errour (as
> it was accordyng).[12]

[11] *Poeticae*, 2. 2, in *Select Translations from Scaliger's Poetics*, trans. F. M.
Padelford (New York: Holt, 1905), p. 15.
[12] Romans 1:22-27. The text is that of the "Bishops' Bible," with which
Marlowe would have been familiar. The relevance of this passage to Or-
pheus and Musaeus is pointed out by Gianfrancesco Pico della Mirandola in

What is particularly interesting here is the linkage of polytheism and homosexuality, as if in Paul's mind one depravity of nature led directly to the other. Indeed, both have been learned from a single source, the inspired poets. It was Orpheus who first instituted among the Greeks the worship of many gods, and his pupil Musaeus who, according to Diogenes Laertius (1. 3), composed the first *Theogony*. It was Orpheus also who, according to both Pausanias and Ovid, first taught the Thracians about the love of young boys.[13] "Whom, then, ye men of Greece, do ye call your teachers of religion?" asked Justin. "The poets? It will do your cause no good to say so to men who know the poets; for they know how very ridiculous a theogony they have composed."[14] Such things are inspired not by God but by the devil, who invented the Greek legends, especially those parts analogous to Christian doctrine, "to produce in men the idea that the things which were said with regard to Christ were mere marvellous tales, like the things which were said by the poets."[15]

Like Orpheus and Musaeus, Marlowe preaches homosexuality and heresy. "All they that love not tobacco & Boyes," he told Richard Baines, "were fooles." "I cover it with reverence and trembling," laments Kyd, that he said that Christ loved St. John "with an extraordinary love." If Marlowe were, like Orpheus, to found a religion, he would, reported Baines, "undertake both a more Excellent and Admirable methode" than Christianity, for "all the new testament is filthily written." Indeed, religion was first invented "only to keep men in awe."

---

his *Examen Vanitatis Doctrinae Gentium* [1520]. See D. P. Walker, *The Ancient Theology* (Ithaca: Cornell University Press, 1972), pp. 33-35.

[13] Pausanias, *Description of Greece*, 9. 30. 5; Ovid, *Metamorphoses* 10. 83-85.

[14] *Cohortatio ad Graecos*, chap. 1, in *The Ante-Nicene Fathers*, ed. Alexander Roberts and James Donaldson, 10 vols. (New York: Scribner's, 1913), 1:274. The attribution of the *Cohortatio* to Justin, though dismissed today, was accepted in the Renaissance.

[15] Justin, *Apologia Prima*, chap. 54, in *The Ante-Nicene Fathers*, 1:181.

This last charge is of course nothing Marlowe couldn't have learned out of the first book of Lucretius, and was picked up by no less than Clement of Alexandria and Lactantius to fling at their pagan adversaries.[16] As a student of theology and of the classics, Marlowe would have needed only an ounce of imagination and a pound of bravado to turn this and other such objections against Christianity itself. His sneer at the rough style of the Gospels merely inverts the incessant boast of the Fathers that their religion needs no rhetoric or sophistry to win belief. Similarly, the tract belonging to Marlowe containing "vile hereticall conceiptes denyinge the deity of Jhesus Christe or Savior," for possession of which Kyd was arrested and tortured, has been shown to consist of passages culled from a quite orthodox treatise on Arianism where they are quoted merely for refutation.[17] While no one of these lurid episodes can be certified as revealing the "real" Christopher Marlowe, they show with remarkable consistency a Marlowe that some men knew. Whether he fashioned himself as the "mad and scoffing poet," or his fellow Elizabethans merely perceived him according to a familiar frame of reference does not much matter; either way "Christopher Marlowe" is a person made up of scraps torn from the books of poets and theologians.[18]

The advantage of seeing Marlowe as the embodiment of a Renaissance behavioral type is that the type is a literary creation every bit as much as his plays and poems and is directly continuous with the persona who lies behind the works. By echoing the *Hero and Leander* of Musaeus in the

[16] Clement, *Protreptikos Pro Hellenas*, 1. 1; Lactantius, *Institutae Divinae*, 1. 22.

[17] William Dinsmore Briggs, "On a Document Concerning Christopher Marlowe," *Studies in Philology* 20 (1923):153-59.

[18] Though our conclusions are radically different, my argument about Marlovian "self-fashioning" is indebted to Stephen J. Greenblatt, "Marlowe and Renaissance Self-Fashioning," in *Two Renaissance Mythmakers*, ed. Kernan, pp. 41-69; and idem, "Marlowe, Marx, and Anti-Semitism," *Critical Inquiry* 5 (1978):291-307.

first lines of his own poem, Marlowe firmly places it in the
orbit of the primeval poet:

> On Hellespont, guilty of true love's blood,
> In view and opposite two cities stood,
> Sea-borderers, disjoin'd by Neptune's might:
> The one Abydos, the other Sestos hight.
>
> [1. 1-4]

> Sestus erat et Abydus è regione, propre mare,
> Vicinae sunt urbes.[19]

"Mousaios is indisputably the principal and direct source,"
Gordon Braden has recently concluded; "his very wording
provides Marlowe with, almost literally, his starting point."[20]
"*Almost* literally," because Marlowe has omitted Musaeus's
opening lines invoking the Muse. He begins with a line of
his own invention, "On Hellespont, guilty of true love's
blood," declaring his erotic tone and foreshadowing its tragic
outcome. Only then does he echo Musaeus, as if restoring
the Homeric pattern of *narratio* before *invocatio*, and calling
on Musaeus rather than the Muse for inspiration.

Such deference is appropriate, for, as Socrates explained to
Ion, the Muse is like a magnet, working indirectly:

> She first makes men inspired, and then through these
> inspired ones others share in the enthusiasm, and a chain

---

[19] Musaeus, *Hero and Leander*, ll. 16-17; the Latin text cited is that given
in the Aldine edition, commonly attributed to Marcus Musurus. In *The
Classics and English Renaissance Poetry* (New Haven: Yale University Press,
1978), Gordon Braden finds that "as the primary vehicle by which *Hero and
Leander* reached Renaissance readers, the Aldine translation is a distinguished
and serviceable achievement. For despite its somewhat slipshod approach to
the individual words, it is almost ferociously honest and literal about some-
thing scarcely less important, the structure of statement in the poem"
(p. 87).

[20] Braden, *The Classics*, p. 125; cf. T. W. Baldwin, "Marlowe's Musaeus,"
*Journal of English and Germanic Philology* 54 (1955):478-85.

is formed, for the epic poets, all the good ones, have their excellence, not from art, but are inspired, possessed, and thus they utter all these admirable poems. . . One poet is suspended from one Muse, another from another; we call it being "possessed," but the fact is much the same, since he is *held*. And from these primary rings, the poets, others are in turn suspended, some attached to this one, some to that, and are filled with inspiration, some by Orpheus, others by Musaeus. But the majority are possessed and held by Homer.

[*Ion* 533e-536b]

Hence inspiration is a state in the audience as well as in the poet, as Socrates proved by his own experience in the *Phaedrus* (234d). In the descriptions of Hero and Leander that follow his invocation, Marlowe's narrator—I might as well call him "Marlowe"—establishes a chain of frenzy running from Musaeus and the gods through Marlowe himself, to the audience.

The chain begins in the opening lines as Marlowe is possessed by Musaeus. Then Hero appears:

At Sestos Hero dwelt; Hero the fair,
Whom young Apollo courted for her hair,
And offer'd as a dower his burning throne,
Where she should sit for men to gaze upon.

[1. 5-8]

Marlowe's poetic fury changes to an erotic fury as he breathlessly repeats her name, and to a mystic revelation of the divine as the god Apollo, patron of the oracle and the lyre, is also caught. Marlowe then yields to his own desire to gaze on Hero and describe her beauty:

The outside of her garments were of lawn,
The lining purple silk, with gilt stars drawn;
Her wide sleeves green, and border'd with a grove,

> Where Venus in her naked glory strove
> To please the careless and disdainful eyes
> Of proud Adonis that before her lies.
>
> [1. 9–14]

As Apollo has desired not Hero herself but the metonymic hair, so Marlowe's fixation is on her splendid robes. At each link in the chain, erotic rapture is centered on substitute objects, fetishes, which are adored through the essentially passive act of gazing.[21] Venus and Adonis, as they are depicted in Hero's robes, complete the chain as the female becomes active, "striving" in her exhibitionism, and the male becomes narcissistic, "careless and disdainful."

The visual basis of erotic rapture was a Renaissance commonplace whose *locus classicus* once again was Plato. In the *Phaedrus*, Socrates explains how the flood of passion seizes the lover much as the aquiline Zeus seized Ganymede. First, love comes in at the eye:

> Part of it is absorbed within him, but when he can contain no more the rest flows away outside him, and as a breath of wind or an echo, rebounding from a smooth hard surface, goes back to its place of origin, even so the stream of beauty turns back and re-enters the eyes of the fair beloved. And so by the natural channel it reaches his [the beloved's] soul and gives it fresh vigor, . . . whereby the soul of the beloved, in its turn, is filled with love.
>
> [*Phaedrus*, 255c–d]

In his account of the mutual ravishment of Hero and Leander, Marlowe fulfills the Platonic formula point by point:

> [Hero] Vail'd to the ground, vailing her eyelids close,
> And modestly they open'd as she rose:
> Thence flew Love's arrow with the golden head,

---

[21] Braden has an insightful discussion of the interaction of *ekphrasis* and visual eroticism in *Hero and Leander* (*The Classics*, pp. 137–44).

And thus Leander was enamoured.
Stone still he stood, and evermore he gazed,
Till with the fire that from his count'nance blazed
Releting Hero's gentle heart was strook:
*Such force and virtue hath an amorous look.*

[1. 159-66]

Love at first sight is an astonishment; "So he loves," says
Socrates, "yet knows not what he loves; he does not under-
stand, he cannot tell what has come upon him; like one that
has caught a disease of the eye from another" (*Phaedrus,*
255d). He mistakes the external beauty of the beloved as the
source of his divine rapture and is incited to worship the
beloved as a deity. St. Paul was not altogether wrong to
associate unbridled passion with idolatry.

The visual rapture first aroused by Hero recurs in the bla-
zon of Leander, which also begins with a fetishistic adoration
of hair and where again the youth enthralls gods with his
beauty. While the adoration of Hero is limited to the gaze,
Leander is touched and tasted. It has frequently been sug-
gested that the physicality of Marlowe's description of Lean-
der (as opposed to his focus on Hero's clothing) is a reflec-
tion of Marlowe's homosexuality, and it may be, but its
significance in the chain of possession is more elaborate.
Marlowe never makes any distinction between the nature of
the desire directed toward Hero and that toward Leander.
They are similar objects of similar raptures and their gender
at this level is quite accidental. The shift from the blazon of
Hero to the blazon of Leander is a progression through the
substitute symbols of eroticism toward its true object, a pro-
gression that ends, inevitably, with intercourse. While Hero
is desired from afar and through her hair and ornaments,
Leander is stripped naked, exposed to the eye, his hand and
neck and breast sipped, tasted, and touched first by the gods
and then by Marlowe himself:

His body was as straight as Circe's wand;
Jove might have sipp'd out nectar from his hand.

Even as delicious meat is to the taste,
So was his neck in touching, and surpass'd
The white of Pelops' shoulder. I could tell ye
How smooth his breast was, and how white his belly,
And whose immortal fingers did imprint
That heavenly path with many a curious dint,
That runs along his back.
                          [1. 61-69]

Still, this is not full possession, but foreplay. Marlowe's
fear is precisely that Leander will play the Narcissus, that,
like the passive Hero or the proud Adonis, he will consent
only to be the object and not the actor of desire. As in Shake-
speare and Fletcher (see Chapter 2 above), the pubescent
male is the middle term between male and female, between
desire and its object. His blazon is placed in the poem be-
tween the opening adoration of Hero from afar and the final
revelation of her nakedness. He is possessed by the gods, by
Marlowe, and by "us"—the presumed male readers—and in
turn possesses Hero for us. Each actor in the chain of desire
moves from astonishment through adoration to action.

In its first few lines, *Hero and Leander* establishes itself as
a poem begot in fury and designed to incite fury. As such,
it is a model enactment of what amounts to a Renaissance
theory of reading. Those who considered poetic fury to be
the mark of the divine were eager for its ravishment. Hence
Ficino wrote to a poet friend that his songs could "rouse
both singer and audience," and Pontus de Tyard observes in
the *Solitaire Premier* that divine inspiration is transmitted
from the poet to those who recite and interpret and thence
to the audience.[22] "Such a situation," Grahame Castor con-

---

[22] Ficino, *Epistolae*, 1. 130 in *The Letters of Marsilio Ficino*, trans. members
of the Language Department of the School of Economic Science, London
(London: Shepheard-Walwyn, 1975), p. 198; Pontus de Tyard, *Solitaire pre-
mier, ou Prose des Muses, et de la fureur poëtique* (1552), p. 26. Cf. Frances
Yates, *The French Academies of the Sixteenth Century* (London: Warburg In-
stitute, 1947), pp. 77-85.

cludes, "would in any other circumstances be exceedingly dangerous. The effect of the poetic fury upon a person is very similar to that of the unbridled passions or of madness, sweeping the reason headlong in a riotous, uncontrollable tumult."[23] There were plenty who considered it dangerous in any circumstances and warned of its pernicious effects on the young and the injudicious, who, misled by the resemblance of the poetic and erotic furies, would be aroused by the poets to erotic acts. Bernard Weinberg summarizes his discussion of the Platonic tradition in sixteenth-century Italian criticism by observing that "the opponents of poetry . . . assume that one reason why poetry is dangerous is that it exercises upon the reader or hearer a kind of irresistible power, a superior rhetorical force which sways his passions and imposes upon him the teachings of the poem."[24]

In its inverted way, then, the idea of inspiration grows in the Renaissance from an epithet into a theory—a theory for discussing poetry that is essentially emotional in its appeal and therefore potentially antisocial, a theory able to account for pornographic and subversive literature. That this theory was chiefly advanced by the enemies of poetry is of little consequence, for anyone likely to write such verse would not likely be reluctant to fulfill the worst suspicions of the greybeards. For the modern reader, the appeal of such a theory is that it comes closer than our usual accounts of Renaissance poetics to describing that combination of delight and strangeness that makes *Hero and Leander*, alone among the Elizabethan minor epics, still widely read today. It lets us talk about desire as well as meaning in the text, which seems particularly appropriate for a poem that not only arises from fury but examines fury throughout.

The revelation of the nature of poetic and erotic fury begins in the contrary movements of the opening description of Hero. Marlowe describes a perfectly eroticized universe

---

[23] Grahame Castor, *Pléiade Poetics* (Cambridge: Cambridge University Press, 1964), p. 36.

[24] Weinberg, *Italian Renaissance*, p. 294.

with Hero at the center, but when among the ornaments that adorn her body he comes to her shoes, "such as the world would wonder to behold," he suddenly shifts his posture. In a ludicrous image he describes how they are filled with water to "chirrup" as Hero walks about; his hyperbolic fetishism breaks down into a comic absurdity that releases erotic tension.

The description of Leander similarly confronts nagging questions about the nature of love's rule. While Hero sat passively on the throne of Apollo, Leander actively controls those who adore him:

> Had wild Hippolytus Leander seen,
> Enamour'd of his beauty had he been;
> His presence made the rudest peasant melt,
> That in the vast uplandish country dwelt.
> The barbarous Thracian soldier, mov'd with nought,
> Was mov'd with him, and for his favour sought.
>                                     [1. 77-82]

As the male beloved, Leander, not his suitor, rules and the erotic furor he inspires is, like the poetic furor of Thracian Orpheus, an ordering and civilizing force. Still, hovering over the entire blazon is a sense of doom, suggested by the fate of Narcissus or of Pelops and explicitly invoked at the outset:

> Amorous Leander, beautiful and young,
> (Whose tragedy divine Musaeus sung) . . .
>                                     [1. 51-52]

The paradox of fury is that it can beget barbarity as well as tame it. Orpheus himself is ripped to shreds by the Bacchantes when they are mad with wine.

When in the next section we enter an entire city in the grip of passion, Hero's position as the adored icon becomes such a source of violence. The section opens again with false worship, the festival of Adonis at Sestos, and again idolatry is an occasion for sexual arousal:

> Thither resorted many a wand'ring guest
> To meet their loves; such as had none at all,
> Came lovers home from this great festival.
>
> [1. 94-96]

As Hero is worshipped on her throne, she assumes the haughty control over her suitors that characterized Leander and Adonis. But where Leander's amorous control had assuaged violence, Hero's incites it:

> Even as, when gaudy nymphs pursue the chase,
> Wretched Ixion's shaggy-footed race,
> Incens'd with savage heat, gallop amain
> From steep pine-bearing mountains to the plain:
> So ran the people forth to gaze upon her.
>
> [1. 113-17]

Again, as the beloved rides the crest of fury, Marlowe calms the overwrought passions with irony and absurdity:

> So at her presence all surpris'd and tooken
> Await the sentence of her scornful eyes;
> He whom she favours lives, the other dies.
> There might you see one sigh, another rage,
> And some (their violent passions to assuage)
> Compile sharp satires, but alas too late,
> For faithful love will never turn to hate.
> And many seeing great princes were denied,
> Pin'd as they went, and thinking on her died.
>
> [1. 122-30]

In these three sections, then, the dynamics of the text are established: the lovers are placed at the crossroads where desire leads either toward fulfillment and satisfaction or toward violence and death. At this moment, as so often happens in the minor epic, the poet introduces an *ekphrasis*, describing the mosaic or "Venus' glass" that decorates her temple. It is of course a condensed image of all that has been told through character and narrative, a revelation of the nature of erotic fury:

> There might you see the gods in sundry shapes,
> Committing heady riots, incest, rapes:
> For know, that underneath this radiant floor
> Was Danae's statue in a brazen tower,
> Jove slyly stealing from his sister's bed,
> To dally with Idalian Ganymede,
> Or for his love Europa bellowing loud,
> And tumbling with the Rainbow in a cloud,
> Blood-quaffing Mars, heaving the iron net
> Which limping Vulcan and his Cyclops set;
> Love kindling fire, to burn such towns as Troy.
>                                        [1. 143-53]

One need not linger over these ominous images except to note that they recount the very tales of heavenly crimes for which Plato banished the poets from his Republic. What is startling and unusual is the way that Marlowe refuses to set off the action of the poem from the *ekphrasis*; instead of being a distancing device, it is a device of enthrallment, for "in the midst a silver altar stood, / There Hero sacrificing turtles' blood" (1. 157-58). Literally Marlowe means that Hero and her altar are in the midst of the floor decorated by the mosaic, but the effect is to place her in the midst of the "heady riots, incest, rapes." At that moment, in an unparalleled economy of seven lines, both Hero and Leander are seized by love.

The immediate result of their desire, as we have seen, is to deify the beloved:

He kneel'd, but unto her devoutly pray'd;
Chaste Hero to herself thus softly said:
'Were I the saint he worships, I would hear him.'
                                         [1. 177-79]

She offers up herself a sacrifice,
To slake his anger, if he were displeas'd.
O what god would not therewith be appeas'd?
                                         [2. 48-50]

Now Socrates has dealt throughout the *Phaedrus* with just
this possibility of mortals rising through the power of frenzy
to communion with the gods. And he has lingered time and
time again on the link between this religio-erotic fury and
the power of speech, both the philosopher's dialectic and the
poet's madness. The link is important because the subject of
the *Phaedrus* is ultimately not love or madness but language;
it examines how the philosopher pursues the dialectic only
to abandon it in an ecstatic vision. The dialogue is ironic in
that the putative subject of Socrates' speech is the question
of whether a young man should love another who loves him
in return, or should love another who does not love him.
Phaedrus has recited the speech by Lysias in favor of the
latter proposition. Socrates has demolished it and given a
better one defending the same position, only to switch sides
finally and praise mutual love. The rhetorical combat thinly
veils a struggle between Lysias and Socrates for the love of
Phaedrus himself, whom the philosopher hopes to lead by
the power of his words from an appetite for the flesh to the
higher lust for the divine.

Similar subtleties circulate through Marlowe's text. The
immediate effect of love on Leander is to forge in him the
link between dialectic, desire, and divinity:

The air with sparks of living fire was spangled,
And Night, deep-drench'd in misty Acheron,

Heav'd up her head, and half the world upon
Breath'd darkness forth (dark night is Cupid's day).
And now begins Leander to display
Love's holy fire, with words, with sighs and tears,
Which like sweet music enter'd Hero's ears,
And yet at every word she turn'd aside,
And always cut him off as he replied.
At last, like to a bold sharp sophister,
With cheerful hope thus he accosted her.
[1. 188-98]

While Leander then sails into a hundred-line fantasia of aphorisms and arguments persuading Hero to love, Marlowe has himself been already seized by "love's holy fire." Here and with obsessive frequency through the narrative he makes dangerous leaps of imagery between the earth and heavens. In the Introduction we saw that such catachretic images, violently yoking unrelated objects, are particularly suited for Marlowe's ambiguous mixture of praise and blame. It is worth adding that the catachretic image was particularly associated with prophetic poetry.[25] These occur over and over at moments of rapture in the text, and with them come bundles of aphorisms:

It lies not in our power to love, or hate,
For will in us is over-rul'd by fate.
When two are stripp'd, long ere the course begin,
We wish that one should lose, the other win;
And one especially do we affect
Of two gold ingots like in each respect.
The reason no man knows: let it suffice,
What we behold is censur'd by our eyes.
Where both deliberate, the love is slight;
Who ever lov'd, that lov'd not at first sight?
[1. 167-76]

---

[25] Rosemond Tuve, *Elizabethan and Metaphysical Imagery* (Chicago: University of Chicago Press, 1947), pp. 130-33.

Like the *ekphrasis* just preceding it, the aphorisms seem to be devices not of distance but of passionate insight—"saws of might," Rosalind calls them—encapsulating wisdom wrung by Marlowe from his moment of vision. And what judgment does he make in his moment of passion but that passion must always overrule judgment. So Leander reasons with Hero, who yields to his arguments "that was won before." Seeking to conceal her passion, she describes her tower. " 'Come thither.' As she spake this, her tongue tripp'd, / For unawares 'Come thither' from her slipp'd" (1. 357-58). At every level, speech is subordinate to desire.

This ravishment of the text is crucial to what we make of the "Mercury digression," for Marlowe there confronts most directly the question of whether his lovers will attain death or divinity, and most clearly tempts us with the possibility that his poem will achieve a prophetic strain. Clearly it is in some way parallel to the story of Hero and Leander itself. Like Apollo, Mercury is captivated by a mortal girl "Whose careless hair, instead of pearl t'adorn it, / Glister'd with dew" (1. 389-90), and like Leander woos her "with smooth speech." Again like Leander, he is himself the object of desire, for the Destinies dote upon him. At first words are a means to control erotic violence, for when Mercury is about to rape the country maid, she cries out and "Herewith he stay'd his fury," and instead wins her with fair speeches. When Mercury is punished by Jove for stealing a draught of nectar for her, his glibness persuades Cupid to make the Destinies love him.

> They granted what he crav'd, and once again
> Saturn and Ops began their golden reign.
> Murder, rape, war, lust and treachery
> Were with Jove clos'd in Stygian empery.
> [1. 455-58]

Again the control of fury is brief, for the "careless and disdainful" Mercury neglects the Destinies, their love is turned to spite, and Jove is returned to power. Likewise Leander is inattentive to the seductive advances of Neptune, who as a result "in his heart revenging malice bare" (2. 208).

There is, in a sense, no limit to how this may be construed. One may, for instance, attempt a Neoplatonist reading by pondering on the peculiar choice of Mercury as protagonist, for Mercury of all the male Olympians is least involved in sexual escapades. If one is guided by the Musaean atmosphere of the tale, one will recall Plato's claim that Musaeus was the poet who best revealed the fate of souls in the other world (*Republic* 2. 363c), or the statement of Diodorus Siculus that Musaeus officiated at the Eleusinian mysteries (4. 25. 1). "Musaeum ante omnis," declared Vergil in the sixth book of the *Aeneid* when Musaeus pointed the way for Aeneas to the Elysian fields. The Church Fathers (including Justin, Clement, and Lactantius) never tired of noting on the evidence of the pseudo-Orphic *Testament* that Orpheus had visited Egypt, learned the teaching of Moses from Hermes (or Mercury) Trismegistus, and led his pupil Musaeus to a recantation of polytheism.[26] Boccaccio even notes the speculation begun by Eusebius that the name Musaeus conceals that of Moses himself.[27] Hence Mercury appears in *Hero and Leander* in his role of *psychopompos* to bring the soul (the country maid) to the upper world and bequeath to it the gift of divine knowledge, which is most commonly figured as nectar. Mercury is clearly Christ himself, who wins the soul by his fair words (the Gospel), but then is crucified ("thrust down from heaven"). Aided by the love of God the Father, who can be known only dimly to the pagan mind as

[26] Pseudo-Justin, *Cohortatio*, 15; Clement, *Protreptikos*, chap. 7; Tatian, *Oratio adversus Graecos*, chap. 8; Theophilus, *Ad Autolycum*, 3. 2; Lactantius, *Institutae Divinae*, 1. 5. The history of the *Testament* is recounted by D. P. Walker, *The Ancient Theology*, pp. 26–33. See also Otto Kern, *Orphicorum Fragmenta* (Berlin, Weidmann, 1922), frr. 245–47.

[27] *Boccaccio on the Art of Poetry* (*Genealogia Deorum Gentilium*, bks. 14–15), trans. Charles G. Osgood (Princeton: Princeton University Press, 1930), pp. 46, 163; cf. Eusebius, *Praeperatio Evangelicae*, 9. 27; and Kern, *Orphicorum Fragmenta*, test. 44.

Destiny, Christ triumphs over Satan (Jove, chief of the pagan gods), and, reunited with the soul, dwells in everlasting bliss. Hence Marlowe, like Musaeus, has under the veil of his erotic paganism concealed the most holy truths of Christian orthodoxy.

Obviously I do not mean this to be taken seriously as an interpretation of *Hero and Leander*. I do mean it seriously as an illustration of "how doubtfully all Allegories may be construed." Spenser's phrase recalls the fundamental problem of the inspired poem that Plato pointed out: the poet is out of his mind and doesn't know what he is saying. How then can we know what he is saying? An inspired poem may be opaque, concealing the most sacred and secret mysteries beneath a veil that is impenetrable to the common understanding, and so requiring an elaborate exegesis. Marlowe, on the other hand, is above all transparent. However ambivalent many of the things he describes may be, he is without ambiguity; all is seen in crisp and sure outline. To Drayton, "his raptures were, / All ayre, and fire, which made his verses cleere."

Insofar as Marlowe's verse is clear it demands no exegesis, and insofar as it is demented its fury is quite simply beyond the control of the exegete. There is no way to pin down a single lost or hidden meaning, either orthodox or heretical, for the poem—like one by Orpheus, Musaeus, or Ovid—tells lascivious stories of the pagan gods, but in the process it exposes the moral failings of those gods to mocking laughter. Marlowe is always downwind of the law. *Doctor Faustus* works in much the same way, for all its impeccable orthodoxy, since it is, like an apology by Justin or Clement, our best source of the very sins it purports to refute. So too *Tamburlaine*: to argue that the play is orthodox, one must imagine that Tamburlaine is punished either by Providence or Nature for "daring God out of Heaven" when he burns the Scripture. But the book he burns is the Koran and the God he defies is Allah; these are arguably the very things in the play of which a rabid Christian might most approve. If the wise reader can find in such works the truths of Christianity, this is evidence not of the author's orthodoxy but of, quite simply, a miracle. Though Jerome had objected to the wresting of pagan verses to disclose pious meanings they never intended, Coluccio Salutati could quite confidently declare that such truths are placed there by the Holy Spirit without the awareness or understanding of the infidel poet.[28] But no more miraculous is the career of Tamburlaine himself, the scourge of God, who rescued Christian Europe from the Turk without the least pious intention.

   Those of us who suspect that such critical miracles are, to use Marlowe's phrase, "mere jugglery" may recall Milton's claim that the right poet is "simple, sensuous, and passionate." To Milton, poetry seems closer to the grace and ornament of rhetoric than to the closely woven topics of logic, and its very openness best shows its "glorious and magnificent use . . . both in divine and human things."[29] One can, if one must, search any text, sacred or profane, for the dense statements of logic, and any text, *sub specie aeternitatis*, can be made orthodox, as a praise of virtue or an exposure of vice. But Marlowe's text, when read in the present tense as impassioned speech, simply refuses to admit the kind of abstracted allegorization that I attempted. To reveal the lesson of our parable, the "Mercury digression" turns away from the act of explanation it began. First Marlowe uses it to explain, rather irrelevantly, why all scholars are poor. Then he instructs us to "muse not Cupid's suit no better sped, / Seeing in their loves the Fates were injured" (1. 483-84). Yet the Fates are no less fickle, irrational, and moody in their behavior than the things they are used to explain. The digression is just one of a series of false aetiologies in the poem, explaining why Cupid is blind, why half the world is

---

[28] Witt, "Coluccio Salutati," 555-56. Witt notes that Salutati's opinion changed over the years; that cited dates to c. 1390.

[29] John Milton, *Of Education,* in *Complete Poems and Major Prose,* ed. Merritt Y. Hughes (New York: Odyssey Press, 1957), p. 637.

black, or why the moon is pale. There is no escaping from the world of passion into the world of logic.

The argument between those who impose moral allegory on pagan poets and those who damn them at their word is a debate between two different concepts of written language. One finds it opaque and responsive to exegesis; the other finds it clear, a similitude of the inspired Word of God, be it true (as for Milton) or false (as for Marlowe), with a fullness, presence, and literalness of meaning. In concluding the *Phaedrus*, Socrates makes a similar distinction between the absence of written language and the presence of the spoken word:

> Then anyone who leaves behind him a written manual, and likewise anyone who takes it over from him, on the supposition that such writing will provide something reliable and permanent, must be exceedingly simple-minded; he must really be ignorant . . . if he imagines that written words can do anything more than remind one who knows that which the writing is concerned with . . . written words . . . seem to talk to you as though they were intelligent, but if you ask them anything about what they say, from a desire to be instructed, they go on telling you just the same thing forever. And once a thing is put in writing, the composition, whatever it may be, drifts all over the place, getting into the hands not only of those who understand it, but equally those who have no business with it.
>
> [*Phaedrus* 275c-e]

The language of presence, "living speech," is inspired speech; in the context of the *Phaedrus*, Socrates refers to the words of the dialogue itself, inspired by the deities of the place where Socrates and Phaedrus sit, and by the love between the two men. If Marlowe's poetry denies its opacity, its interpretability, and its orthodoxy, it becomes present, clear, arresting, and—because it speaks of false gods—damnable. As ordinary written speech, it is sibylline in its ambiguity; as an inspired poem, the similitude of impassioned speech, it means what it says. The furious poem is the perfectly self-referential artifact; the idea of inspiration has restored the creator to the poem only to have him swallowed by his creation.

Let me put it another way. The point of Plato's account of the four furies was to tell Phaedrus what he had to go through before he could escape the world of strife, the conflict of the noble and wicked steeds, and the struggle of the dialectic. Marlowe places his lovers again and again in the midst of strife and shows that there is no escape. The nature of erotic fury is to make the promise of transcendence and then to turn into violent struggle. The loves of the gods yield "Mars, heaving the iron net." Neptune adores Leander and drowns him. If Hero and Leander seemed, like Mercury and his maid, to be innocent of the sexual violence practiced by Jove and Mars, they are revealed in their moment of consummation to be no different after all. First Leander is like the son of Jove:

> Leander now, like Theban Hercules
> Enter'd the orchard of th'Hesperides,
> Whose fruit none rightly can describe but he
> That pulls or shakes it from the golden tree.
>                                     [2. 297-300]

Then the two appear as Mars and Venus, trapped by the jealous Apollo:

> For much it griev'd her that the bright daylight
> Should know the pleasure of this blessed night,
> And them like Mars and Erycine display'd,
> Both in each other's arms chain'd as they lay'd.
>                                     [2. 303-6]

Hero, Mercury and Jove all embrace pleasure based on the crime of theft:

> But far above the loveliest Hero shin'd,
> And stole away th'enchanted gazer's mind.
>
> [1. 103-4]

> Jove slyly stealing from his sister's bed,
> To dally with Idalian Ganymede . . .
>
> [1. 147-48]

> He [Mercury] ready to accomplish what she will'd,
> Stole some [nectar] from Hebe (Hebe Jove's cup fill'd)
> And gave it to his simple rustic love.
>
> [1. 433-35]

With each theft comes retribution. The lovers are caught in an up-and-down cycle as they are loved by the gods, elevated, adored, and plunged down again. Each elevation is a moment of revelation into the mysteries of passion that their simple minds had not dreamed of, as when Leander protests to Neptune that " 'You are deceive'd, I am no woman, I.' / Thereat smil'd Neptune" (2. 192-93). The power of Neptune, like the power of the waves that will finally drown Leander, is an erotic force not to be limited by Leander's pretty face or words. The world of the poem is epitomized in those lines cited at the beginning of this chapter, which bear repeating:

> Even as a bird, which in our hands we wring,
> Forth plungeth, and oft flutters with her wing,
> She trembling strove; this strife of hers (like that
> Which made the world) another world begat
> Of unknown joy.
>
> [2. 289-93]

If Marlowe's poetics are Platonic, his cosmology is not. As in a mystical experience, the moment of fullest rapture is the moment of fullest knowledge, but the cosmos these lovers uncover is a purely physical and self-generative universe of Empedoclean strife.[30] What Empedocles actually thought and said is lost to us, but one fragment is recorded by Simplicius:

> And these things never cease from continual shifting, at one time all coming together, through Love, into one, at another each borne apart from the others through Strife.[31]

Marlowe would make only one emendation: the two universal forces of Love and Strife, one creative and one destructive, are identical.

Let me take as an emblem for this universe the last words of the poem *Desunt nonnulla*, "something is lacking." Of course, these words belong not to Marlowe but to the printer Edward Blunt. Marlowe's last image is of Hero revealed in her nakedness to Leander:

> So Hero's ruddy cheek Hero betray'd,
> And her all naked to his sight display'd,
> Whence his admiring eyes more pleasure took
> Than Dis, on heaps of gold fixing his look.
> By this Apollo's golden harp began
> To sound forth music to the Ocean,
> Which watchful Hesperus no sooner heard,
> But he the day's bright-bearing car prepar'd,
> And ran before, as harbinger of light,

[30] The best discussions of Marlovian cosmology are D. J. Palmer's essay on "Marlowe's Naturalism," in *Christopher Marlowe*, ed. Brian Morris (New York: Hill and Wang, 1968), pp. 153-75 (especially for the plays); and Myron Turner, "Pastoral and Hermaphrodite: A Study in the Naturalism of Marlowe's *Hero and Leander*," *Texas Studies in Literature and Language* 17 (1975):397-414 (with an interesting discussion of Leander's bisexuality).

[31] G. S. Kirk and J. E. Raven, *The Pre-Socratic Philosophers* (Cambridge: Cambridge University Press, 1957), p. 324.

And with his flaring beams mock't ugly Night,
Till she, o'ercome with anguish, shame, and rage,
Dang'd down to hell her loathsome carriage.
                                                    [2. 323-34]

The poem breaks off as it began, with scopophilia, the universal gaze linking human beings to the spheres amid the contrary movements of adoration and laughter. Blunt's words are an act of interpretation and, I think, a correct one.[32] There is no way for such a poem to be complete, no way to release the lovers, the poet, the reader. For something besides an ending is lacking from the poem—any sense of serenity, harmony, or rest.

Perhaps "unfinished" is the wrong word for *Hero and Leander*; perhaps "fragmentary" would be more apt. If Marlowe really is imitating the primeval poets, what—and this is sheer speculation—would be more correct than an Empedoclean fragment?[33] After all, a legend existed in his lifetime that Michelangelo had carved a statue of Bacchus, knocked off its arm, and buried it.[34] When it was "discovered" and celebrated as an archeological find, he stepped forward to

---

[32] Since Louis Martz's edition of *Hero and Leander* (Washington, D.C.: Folger Library, 1972), the idea has taken hold that Marlowe's poem is finished, a thesis now endorsed by the *Norton Anthology*. There is no positive external evidence in its favor, and it requires the dismissal of Blunt's repeated assertion to the contrary. Martz's case is based on a formal analysis that finds in the poem "a symmetrical, triadic design" with "the structure of a triptych," the meeting and consummation of the lovers forming two side panels with the Mercury digression as the center panel. As is evident from my suggestion that the poem may be "finished" but incomplete, I do not find the unity, balance, and control Martz does. The imperfection of Martz's analogy is worth noting: the wings of his triptych are too wide to close. With Martz's characterization of Chapman's poem as a "poetical commentary upon Marlowe's treatment of the legend," I have no quarrel.

[33] For that matter, Marlowe may have composed any number of "Lost Works." In the *Ion*, Socrates quotes a few lines from the "unpublished verse" of Homer.

[34] Edgar Wind, *Pagan Mysteries in the Renaissance*, rev. ed. (New York: Norton, 1968), pp. 180-81.

receive credit as the equal of the antique artists. So perhaps Marlowe left the poem unfinished on purpose; perhaps even the famous misarrangement of lines in the consummation passage is a deliberate mutilation. Or perhaps he did manage after all to get himself killed before he could bring Hero and Leander to their intended deaths. Either way, we may place as his epitaph Horace's last words on the inspired poet:

> I'll tell the tale of the Sicilian poet's end.
> Empedocles, eager to be thought a god immortal,
> coolly leapt into burning Aetna. Let poets have
> the right and power to destroy themselves.[35]

## CHAPMAN'S LEARNED FIRE

To argue that *Hero and Leander* is in any way finished would seem to dethrone George Chapman's four sestiads from their position as the best available ending to the poem. I suspect that the opposite is true, for Chapman, the translator of Homer, Hesiod, and Musaeus, and the affector of prophetic airs in the *Shadow of Night*, knew more about inspired poetry than anyone else in Renaissance England. Someone able to penetrate the conundrum of *Ovids Banquet of Sense* would not be puzzled by an oracular trifle like *Hero and Leander*. Chapman's invocation of Marlowe in the third sestiad demonstrates clearly enough that he knew what game was afoot:

> Then thou most strangely-intellectual fire,
> That proper to my soul hast power t'inspire
> Her burning faculties, and with the wings
> Of thy unsphered flame visit'st the springs
> Of spirits immortal; now (as swift as Time
> Doth follow Motion) find th'eternal clime

[35] Horace, *Ars Poetica*, ll. 463–66, trans. H. Rushton Fairclough, Loeb ed. (London: Heinemann, 1926).

Of his free soul, whose living subject stood
Up to the chin in the Pierian flood,
And drunk to me half this Musaean story,
Inscribing it to deathless Memory:
Confer with it, and make my pledge as deep,
That neither's draught be consecrate to sleep.
Tell it how much his late desires I tender
(If yet it know not), and to light surrender
My soul's dark offspring, willing it should die
To loves, to passions, and society.[36]

With teasing ambiguity, Chapman suggests that a divine
fury flows from the "Pierian flood" sacred to Apollo and the
Nine, a suggestion echoed by the "unsphered flame" of
Chapman's own "strangely-intellectual fire." On the other
hand, the alcoholic overtones of "drunk," "pledge," and
"draught" suggest a less holy sort of frenzy, as does Chap-
man's claim that the fire is "proper to my soul." If Chap-
man's inspiration is divine in origin, he at least hints that it
may be natural in its operation, and if (as he remarks in the
dedicatory epistle) he acquires a "strange instigation" from
Marlowe's verse, he is the possessor of his own fire and not
wholly derivative of the inspiration of his predecessor.

Chapman's invocation, then, is a declaration of the rela-
tion of his poem to Marlowe's, a declaration simultaneously
of dependence and independence; he drinks from the same
spring as Marlowe, but his draught is his own.[37] What he

[36] *Hero and Leander*, 3. 183-98. Chapman's poem is regularly included in
editions of Marlowe, as is the case here. All references are to the MacLure
edition of Marlowe (see "A Note on Texts").

[37] I must state explicitly my affiliation with three insightful Chapman
scholars, to all of whom I am indebted, even though their positions on *Hero
and Leander* are contradictory, if not mutually exclusive. I have relied heavily
on D. J. Gordon's analysis of the meaning of "form" and "Ceremony" in
"The Renaissance Poet as Classicist: Chapman's *Hero and Leander*," in *The
Renaissance Imagination*, ed. Stephen Orgel (Berkeley: University of Califor-
nia Press, 1975), pp. 116-29. I accept Raymond Waddington's view in *The
Mind's Empire: Myth and Form in George Chapman's Narrative Poems* (Balti-

declares outright in the invocation is scarcely more oblique
in his opening lines:

New light gives new directions, fortunes new,
To fashion our endeavours that ensue;
More harsh (at least more hard) more grave and high
Our subject runs, and our stern Muse must fly;
Love's edge is taken off, and that light flame,
Those thoughts, joys, longings, that before became
High unexperienc'd blood, and maids' sharp plights,
Must now grow staid, and censure the delights,
That being enjoy'd ask judgment; now we praise,
As having parted: evenings crown the days.
                                         [3. 1-10]

The studied ambiguity of the paragraph lies in the syntactic
puzzle of line 8: the verbal phrases "grow staid" and "cen-
sure the delights" appear at one glance as imperatives to the
reader, who must now put off his delight at the lovers and
join in the "grave" sentiment of the poet. Actually, their
subject is the string of nouns describing the erotic joys of
Hero and Leander: "thoughts, joys, longings." Chapman
shifts the tone of the poem simply because it is the nature of
desire to recoil on itself in judgment and censure. Nothing
arbitrary is being imposed on the poem, he insists. He "ten-

---

more: Johns Hopkins University Press, 1974), pp. 153-80, that Chapman is
correcting Marlowe. Although I place both of them in a Musaean context
rather than the Ovidian context Waddington suggests, I am at some pains
to show that Ovid himself can be located in the Musaean tradition. While
I have disagreed with John Huntington's thesis about the stylistic similarity
of Marlowe and Chapman, I have repeatedly had recourse to his description
of the irony of Chapman's poetry. He alone has seen that the density of
Chapman's language is an active force in the poem and not just a fog to be
pierced by the lantern of learning. See "Condemnation and Pity in Chap-
man's *Hero and Leander*," *English Literary Renaissance* 6 (1977):307-23; and
"The Serious Trifle: Aphorisms in Chapman's *Hero and Leander*," *Studies in
the Literary Imagination* 11 (1978):107-13.

ders" Marlowe's desires, either holding them tender, or presenting them formally in the act of publication, "they" being both Marlowe's desires or intentions for the poem and his erotic desires as expressed in the poem. The changes are part of an inevitable natural process: "evenings crown the days." If Marlowe is the demented poet, then Chapman's right to revise is based on his fuller knowledge of the world. No less inspired than Marlowe, he claims to add wisdom to his verse as well.

Corollary to the turn in erotic force from delight to gravity is a development in the nature of erotic language, in which an opaque language allowing ironic distance and the play of judgment replaces the impassioned clarity of Marlowe's verse:

> And as amidst th'enamour'd waves [Leander] swims,
> The god of gold of purpose gilt his limbs,
> That this word gilt including double sense,
> The double guilt of his incontinence
> Might be express'd, that had no stay t'employ
> The treasure which the love-god let him joy
> In his dear Hero, with such sacred thrift
> As had beseem'd so sanctified a gift;
> But like a greedy vulgar prodigal
> Would on the stock dispend, and rudely fall
> Before his time, to that unblessed blessing,
> Which for lust's plague doth perish with possessing.
> *Joy graven in sense, like snow in water wastes;*
> *Without preserve of virtue nothing lasts.*
> [3. 23-36]

The "god of gold" is Phoebus, lord of that new light which has given new directions. As he enviously exposed Mars and Venus when they lay together, so he has at the end of Marlowe's verses interrupted Hero and Leander, and now in the commencement of Chapman's his new light is "of purpose" used to expose shadowed meanings. The sensual surface of language dissolves "like snow in water" to reveal truth preserved in virtuous aphorism.

While Renaissance ideas of reading presumed that an inspired text could rouse the impressionable reader to heresy, lust, or sedition, a second basic assumption held that "others are quite capable of resisting, and hence are out of danger . . . the old and the wise, blessed with intelligence, refuse to be duped by appearances and extract from the core of poetry the most abstruse and recondite teachings."[38] Chapman's novel project is not to reject the lascivious reader on behalf of the wise, but to turn the one into the other:

> And now ye wanton Loves and young Desires,
> Pied Vanity, the mint of strange attires,
> Ye lisping Flatteries and obsequious Glances,
> Relentful Musics and attractive Dances,
> And you detested Charms constraining love,
> Shun love's stol'n sports by that these lovers prove.
> [3. 11–16]

Every noun in his catalogue is inflected with an adjective: "wanton," "young," "Pied," "strange," and so forth. Chapman's battle is not with the nouns themselves, the "Loves" and "Desires," the "Musics" and "Dances" (though admittedly it is with "Flatteries" and "Glances")—that is, not a quarrel with sense and appearance in themselves, but with how they are understood, and consequently, how they are used. "The use of time is Fate," Chapman remarks a few lines later, and to use time, his reformed reader must have one foot on the timeless shore. Chapman's revision of Marlowe's poetic language simply moves his reader to a position where he looks at the poem not *sub specie saecularis* but *sub specie aeternitatis*; the difference between his and Marlowe's poem is less a contrast than a transformation in perception.

[38] Weinberg, *Italian Renaissance*, pp. 294–95.

The most subtle metamorphosis occurs in Marlowe's own lines with the division of the poem by Chapman into sestiads and the addition of arguments at the beginning of each sestiad. The immediate effect is to elevate Marlowe's poem, to ennoble it with the implicit comparison with the *Iliads* of Homer. The change recalls the concern Chapman expressed in his dedication to Lady Walsingham about dealing with trifles like Marlowe's poem and its Musaean original:

> I present your Ladyship with the last affections of the first two lovers that ever Muse shrined in the Temple of Memory; being drawn by strange instigation to employ some of my serious time in so trifling a subject, which yet made the first Author, divine Musaeus, eternal. And . . . [yet] it goes much against my hand to sign that for a trifling subject, on which more worthiness of soul hath been showed . . . But he that shuns trifles must shun the world; out of whose reverend heaps of substance and austerity I can, and will ere long, single or tumble out as brainless and passionate fooleries as ever panted in the bosom of the most ridiculous lover.

The word "trifle" is a fair translation of the Latin "nuga," one of the epithets most frequently applied to the *Hero and Leander* of Musaeus. The Greek poem posed a dilemma for the critic in the obvious contrast between its sensuous elaboration and its supposed antiquity. Chapman recognizes that sensuousness in his resolution to play the amorous fool, yet still admires the resultant fame of Musaeus. The conflict was faced most squarely by J. C. Scaliger, who bears an undeserved reputation of obtuseness for his infamous preference for Musaeus over Homer. What Scaliger actually said was that "if it were not for the historical records, one could fancy that Musaeus was later than Homer, for he is more polished and refined."[39] Like so many critics, he prizes the poem, as

---

[39] Scaliger, *Poeticae*, 1. 2, trans. Padelford, p. 15.

Ovid's was prized, for its rhetorical surface. In his *editio prin-ceps* of *Hero and Leander* of around 1490, Aldus Manutius identifies Musaeus as one of the most ancient poets, yet praises his "little poem" not for its wisdom but for its charm and eloquence, which make it suitable material for Ovid to imitate in the *Heroides*. To later editors, *Hero and Leander* is an "opusculum," like Virgil's *Culex* or Homer's *Batracho-myomachia*, and was suitably bound with them or more often with Aesop's *Fables*; yet even from such a slender work we can recognize the divinity of its maker, for nothing is more "elegant," "pure," and "ornate."

Another strand of criticism saw Musaeus as potentially more dignified. Scaliger implies as much in his comparison with Homer and goes on to call the poem a "tragedy" (3. 96). To Torquato Tasso, the poem was vital evidence that love could be a fit subject for heroic poetry. Drawing on Plato's *Phaedrus* and *Symposium*, he argues that the ancients honored love as a divine virtue. "Let us grant then that the epic poem may use such amorous subjects as the love of Hero and Leander, of which the ancient Greek poet Musaeus sang." Even homosexuality may be included, or more guardedly, "love and friendship . . . if we are willing to call the relation between Achilles and Patroclus friendship, [for] no other has supplied the material for a more heroic vein of poetry."[40] Chapman's elevation of Marlowe's poem moves it from one end of the Musaean spectrum to the other. He lifts an elegant trifle to the status of a minor epic, a shift akin to that from clarity to opacity and from Pied Vanity to judgment.

The division into sestiads has a second, less visible, effect in that it reorganizes Marlowe's poem as well. The rapid flow of his couplets is segmented, the Mercury digression is made to stand even more apart from the main narrative, the parts are marked off and a promise of order is brought into

---

[40] Tasso, *Discourses on the Heroic Poem*, trans. Mariella Cavalchini and Irene Samuel (Oxford: Clarendon Press, 1973), p. 48-49.

a chaotic universe. The change is less stylistic than formal, and again J. C. Scaliger raised exactly this issue in his discussion of Musaeus. All poetry, he argues, is judged by reference to the form of epic, which is divided into chapters in imitation of nature, which divides living bodies into parts "so related that they constitute an organic body. . . . Nor is Musaeus to be condemned because in his altogether charming story of Leander he does not follow the same practice, for that story is, as it were, a tragedy, so that the narrative properly begins and ends with the immediate tale of Leander.[41] A purely epic poet like Vergil brings in subsidiary matters concerned with kings, heroes, gods, war and peace. Hence by restricting his subject to the single story of the two lovers, Musaeus avoids the narrative complexity that requires division into books.

Chapman of course knew Scaliger's opinions and detested them, alluding to these very passages in his denunciation of Scaliger in his prefaces to Homer. By dividing *Hero and Leander*, he may appear to be correcting the deficiencies of a Musaean poem by bringing it into conformity with a Homeric pattern. As appealing as this idea is, it is disturbed by the fact that at some point Chapman came to see a distinct difference in the "matter" of Marlowe and Musaeus.[42] Since "matter" is the subject of the work, the received story, one may wonder how two poems, both telling of Hero and Leander, could differ. The only explanation I can see is that Marlowe introduces new matter, specifically in the tale of Mercury and the country maid and perhaps also in his elaboration of Neptune's role. If this guess is correct, it would further motivate the division into sestiads, since by adding secondary plots Marlowe has removed himself from the dis-

---

[41] Scaliger, *Poeticae*, 3. 96, trans. Padelford, pp. 55-56.

[42] Cf. Chapman's "Epistle" to the reader in his translation of Musaeus (date of composition uncertain; printed London, 1616). He refers to Marlowe's poem as "partly excellent," meaning excellent in some parts but not in others, or perhaps excellent throughout the part Marlowe finished.

pensation Scaliger gave Musaeus from the requirement that
the poet divide his book into chapters. Hence the sestiads are
the mark of a poem conceived of as multiple in its matter.
Chapman's gesture demonstrates that he is endowed with art
as well as knowledge, able to correct the formal lapses of his
predecessor. The division into sestiads also licenses Chap-
man's own rather extensive digressions, with the tale of Hy-
men in the fifth sestiad and the smaller *ekphraseis* and em-
blems throughout the poem.

This divisive, emblematic method reveals itself in the way
the two poets construct images. While Marlowe would
strike an image and shows its significance to his narrative by
a single point of comparison, Chapman uses his digressive
style to linger over the image, forcing us to look and look
again as its significance is teasingly revealed. For instance,
when Leander returns to Abydos after his night with Hero,
the water runs from his body onto the earth:

> . . . like a shower he flew,
> Sprinkling the earth, that to their tombs took in
> Streams dead for love to leave his ivory skin,
> Which yet a snowy foam did leave above,
> As soul to the dead water that did love;
> And from thence did the first white roses spring
> (For love is sweet and fair in every thing).
> [3. 74-80]

The eroticization of nature, the false aetiology, and the sen-
tentious conclusion could all have been written by Marlowe.
Un-Marlovian are lines 77-78, where Chapman, lingering
over his image, forces a re-vision of it, focusing on the detail
of the foam that unexpectedly takes on significance.

Chapman's revising of images is done on a grand scale in
the subsequent appearance to Leander of the goddess Cere-
mony, who requires him to re-view his entire experience up
to that moment and to see that he has omitted the marriage

rite that would bless his union with Hero. While Ceremony
is a divinity, Leander's vision is not in the final sense mystic:

> All her body was
> Clear and transparent as the purest glass:
> For she was all presented to the sense.
>
> [3. 117-19]

In completing Marlowe's poem, Chapman seems to have
recognized that the search beneath the veil of words for re-
condite meaning is ultimately an attempt to reveal truth to
the physical eye with all the clarity and sensuousness of Cer-
emony. The effect of Leander's vision is for him to see a
different purpose to his past actions. Consummation is no
longer an end in itself, but part of a larger union of marriage,
a union which is itself part of a general social and natural
order. Leander's revision, like Chapman's own, affects both
the future and the past, both what he shall do and what has
been done.

For Hero, the process of revision is more complex, for she
must correct not only her actions but their concomitant
emotions as well. While Ceremony has chastized Leander for
his hastiness in love, she has implied that sexual consum-
mation is perfectly all right as long as the holy nuptials come
soon enough afterward. Hero sees a greater incompatibility
of the erotic and religious furies and tries to use the second
to purify the first:

> Now from Leander's place she rose, and found
> Her hair and rent robe scatter'd on the ground;
> Which taking up, she every piece did lay
> Upon an altar, where in youth of day
> She us'd t'exhibit private sacrifice.
> Those would she offer to the deities
> Of her fair goddess and her powerful son,
> As relics of her late-felt passion;

And in that holy sort she vow'd to end them,
In hope her violent fancies that did rend them
Would as quite fade in her love's holy fire,
As they should in the flames she meant t'inspire.
[4. 1-12]

Hero's resolution to burn her hair and robes as a sacrifice
appears on the surface as a vow to end the passions of which
they are relics. But the clarity of the first few lines is then
disturbed by slippery pronoun references and odd verb
choices. The opacity becomes misleading at the phrase "her
late-felt passions" in line 8 if one takes it to mean her love
for Leander, since the last three lines make clear that Hero
does not disavow eroticism itself—her prayer, after all, is to
Venus and Cupid—but only that passionate aspect of it that
leads to psychological turbulence.

Hero's repentence leaves intact the confusion of erotic and
religious furies that it seemed momentarily to clarify. Chap-
man is quick to insist, however, that Hero knows intuitively
that she will not escape so easily the dangers inherent in that
confusion. She sews a scarf filled with emblems of the dis-
aster to come: a changing moon, shooting stars, a fisherman
who draws in his nets and is stung by the serpent he has
caught in them, a country virgin snaring grasshoppers while
her picnic lunch is stolen away by foxes:

These ominous fancies did her soul express,
And every finger made a prophetess,
To show what death was hid in love's disguise,
And make her judgment conquer destinies.
O what sweet forms fair ladies' souls do shroud,
Were they made seen and forced through their blood;
If through their beauties, like rich work through lawn,
They would set forth their minds with virtues drawn.
[4. 108-15]

To Hero the scarf is an "ominous fancy," depicting what she dreads but does not yet know must come. To the poet, who does know, it is a sign that Hero has at this moment shown a judgment superior to that even of Destiny in her understanding of the transience of pleasure (I think the sense of the line is the same whether "destinies" is genetive singular or accusative plural). What he does not make clear at this point is the implication of "conquer." Can Hero alter her destiny and Leander's by correct judgment? Or is she already doomed and able only to win an ethical superiority in death?

Rather than answer right away a question so enigmatically posed, Chapman shifts to a different level of discussion in his analogy between sewing and prophesy, making the "ominous fancies" a metaphor for the revelation of form in the outward beauties of the material world. Form is "shrouded" in the soul and must be forced to the surface by virtuous art. With that metaphor, Chapman raises Hero's scarf into a mirror of his own poem. In their attention to the sensuous surface of things, both Marlowe and his lovers have understood only a part of what they see. Chapman's opaque style is necessary to express the full nature of their experience and hence to control the sensuous realm by the power of virtuous understanding—to give it "form." In his art he is like the ladies sewing:

> . . . their needles leading
> Affection prisoner through their own-built cities,
> Pinion'd with stories and Arachnean ditties.
> [4. 119-21]

Hero rests beneath Chapman's interpretative gaze as one who sees and is seen. She knows the significance of the scarf but does not fully know the significance of her making the scarf. Her half-understanding is reiterated when she lapses again into a confusion of erotic and religious desire:

She would the faith of her desires profess:
Where her religion should be policy,
To follow love with zeal her piety;
Her chamber her cathedral church should be,
And her Leander her chief deity.
For in her love these did the gods forego;
And though her knowledge did not teach her so,
Yet did it teach her this, that what her heart
Did greatest hold in her self greatest part,
That she did make her god.
                    [4. 177-86]

This idolatrous confusion leads her to invert the proper re-
lationship of soul to outward form. Instead of continuing to
make visible her inward beauty, she resorts again to "love's
disguises," and resolves to mask the erotic basis of her piety
under the appearance of conventional devotion. Far more
complex psychologically than Leander, Hero nearly attains
the maguslike stature of the prophetic poet able to formalize
the material universe and so to bring order into the unstable
flux of actions and emotions. To do so she must become like
the goddess Ceremony, "transparent," with the inner truth
made present to the senses by the outward, sensual material
of her appearance and behavior. It is her fatal decision to
embrace the doubleness of dissimulation that prevents the
elevation of her experience—and of the poem recording it—
into the realm of clarity, and which seals the doom of the
two lovers.

Chapman's insight and Hero's blindness to the similar or-
ders of art, love, and fate are elaborated in the digression of
Hymen that makes up the fifth sestiad. Here Chapman pre-
sents us with an inspired poet, the nymph Teras, who is, like
Musaeus, especially associated with prophecies:

. . . never was propos'd
Riddle to her, or augury, strange or new,
But she resolv'd it; never slight tale flew

From her charm'd lips without important sense,
Shown in some grave succeeding consequence.
[5. 72-76]

Her skill is at the resolution of dark sayings propounded by
others, and her tale of the marriage of Hymen and Eucharis
is, appropriately enough, an explanation of Hero's plight. It
approaches the problem from the opposite end, telling of a
well-ordered love affair and meditating on the proper order
of sight, erotic fury, and the consummation of desire. Like
Leander, Hymen is captivated by the sight of his mistress
and in the best fashion of the foolish lover he dresses up in
women's clothes to come near Eucharis. When this prox-
imity allows him to rescue her from peril, she learns to love
him in return:

And thus came Love with Proteus and his pow'r,
T'encounter Eucharis: first like the flow'r
That Juno's milk did spring, the silver lily,
He fell on Hymen's hand, who straight did spy
The bounteous godhead, and with wondrous joy
Offer'd it Eucharis. She, wondrous coy,
Drew back her hand: the subtle flow'r did woo it,
And drawing it near, mix'd so you could not know it.
As two clear tapers mix in one their light,
So did the lily and the hand their white.
She view'd it, and her view the form bestows
Amongst her spirits: for as colour flows
From superficies of each thing we see,
Even so with colours forms emitted be,
And where Love's form is, Love is; Love is form.
[5. 213-27]

What could be less like Marlowe's description of the erotic
fury of Hero and Leander? Yet Chapman is performing no
idle elaboration. As D. J. Gordon has shown, "Proteus is
allegorically the *materia prima*, the prime matter, and the *in-*

*formis rerum materia* . . . which, for both Aristotle and Ficino, is pure potentiality. This achieves the form of love: and takes visible shape as the lily. . . . Eucharis receives this form through the eye—and loves because this form is love: and love *is* form."[43]

The transformation of erotic fury into form itself is emblematized in Chapman's comparison of the "sacred storm of love" that seizes Eucharis to the Hellespont raging in a tempest:

> It stirr'd her blood's sea so, that high it went,
> And beat in bashful waves 'gainst the white shore
> Of her divided cheeks; it rag'd the more,
> Because the tide went 'gainst the haughty wind
> Of her estate and birth. And as we find
> In fainting ebbs, the flow'ry Zephyr hurls
> The green-hair'd Hellespont, broke in silver curls
> 'Gainst Hero's tower, but in his blast's retreat,
> The waves obeying him, they after beat,
> Leaving the chalky shore a great way pale,
> Then moist it freshly with another gale:
> So ebb'd and flow'd the blood in Eucharis' face.
>                                          [5. 230–41]

There is a cut-glass prettiness about the "flow'ry Zephyr," "green-hair'd Hellespont," and "silver curls" of lines 236–37. Half the actions—"fainting ebbs," "retreat," "obeying," break the violence of "beat," "rag'd," "hurls," and "beat" again. The whole description of the storm, foreshadowing the imminent death of Leander, is held suspended between the "so" of line 230 and the "so" of line 241. The whole tempest is no more than a flush on a lover's cheek, the whole tale the occasion for a well-wrought simile.

What Marlowe made clear, erotic desire and act, Chapman obscures. What Chapman does instead is to make visible the

---

[43] Gordon, "The Renaissance Poet as Classicist," p. 126.

2. *Homer and Chapman*. Title page, Homer, *Batrachomyomachia*, trans. George Chapman (London, 1624?). Huntington Library, San Marino, California.

process by which passion becomes poetry, the process which in Marlowe's poem is rendered mysterious and irrational. Chapman makes no less of a vatic claim than Marlowe, indeed more, for he claims mastery over a process of which Marlowe's highest praise was total deference, the submersion of his own personality into the role of poetic madman. The self-image Chapman is trying to project, and the relation of that self to his predecessor, is perhaps best illustrated by that other "trifle" to which the *Hero and Leander* of Musaeus was so often compared, the pseudo-Homeric *Batrachomyomachia*. On the title page of his translation [fig. 2], Chapman showed Homer, blind and bearded, turning his sightless eyes toward the heavens. Below is the portrait of Chapman himself, also bearded and his head wreathed in clouds, but his eyes clear and gazing steadily outward at the world.

At the beginning of this chapter, I observed that the idea of inspiration seems on the surface to put a stop to any further critical discussion. This would seem especially true if one wished to discuss genre, for an inspired poem would by definition be sui generis. Chapman's great contribution, for good or ill, is nothing less than the domestication of inspiration. By seeing in it an impulse to formality, he moves the inspired poem back into the generic system of Renaissance verse. Chapman finds the poet's gift to be a special insight into the realm of the spirit, joined with the ability to make that insight manifest in the realm of matter. For this reason, his poetry perhaps more than any other's exemplifies the notion of genre suggested by Rosalie Colie: "a set of interpretations, of 'frames' or 'fixes' on the world." To other poets, genre may be a fix on poetry; to Chapman, it is a philosophic manifesto, a statement about the form of the universe.

# Chapter 4

# Shakespeare, Poet and Painter

Although the Renaissance prided itself on the rebirth of letters, its cultural achievement was as great in other areas, notably the fine arts, as it was in literature. Indeed, one could argue quite easily that the modern conception of the Renaissance depends far more on the Italian painters than on anything else. Any attempt to make sense of the Renaissance must find some connections among the achievements in various fields, especially when one is considering something like the Elizabethan minor epic, which shared so large a body of subject matter with painting. Casual comparisons abound between such poems as *Venus and Adonis* and *Lucrece* on one hand, and familiar paintings by Botticelli and Titian on the other, but rarely do they go beyond a superficial level of coincidence in date and subject matter.

In fact, knowledge of Italian, French, or even Netherlandish painting in sixteenth-century England was extremely limited. Sidney was unusual in visiting northern Italy and having his portrait painted by Veronese. Spenser refers to Michelangelo as a proverbial master, while Shakespeare names just one modern painter, Giulio Romano, in all his works, citing him as a decorator of wax effigies. A cunning historian has discovered that Giulio did in fact once paint an effigy, but this, I think, is sheer coincidence, and Shakespeare's remark shows his colossal ignorance of Continental art. Nor did the Elizabethans find much at home to inspire them. Despite the noble efforts at resuscitation by Roy Strong and others, one must admit that Elizabethan painting is pedestrian, narrow, and derivative, overwhelmingly consisting of portraiture commissioned for nonaesthetic reasons, and making a significant achievement only in the miniatures of Hilliard and Oliver. Visits from distinguished foreigners such as Antonis Mor or Federico Zuccaro and the occasional importation of paintings or etchings may have brought glimpses of Continental sophistication, but not until the advent of the Stuarts did England enter the mainstream of European painting.

The more promising avenue of exploration is to ask not what Elizabethan poets saw, but how they saw it. The search for a specific painterly source for a poem is almost always in vain. More important, and not only because it is more accessible, is the way the poet thinks about painting, his conception of what it shares with his own medium and how it differs. Merely posing this question uncovers a vast body of subliterary and subartistic material that forms the common ground between poetry and painting in the Renaissance: emblem books, mythological handbooks and commentaries, treatises on art theory, and treatises on rhetoric and poetics. Such works are the symptoms of poetry and painting as humanist disciplines, and the manifestations of their common humanist heritage. Collectively they make up a body of theory, epithet, and commentary such as we have seen in the Renaissance idea of inspiration and will see again in Renaissance ideas of history. It is this body of ideas on which poet and painter alike based their treatment of mythological and historical subjects, and which establishes connections between them even if they were ignorant of one another's work.

For no poet is this conflict of knowledge and ignorance more acute than for William Shakespeare. With neither a university education nor, to our knowledge, the experience of foreign travel, he published two poems, *Venus and Adonis* and *Lucrece*, that epitomized for his contemporaries the new classicizing and Italianate culture. Although he may have never seen anything more *au courant* than a Hilliard miniature or the occasional imported tapestry or etching, his minor epics are a painter's poems, founded on a subtle understanding of the creation and interpretation of visual images. More than one modern art historian has come away impressed by the profundity of the poet's visual culture. Two aspects of that culture in particular beg for attention. In *Venus and Adonis*, like a host of painters before him, Shakespeare draws on traditions of iconography in his manipulation of Greek myth. In *Lucrece*, he turns to the rhetorician's device of *ekphrasis* in his creation of a monumental visual scene of the fall of Troy that decorates the house of Lucrece. While I have dealt in passing with both iconography and *ekphrasis* earlier, now with Shakespeare's poems it is possible to consider them in some technical detail as formal elements in the shaping of the minor epic. Together they demonstrate that the generic barrier between the arts could itself be crossed, and that the Renaissance took as a living truth the old saying that painting is mute poetry and poetry a speaking picture.

## THE ICONOGRAPHY OF *Venus and Adonis*

The most remarkable thing about Shakespeare's treatment of the myth of Venus and Adonis is his elimination of its central erotic action. Instead of being Love's lover, as in ancient literary sources,[1] Adonis leaves Venus flat on her back and runs off to hunt with the boys. There is some debate as to Shakespeare's originality here, centering around Titian's painting of *Venus and Adonis* at the Prado [fig. 3]. Titian shows the seated Venus restraining Adonis as he pulls away to join the boar hunt. A number of people, most notably Erwin Panofsky, have interpreted the scene as Adonis refusing Venus and have proposed it as Shakespeare's source, but recently David Rosand has persuasively argued that Titian

---

[1] *Orphic Hymns*, 65; Theocritus, 1, 3, 15; Bion, "Epitaphium Adonidis"; Ovid, *Metamorphoses*, 10; also Cicero, *De Natura Deorum*, 3. 59; Servius, commentary on Vergil's *Aeneid*, 7. 761; Hyginus, *Fabulae*, nos. 164, 271; Fulgentius, *Mythologia*, 3.

3. Titian. *Venus and Adonis*. 1554. Canvas. Museo del Prado, Madrid.

drew on a sarcophagus tradition older than Ovid to depict
the parting of the lovers at dawn.[2] In his own day Titian was
criticized by Raffaelo Borghini for making Adonis refuse
Venus,[3] and Shakespeare may have similarly misinterpreted
the tension evident in Titian's intertwined figures or have

[2] Erwin Panofsky, *Problems in Titian, Mostly Iconographic* (New York: New
York University Press, 1969), pp. 149-54. David Rosand, "*Ut Pictor Poeta*:
Meaning in Titian's *Poesie*," *New Literary History* 3 (1972):527-46; idem,
"Titian and the 'Bed of Polyclitus,' " *Burlington Magazine* 117 (1975):242-
45; and idem, *Titian* (New York: Abrams, 1978), p. 132.

[3] Panofsky, *Titian*, p. 151.

4. Giulio Sanuto after Titian. *Venus and Adonis*. 1559. Etching. British Museum, London.

projected that tension back onto earlier parts of the story. All this assumes that Shakespeare had in fact seen the painting, which was shipped to Philip II in England in 1554, or had at least seen one of the etchings of it by Martino Rota or Giulio Sanuto [fig. 4]. But Philip presumedly took the painting with him upon his return to Spain, and the traffic in etchings is notoriously hard to trace.

As a source for Shakespeare, Titian is at best highly equivocal, and there are a myriad of other candidates for the honor. Perhaps Shakespeare's invention owes something to the stories of Narcissus and of Salmacis and Hermaphroditus, or to the special tastes of the Earl of Southampton.[4] In *Hero and Leander* Marlowe describes how

> . . . Venus in her naked glory strove
> To please the careless and disdainful eyes
> Of proud Adonis that before her lies.
> [1. 12-14]

If this is not just a remarkable coincidence, Shakespeare may have radically expanded a casual hint by Marlowe. But it seems unlikely that Marlowe would have made so startling an innovation in so offhanded a form without developing it, and his lines look more likely to be an allusion to Shakespeare's poem. The most sensible conclusion, then, seems to be that Shakespeare had no particular source, and actually thought of the idea himself.

Whatever its origin, and despite the casualness with which it is introduced, the change from the love of Venus and Adonis to the refusal of Venus by Adonis threatens to make hash of Shakespeare's poem. Advancing on Adonis in the

---

[4] Southampton's role is discussed by A. L. Rowse in *Shakespeare's Southampton: Patron of Virginia* (New York: Harper, 1965), pp. 74-81; and, more judiciously, by G.P.V. Akrigg, *Shakespeare and the Earl of Southampton* (Cambridge: Harvard University Press, 1968), pp. 33-34, 195-98. Other classical and Renaissance sources of Shakespeare's poems are examined in the New Variorum Edition by Hyder Rollins (Philadelphia: Lippincott, 1938), pp. 390-400; Douglas Bush, *Mythology and the Renaissance Tradition in English Poetry* (1932; rev. ed. New York: Norton, 1963), pp. 137-45; T. W. Baldwin, *On the Literary Genetics of Shakespeare's Poems and Sonnets* (Urbana: University of Illinois Press, 1950), pp. 2-48; and Geoffrey Bullough, *Narrative and Dramatic Sources of Shakespeare*, 10 vols. (New York: Columbia University Press, 1957), 1:161-65.

first lines, Venus seems to become a sweaty, muscular rapist. In the middle, as Adonis resists her, the sweet couple falls into a philosophic bicker over whether Venus or Diana is the author of death. At the end, Venus bursts into a passionate lament over the dead Adonis that is admirable poetry but is utterly inconsistent with her earlier characterization as a comic seducer and immoral lecher. And why is Adonis killed for what he doesn't do, or worse yet, why doesn't he do it? The modern reader, as J. W. Lever summed it up, usually takes the poem as "a very funny story which somehow forgets the joke; or as a highly cautionary tale which, in showing the dangers of caution, does not point the moral at all well."[5]

A famous poet has remarked that it is hard to applaud *Venus and Adonis* unless one knows the rules of the game.[6] Shakespeare is playing far more than we have realized by the rules of a highly sophisticated tradition of allegorical poetry and painting, so that the various aspects of Venus portray alternately the comic and serious qualities of physical love while the death of Adonis suggests the internal contradictions of earthly beauty, whose splendor comes at the price of transience.[7] Yet the poem adds up to no homily on love. In

[5] J. W. Lever, "Venus and the Second Chance," *Shakespeare Survey* 15 (1962):81-88. See also Lever's review of modern criticism in the same volume (19-22).

[6] Richard Wilbur, Introduction to the narrative poems, *The Pelican Shakespeare*, ed. Alfred Harbage (Baltimore: Penguin, 1969), p. 1401.

[7] Steps in this direction have been taken by Lever and by A. C. Hamilton, *The Early Shakespeare* (San Marino, Ca.: Huntington Library, 1967), who attempt to deal seriously with Venus and Adonis as mythic rather than dramatic characters. My partners in the new orthodoxy of an ambivalent *Venus and Adonis* are Kenneth Muir, "*Venus and Adonis*: Comedy or Tragedy?" in *Shakespearean Essays*, ed. Alwin Thayer and Norman Sanders (Knoxville: University of Tennessee Press, 1964), pp. 1-13; Norman Rabkin, *Shakespeare and the Common Understanding* (New York: Free Press, 1967), pp. 150-62; William Keach, *Elizabethan Erotic Narratives* (New Brunswick: Rutgers University Press, 1977), pp. 52-84; and Donald G. Watson, "The Contrarieties of *Venus and Adonis*," *Studies in Philology* 75 (1978):32-63. Most recently, A. Robin Baumann has attacked us as "modern critics of a fashion-

the strife between Venus and Adonis, Shakespeare holds his
conflicting attitudes toward earthly love in an aesthetic bal-
ance through a form which, in the same iconographic tradi-
tion, is both narrative and pictorial.

Of the elements of iconography, most significant for
Shakespeare's poem was the development of the attribute
system as a way of representing mythic characters in alle-
gorical poetry and painting. A description of a god or god-
dess in, say, Vincenzo Cartari's *Le imagini de i dei de gli antichi*
(1556; first illustrated edition 1571) will show a unitary fig-
ure—suitable for a painting, emblem, or medallion—deco-
rated and embellished with various attributes, each of which
is the relic of a story about the deity and the symbol of an
abstract quality. Venus, for instance, is described with a rose,
which recalls how she cut her foot as she ran to the dying
Adonis and represents the painful side of love.[8] In a version
of *The Death of Adonis* now in the Uffizi [fig. 5], Sebastiano
del Piombo shows Venus inspecting her wound with the of-
fending flowers just visible below her foot. Cupid and her
nymphs rush to attend her while Adonis lies neglected in the
background.

This iconographic technique is of course not restricted to

---

ably pluralistic bent," arguing that the poem must be read in light of "the
concept of moral didacticism so prevalent in Renaissance literary theory"
(" 'Hard Armours' and 'Delicate Amours' in Shakespeare's *Venus and
Adonis*," *Shakespeare Studies* 12 (1979):1-23). In general agreement with Bau-
mann's position is David N. Beauregard, "*Venus and Adonis*: Shakespeare's
Representation of the Passions," *Shakespeare Studies* 8 (1975):83-98. We need
not, however, reject an ambivalent reading of a poem merely because it
coincides with modern thinking. The arguments of this and the preceding
chapter will, I hope, demonstrate that such pluralism is perfectly consonant
with an informed understanding of Renaissance poetics.

[8] Vincenzo Cartari, *Le imagini de i dei de gli antichi* (Venice, 1571), pp. 536-
37. The aetiology originates with Bion's "Epitaphium Adonidis" and is re-
peated in Jacobus Micyllus's commentary on Ovid, *Metamorphoseos* (Basel,
1543), p. 243; and in Natali Conti, *Mythologia* (Venice, 1568), p. 230a. Its
allegorical significance is expounded by Fulgentius, *Mythologia* (Paris, 1578),
p. 136a; quoted by Giovanni Boccaccio, *Genealogie Deorum Gentilium*, bk.
3, chap. 23, ed. Vincenzo Romano, 2 vols. (Bari: Laterza, 1951), 1:152.

5. Sebastiano del Piombo. *The Death of Adonis.* c. 1512. Canvas. Galleria degli Uffizi, Florence. (Photo: Alinari).

pagan subjects. The archangel Raphael, for instance, is regularly depicted with a youth carrying a fish, recalling the tale of Tobias and signifying Raphael's quality as the "affable archangel" who aids and protects men.[9] In Verrocchio's portrayal [fig. 6] Tobias is the attribute of Raphael and the fish is the attribute of Tobias, just as the rose is Venus's or the caduceus is Mercury's. Iconography, then, is not just a content but a *process* of representation, a continual infolding and unfolding of pictorial and narrative forms. It mediates between two different modes of conception, between discursive and nondiscursive thinking: the material of the visual world is made into narrative, narrative into argument, and argument into vision.

That Shakespeare uses iconography as a formal constituent

[9] E. H. Gombrich, "Tobias and the Angel," in his *Symbolic Images: Studies in the Art of the Renaissance* (London: Phaidon, 1972), pp. 26-30.

6. Follower of Verrocchio. *Tobias and the Angel*. c. 1470. Panel. National Gallery, London.

of his poetry is amply illustrated by the figure of Adonis. Arthur Golding, Shakespeare's favorite translator of Ovid, wrote in his "Dedicatory Epistle" to the Earl of Leicester that Book 10 of the *Metamorphoses* "chiefly doth containe one kind of argument, / Reprooving most prodigious lusts."[10] The same argument springs to the lips of Adonis when he rejects Venus. Yet she has a word or two of answer, and anyway, Adonis's refusal means that the pair will enact no lusts worthy of reproof, so Shakespeare's own position must go beyond Golding's simpleminded moral. Golding's source, the Regius-Micyllus Ovid, indeed offers more varied allegory. Historically, the myth recalls ancient religious festivals in Assyria.[11] Physically interpreted, Adonis represents the crops of the earth, as Micyllus learned from scholia in Theocritus, *Idyll* 3.[12] Or, in Boccaccio's version, Adonis is the sun and Venus the earth; their love brings forth lush flowers, leaves, and ripe fruit. But winter is like the boar that slays the beautiful Adonis, for then the sun seems banished from our world, Venus mourns, the earth lies barren.[13]

The most common interpretation, though, is suggested by Ovid himself. When Adonis is turned into a flower at the end of his tale, he writes:

[10] Arthur Golding, *The XV. Bookes of P. Ovidius Naso, Entituled Metamorphosis* (London, 1593), sig. A4ʳ. This is a common understanding of the myth, shared by Georgius Sabinus in the commentary to his edition of Ovid's *Metamorphoses* (Cambridge, 1584), p. 419; by an early commentary on Bion in *Opera* (Bruges, 1565), p. 38; by Abraham Fraunce, *The Third Part of the Countesse of Pembrokes Yvychurch* (London, 1592), p. 45b; and by Claude Mignault in his commentary on the *Emblemata* of Andraea Alciati (Antwerp, 1577), p. 288.

[11] Micyllus, *Metamorphoseos*, p. 243; based probably on Lucian. A much fuller account, based on Pausanias, is given in Bartholomew Merula's commentary on the *De Arte Amandi*, ed. Micyllus (Basel, 1549), p. 379. Theocritus, 15 describes an Alexandrian festival, cited in Lilio Gregorio Giraldi, *De Deis Gentium* (Basel, 1560), p. 397. Cf. Conti, *Mythologia*, p. 161b; Cartari, *Le imagini*, p. 553.

[12] Micyllus, *Metamorphoseos*, p. 243. Cf. Giraldi, *De Deis Gentium*, p. 397; Conti, *Mythologia*, p. 162a.

[13] Boccaccio, *Genealogie*, bk. 2, chap. 53, ed. Romano, 1:102. Boccaccio's source is Macrobius, *Saturnalia*, and derives ultimately from the Orphic "Hymn to Adonis." Cf. Conti, *Mythologia*, p. 162a; Cartari, *Le imagini*, pp. 553-54; Fraunce, *Countesse of Pembrokes Yvychurch*, p. 45b; and Sabinus, *Metamorphoses*, p. 418, who attributes the allegory to Giovanni Pontano.

. . . brevis est tamen usus in illo [flore];
namque male haerentem et nimia levitate caducum
excutiunt idem, qui praestant nomina, venti.

(. . . But short-lived is their flower; for the winds
from which it takes its name shake off the flower so
delicately clinging and doomed too easily to fall.)[14]

This sense of transience acquires almost proverbial weight as
it is repeated by mythographers. Boccaccio writes:

> But as to the fact that Adonis is transformed into a
> flower: by that invention I think is shown to us the
> brevity of beauty, which in the morning is richly col-
> ored, but at a late hour, drooping and pale, grows fee-
> ble; and so mankind in the morn, that is, in the time of
> youth, is blooming and splendid; but in the eve, that is,
> in the time of old age, we grow pale, and we fall into
> the shadows of death.[15]

What this philosophical interpretation has in common
with the physical is the importance given to flowers. In one
case, Adonis is *like* a flower; in the other, he *causes* flowers.
Both statements describe the action of Shakespeare's poem.
Its opening lines link Adonis to the purple sun:

---

[14] *Metamorphoses*, 10. 737-39, trans. Frank Justus Miller, Loeb ed., 2 vols.
(London: Heinemann, 1916), 2:116-17.

[15] "Quod autem sit Adon transformatus in florem, ob id fictum puto, ut
nostri decoris brevitas ostendatur, mane quidem purpureus est, sero lan-
guens pallensque marcidus efficitur, sic et nostra humanitas mane, id est
iuventutis tempore, florens et splendida est, sero autem, id est senectutis
evo, pallemus et in tenebras mortis ruimus." Boccaccio, *Genealogie*, bk. 2,
chap. 53, ed. Romano, 1:103. Giovanni dell' Anguillara smuggles this inter-
pretation into his Italian translation of Ovid (Venice, 1578), p. 186b. Cf.
Micyllus, *Metamorphoseos*, p. 243; Sabinus, *Metamorphoses*, p. 418; Fraunce,
*Countesse of Pembrokes Yvychurch*, p. 45b. The garden of Adonis as a pro-
verbial example of transience is cited in Erasmus's *Adagia*.

Even as the sun with purple-colour'd face
Had ta'en his last leave of the weeping morn,
Rose-cheek'd Adonis hied him to the chase.

At the end, his purple blood begets a flower:

And in his blood that on the ground lay spill'd,
A purple flower sprung up, checker'd with white,
Resembling well his pale cheeks and the blood
Which in round drops upon their whiteness stood.
[ll. 1167-70]

Throughout, he is linked to flowers, explicitly as a metaphor
for his beauty:

"Thrice fairer than myself," thus she began,
"The field's chief flower, sweet above compare;
Stain to all nymphs, more lovely than a man,
More white and red than doves or roses are."
[ll. 7-10]

The realization that Adonis is Beauty, which fadeth like
the flower, explains his peculiar, unmotivated death. Beauty
fades, flowers wither, no matter what. His death does not
show a doom that awaits lechery, since he will have none,
and Venus (who he does think is a lecher) has sought to
protect him. Certainly it does not prove that sex is very nice;
it proves simply that beauty fades. In short, the sequence of
the narrative is not finally a causal or argumentative se-
quence; rather, it is an unfolding of Adonis's attributes, a
making explicit of what is implicit in line 8—"the field's
chief flower." Shakespeare can say he *is* a flower, while a
painter would show him *with* a flower; the narrative repeats
this attribute by showing him *becoming* a flower. Narratively,
he must die to become that flower, and what the flower
means is that he must die.

If Shakespeare's portrayal of Adonis is deceptive only be-
cause it is so simple, the portrait of Venus is a genuine prob-
lem. That Venus is Love is axiomatic; that she is earthly love
is quickly apparent. Adonis calls her Lust; she herself claims
to be fruitful and generative; and her hand is moist, the
proper characteristic of a passionate lover. George Wynd-
ham, the first modern critic of the poem, likened her to
Botticelli's Venus, rising from the foam.[16] But if she is born
of the sea, it is in Abraham Fraunce's sense:

> She is borne of the sea, lovers are inconstant, like the
> troubled waves of the sea: Hereof was she called *Aph-
> rodite*, of the froath of the sea, being like to *Sperma*.[17]

Shakespeare's description of her is a metaphoric catalogue
of the characteristics of physical love. When he wishes to
show that love is light, that is, merry and delightful, he says
that Venus does not weigh much:

> "Witness this primrose bank whereon I lie:
> These forceless flowers like sturdy trees support me.
> . . . . . . . . . . . . . . . . . . . . . . . . . . .
>     Is love so light, sweet boy, and may it be
>     That thou should think it heavy unto thee?"
>                                              [ll. 151–56]

The pun is outrageous, and the figure contorted, for its lit-
eral and metaphoric senses have reversed positions. As Car-
tari prescribes, the principal characteristics of the god are
those which signify the god's nature and effects.[18] We are
used to the physical being the literal, but literally Venus is

---

[16] George Wyndham, ed., *The Poems of Shakespeare* (New York: Crowell,
1898), pp. lxxxv–lxxxvi.

[17] Fraunce, *Countesse of Pembrokes Yvychurch*, p. 45a. The etymology de-
rives from Hesiod, *Theogony*, ll. 188–204, allegorized by Fulgentius, *My-
thologia*, p. 135b.

[18] Cartari, *Le imagini*, p. 16.

delightful, and so she is figured as if she were light in weight. But, curiously, this reversal changes the impact of the image; instead of seeing a sylph supported on flowers, we see tree trunks holding aloft an awesome bulk. This is the core of the poem's problem. If one grants that Venus is earthly love, what is the attitude toward earthly love? Is it loathsome, foul lust? Delightful sense? A near-sacred force of natural propagation?

The most casual glance at the sonnets would remind us that Shakespeare is perfectly capable of portraying love in all three ways. *Venus and Adonis* opens in travesty, as if love were something that reduces human beings to the grotesque and foolish:

Over one arm the lusty courser's rein,
Under her other was the tender boy,
[ll. 31-32]

Backward she push'd him, as she would be thrust,
And govern'd him in strength, though not in lust.
[ll. 41-42]

"Were I hard-favour'd, foul or wrinkled old,
Ill-nurtur'd, crooked, churlish, harsh in voice,
O'erworn, despised, rheumatic and cold,
Thick-sighted, barren, lean, and lacking juice,
Then mightst thou pause, for then I were not for thee."
[ll. 133-37]

He wrings her nose, he strikes her on the cheeks,
He bends her fingers, holds her pulses hard.
[ll. 475-76]

She sinketh down, still hanging by his neck;
He on her belly falls, she on her back.
[ll. 593-94]

If the moments of direct physical contact are ludicrous, the passages of enticement reveal the sensuality that led Francis Meres to call Shakespeare "Mellifluous & hony-tongued":

> "Bid me discourse, I will enchant thine ear,
> Or like a fairy trip upon the green,
> Or like a nymph, with long dishevell'd hair,
> Dance on the sands, and yet no footing seen."
>                                        [ll. 145-48]

> "Sweet bottom grass and high delightful plain,
> Round rising hillocks, brakes obscure and rough,
> To shelter thee from tempest and from rain:
> Then be my deer, since I am such a park."
>                                        [ll. 236-39]

These two moods have won the poem its reputation for comic sensuousness. But there is another tone, like to that of Sonnet 129, "The expense of spirit in a waste of shame," in which love is presented as a violent force of destruction:

> Even as an empty eagle, sharp by fast,
> Tires with her beak on feathers, flesh and bone,
> Shaking her wings, devouring all in haste,
> Till either gorge be stuff'd or prey be gone:
>   Even so she kiss'd his brow, his cheek, his chin.
>                                        [ll. 55-59]

> And having felt the sweetness of the spoil,
> With blindfold fury she begins to forage;
> Her face doth reek and smoke, her blood doth boil,
> And careless lust stirs up a desperate courage,
>   Planting oblivion, beating reason back,
>   Forgetting shame's pure blush and honour's wrack.
>                                        [ll. 553-58]

We have, in effect, not one but three Venuses, comic, sensual and violent, all embodying earthly love but differently depicted to reveal different aspects. Venus is the empty eagle, the randy jennet, the tender snail, the anguished milchdoe, and the timid hare. Even the boar is finally her animal. Traditionally, the boar represents jealousy, because Mars took its shape to eliminate his rival.[19] In Shakespeare's version, Mars has been mastered by Venus, who is herself the jealous one, that is, possessive of Adonis. When first the boar is mentioned, she quakes with fear of loss:

"For where love reigns, disturbing jealousy
Doth call himself affection's sentinel;
. . . . . . . . . . . . . . . . . . . . . . . . . .
Distemp'ring gentle love in his desire,
As air and water do abate the fire."
[ll. 649-54]

So when the boar appears, he possesses Adonis with a firm embrace which Venus can only envy:

"And nuzzling in his flank, the loving swine
Sheath'd unaware the tusk in his soft groin.

"Had I been tooth'd like him, I must confess,
With kissing him I should have kill'd him first."[20]
[ll. 1115-18]

[19] Micyllus, *Metamorphoseos* (p. 243) attributes the anecdote to a Greek source; Giraldi, *De Deis Gentium* (p. 397) traces it to Eusebius and Augustine; Conti, *Mythologia* (pp. 121b, 230a) wrongly derives it from *Metamorphoses* 10; cf. Cartari, *Le imagini*, p. 537; and Ronsard's "Adonis," in *The Pastoral Elegy*, ed. T. P. Harrison (Austin: University of Texas Press, 1939), pp. 161-65.

[20] The conceit of the boar kissing Adonis derives from the pseudo-Theocritan "Death of Adonis," accepted as Theocritus, 30 in the Renaissance; see Bush, *Mythology*, pp. 54, 137, and Baldwin, *Literary Genetics*, p. 42. It was translated anonymously into English in *Sixe Idillia* (1588; reprint ed.,

Venus is a series of images, even of puns, like the strange animal-headed figures who inhabit the pages of Cartari [fig. 7]. Contradictory elements require contradictory figures. Cartari depicts Venus five different ways, and once, rather like Shakespeare, groups three different Venuses in the same frame [fig. 8]. Too much can be made of the "character" of Shakespeare's Venus. She is no Lady Macbeth or Prince Hamlet. The idea of character requires a personality continuous over a period of time. But not the allegorical figure, as Dante explained in *La vita nuova*: one "could be puzzled at my speaking of Love as if it were a thing in itself, as if it were not only an intellectual substance, but also a bodily substance. This is patently false, for Love does not exist in itself as a substance, but is an accident in a substance."[21] Shakespeare's mythic goddess is not so much a person as a diverse group of actions inhabiting a single body.

If the characters of Venus and Adonis show the kinship in this case between poetry and the visual arts, they may also remind us of Lessing's warning about the fundamental difference between the arts. Painting, he says, employs figures and colors in space and imitates bodies; poetry articulates sounds in time and imitates actions.[22] The iconographic de-

---

London: Duckworth, 1922); cited by Giraldi, *De Deis Gentium*, p. 374; and imitated by Ronsard and by Minturno, "De Adoni ab Apro Interempto," in *Epigrammata et Elegiae*, pp. 7a-8b, bound with *Poemata* (Venice, 1564).

[21] "Persona . . . dubitare potrebbe di ciò, che io dico d'Amore come se fosse una cosa per sè, e non solamente sustanzia intelligente, ma sì come fosse sustanzia corporale: la quale cosa, secondo la veritade, è falsa; chè Amore non è per sè sì corne sustanzia, ma è uno accidente in sustanzia." Dante, *La vita nuova*, 25. 1, ed. Michele Barbi (Milan, Hoepli, 1907), p. 67. The English version is from *Dante's Vita Nuova*, trans. Mark Musa, rev. ed. (Bloomington: Indiana University Press, 1973), p. 54.

[22] G. E. Lessing, *Laöcoon*, trans. Sir Robert Phillimore (London: Macmillan, 1874), p. 149. The very real difficulties in comparisons between art and literature are demonstrated by René Wellek, "The Parallelism between Literature and the Arts," in *English Institute Annual, 1941* (New York: Columbia

piction of Shakespeare's characters gives them a self-contained unity, a perfect balance of action and physique within each figure. But that very completeness *within* the figures transforms the traditional relationship *between* them: Adonis no longer needs an affair with Venus to define himself. Shakespeare goes further still, making Adonis not just indifferent to Venus but downright disdainful of her. This novel arrangement, we may recall, is hinted at by Titian, in whose *Venus and Adonis* we may find iconographic structures that break down Lessing's dichotomy between pictorial and discursive forms and offer a model for Shakespeare's handling of the affair.

Titian's *Venus and Adonis* [fig. 3] is built around conflict—Adonis pulls away, Venus restrains him. The debate as to whether the subject is the "refusal of Adonis" or the "leave-taking" of Adonis is in a sense a debate about the point in the story at which this conflict takes place. It is less a debate about what is happening in the painting than about what has happened in the previous moments. Either way, Titian has chosen the instant where the desires of Venus and Adonis are opposed and developed the opposition iconographically. Dogs and boar spear are Adonis's attributes; an overturned urn in the left foreground is Venus's. In the background is an inert, winged figure, his bow and quiver hanging from a nearby tree. Panofsky identifies him as a sleeping Cupid, symbolic of cool passions.[23] Ovid and others, though, tell us of the resemblance of Adonis to Cupid. They look so much alike that unless one had wings and the other his quiver you could not tell them apart.[24] This figure, equipped with both

University Press, 1942); and by Svetlana and Paul Alpers, "*Ut Pictura Noesis? Criticism in Literary Studies and Art History*," *New Literary History* 3 (1972):437-58.

[23] Panofsky, *Titian*, p. 151.

[24] "Qualia namque / corpora nudorum tabula pinguntur Amorum, / talis erat, sed, ne faciat discrimina cultus, / aut huic adde leves, aut illi deme pharetras"; *Metamorphoses*, 10. 515-18.

7. *Animal-headed Gods.* Vincenzo Cartari, *Le imagini de i dei de gli antichi.*
(Venice, 1571). Newberry Library, Chicago.

8. *Three Venuses.* Vincenzo Cartari, *Le imagini de i dei de gli antichi.* (Venice, 1571). Newberry Library, Chicago.

9. *The Death of Adonis*. Ovid, *Metamorphoses*, ed. Johannes Sprengius (Frankfurt, 1563). Newberry Library, Chicago.

wings and quiver, lies in the same position as the dying
Adonis in illustrated Ovids of the Renaissance [fig. 9]. It may
also recall the position of Adonis in *The Death of Adonis* by
Titian's follower Sebastiano [fig. 5] or the fresco of *The
Death of Adonis* by Baldassare Peruzzi [fig. 10], which Titian
would have seen in Rome. In Titian's painting it seems likely
that the dead Adonis is fused with the sleeping Cupid so that
we are reminded of the conclusion of the tale at the moment
that Adonis takes his fatal step. A further reminder is con-
tained in the peculiar twist of Adonis's left arm, a position
normally associated with the sleeping Cupid or the dead
Christ.[25] Titian has transformed the departure of Adonis into

[25] Rosand, "Titian and the 'Bed of Polyclitus,' " pp. 242-45.

10. Baldassare Peruzzi. *The Death of Adonis.* c. 1515. Fresco. Villa Farnesina, Rome. (Photo: Alinari).

a moment of choice between the conflicting values of *eros* and *heros* (symbolized, if you like, by the urn and the spear), both of which lead to death. The painting offers no solution to this conflict. Its unity is strictly aesthetic, achieved through synthetic perspective and a balance of horizontals and verticals, which is accented by the single diagonal of the intertwined figures and focused by the brilliant red of Adonis's tunic.

Titian's painting, then, can work as a narrative, much as narratives can work as pictures. He can imply narrative through the depiction of attributes, through gesture, which is itself interrupted action, and through the device of continuous representation, in which the several scenes of a painting depict successive events. He can also use space as an equivalent to logical extension so that the visual relationship of his figures expresses their conceptual relationship. As each figure is allegorized to become an abstraction, so space is allegorized to become a visual syntax.[26] The introduction of temporal and allegorical sequence, though, threatens to fragment the visual realm of imitation. Pictorial success then depends upon the artist's ability to control the tension between visual and rhetorical schemes through the unifying forces of three-dimensional perspective and two-dimensional symmetry, in order to create a "speaking picture," in which the ocular unity of the scene brings a sense of completeness to the story and argument.

In attaining its narrative unity, Shakespeare's poem, like Titian's painting, seems to operate through a reconciliation of tension in which visual images hold together the machinery of an incomplete argumentative sequence. By making Venus and Adonis antagonists instead of lovers, Shakespeare places them physically in a tableau of conflict and transforms this conflict of action into a conflict of ideas, enacted in a formal debate. Why does beauty wither? Venus argues that Diana, goddess of chastity and narcissism, is to blame and that love is the force that preserves:

> "And therefore hath [Diana] brib'd the destinies
> To cross the curious workmanship of nature,
> To mingle beauty with infirmities
> And pure perfection with impure defeature,
>     Making it subject to the tyranny
>     Of mad mischance and much misery."
>                                 [ll. 733-38]

Adonis will have none of it. Venus he sees unequivocally as lust—not Venus Genetrix, but Venus Vulgaris. Passion itself, then, is the force of death:

[26] The rhetorical development of Renaissance painting is examined by Rensselaer W. Lee, *Ut Pictura Poesis: The Humanistic Theory of Painting* (1940; reprint ed. New York: Norton, 1967); John R. Spencer, "*Ut Rhetorica Pictura*: A Study in Quattrocento Theory of Painting," *Journal of the Warburg and*

"Call it not love, for love to heaven is fled,
Since sweating lust on earth usurp'd his name;
Under whose simple semblance he hath fed
Upon fresh beauty, blotting it with blame;
Which the hot tyrant stains and soon bereaves,
As caterpillars do the tender leaves."
[ll. 793-98]

The debate between Venus and Adonis persistently re-solves into the more traditional debate between Venus and Diana, which, in as immediate a source as Book 3 of the *Faerie Queene*, represents warring attitudes toward sexual love. Both goddesses are, in their way, hunters, though of different prey. Ovid tells how Venus,

per silvas dumosaque saxa vagatur
fine genu vestem ritu succincta Dianae
hortaturque canes tutaeque animalia praedae,
aut pronos lepores aut celsum in cornua cervum
aut agitat dammas.

(Over mountain ridges, through the woods, over rocky places set with thorns, she ranges with her garments girt up to her knees after the manner of Diana. She also cheers on the hounds and pursues those creatures which are safe to hunt, such as the headlong hares, or the stag with high-branching horns, or the timid doe.)
[*Metamorphoses*, 10. 535-39]

Ovid lightly parodies the passage in Vergil's *Aeneid* where Venus in the guise of Diana helps Aeneas in his epic quest.[27]

---

*Courtauld Institutes* 20 (1957):26-44; Michael Baxandall, *Giotto and the Orators* (Oxford: Clarendon Press, 1971); and especially pertinent here, Rosand's "*Ut Pictor Poeta.*"

[27] *Aeneid*, 1. 320. The passage became a Neoplatonist allegory of the chaste Venus; see Edgar Wind, *Pagan Mysteries in the Renaissance*, rev. ed. (New York: Norton, 1968), pp. 73-77, 85-88.

The choice between the "hard hunt" for the boar and the "soft hunt" for Wat the hare becomes a choice between the heroic and erotic lives, as Titian knew.[28] Venus tells us how in erotic mastery she subdued the virile Mars:

"Thus he that overrul'd I oversway'd,
Leading him prisoner in a red rose chain:
Strong-temper'd steel his stronger strength obey'd,
Yet was he servile to my coy disdain."
                                        [ll. 109-12]

If Mars here is robbed of heroism, one may recall that to the Neoplatonists the love of Mars and Venus was an allegory of a transcendent concordance of Virtue and Pleasure.[29] Shakespeare too crosses his debate structure with images suggesting a reconciliation between eros and heroism. Adonis's horse is an epic steed, fit for the fields of praise, yet he is also a descendant of Plato's dark horse, the emblem of license.[30] The horse simultaneously breaks his servile bondage and unbridles his lust:

[28] Micyllus, *Metamorphoseos* (p. 239) suggests that Adonis goes to the hunt in pursuit of glory, while Sabinus, *Metamorphoses* (p. 418) concludes that Adonis's death shows that such weaklings should leave the sport to real men. See Don Cameron Allen's classic study of the hunts, "On *Venus and Adonis*," in *Elizabethan and Jacobean Studies Presented to F. P. Wilson* (Oxford: Clarendon Press, 1959), pp. 100-111.

[29] Hesiod, *Theogony*, ll. 934-37; and Plutarch, *De Iside et Osiride*, 48, record that Harmony is the daughter of Venus and Mars. See Erwin Panofsky, *Studies in Iconology* (1939; reprint ed., New York: Harper, 1962), pp. 163-64; and idem, *Titian*, p. 127; Wind, *Pagan Mysteries*, pp. 85-89; and Gombrich, "Botticelli's Mythologies," in *Symbolic Images*, pp. 66-69.

[30] Lever objects that Plato's dark horse is vicious and misshapen, no fit ancestor for Shakespeare's stallion ("Venus and the Second Chance," p. 83). However, Achilles Bocchi, *Symbolicae Quaestiones* (Bologna, 1555), 115, depicts a bridled beast in good point as an emblem of contained lust, as does Titian in the sculptural frieze in the *Sacred and Profane Love*. Sir John Harington sees Renaldo's charger Bayardo as a symbol of lust in *Orlando furioso*, Canto 2. See Guy de Tervarent, *Attributs et symboles dans l'art profane: 1450-1600*, 2 vols. (Geneva: Droz, 1959), 2:418; and Panofsky, *Titian*, p. 118.

> The iron bit he crusheth 'tween his teeth,
> Controlling what he was controlled with.
>
> [ll. 269-70]

Adonis too has been in bondage to Venus:

> Look how a bird lies tangled in a net,
> So fasten'd in her arms Adonis lies.
>
> [ll. 67-68]

Although Venus conquered Mars, Adonis has conquered her, and has a chance to reenact his horse's epic deed:

> Now is she in the very lists of love,
> Her champion mounted for the hot encounter.
> All is imaginary she doth prove;
> He will not manage her, although he mount her.
>
> [ll. 595-98]

The moment of union slips away, love's freedom and bondage still at strife.

The debate structure of the poem permeates not only individual symbols but the syntax of the verse as well, so that images are yoked in warring pairs. At the opening of the poem, red and white appear as a smooth parallel: Adonis's cheek is "more white and red than doves or roses are" (l. 10). It is a familiar Petrarchan trope for the complexion of the beloved, embodying that blend of opposites which defines beauty and linking this master-mistress with the birds and flowers sacred to Venus.

As Adonis demurs, the conceit is inverted to show his unreadiness for love: "He red for shame, but frosty in desire" (l. 36). Syntactically the colors are now in opposition, yet metaphorically they again express parallel sentiments—shame and disdain, both aspects of *pudor*. When the figure is transferred to Venus, its tension is heightened, reflecting a clash of emotions:

> . . . the fighting conflict of her hue,
> How white and red each other did destroy!
> But now her cheek was pale, and by and by
> It flash'd forth fire, as lightning from the sky.
>
> [ll. 345-48]

The figure then goes underground, only to make two startling reappearances, one at the first sight of the boar:

> Whose frothy mouth bepainted all with red,
> Like milk and blood being mingled both together.
>
> [ll. 901-2]

Syntactically the colors are in harmony, but because of its position in the narrative, the conceit is a torturous mockery, death in the garments of love. Then the corpse of Adonis is transformed:

> A purple flower sprung up, checker'd with white,
> Resembling well his pale cheeks and the blood
> Which in round drops upon their whiteness stood.
>
> [ll. 1168-70]

In the dozens of versions of this myth in classical and Renaissance verse and prose, nowhere else is the flower both red and white. Some say Adonis is turned to a rose, some say to an anemone, and some record that each flower formerly was white but now is stained red with the shepherd's blood. Shakespeare's insistence is clear, recalling the antithesis one last time, restored nearly to its original form but applied now to an object which is the negation of the original—a summation of the struggle among Venus, Adonis, and the boar.

The war of red flame and pale frost is echoed by the more elementary strife of fire and water. Ovid, at the opening of the *Metamorphoses*, tells how an unknown god bound in harmony the warring elements.[31] Natali Conti, meditating on a

---

[31] *Metamorphoses*, 1. 16-68. Cf. Plato, *Timaeus*, 32c; Macrobius, *Expositio in Somnium Scipionis*, 6. 24-33.

passage in Euripides, discovers that Harmony is "the off-spring of the elements of all things; and that force which is born from the motion of celestial bodies, whether we call it divine or natural, acting so that the elements themselves are led into this mixture, or rather leading them, that force is called Venus."[32] Shakespeare's Venus strives to harmonize the elements, as they appear in various guises: in climatic terms, they are wind, sun, earth and rain; in emotional terms, sighs, desires, disdain, and tears. As Aphrodite, foam-born, she is already hot and moist:[33]

"My flesh is soft and plump, my marrow burning.
My smooth moist hand, were it with thy hand felt,
Would in thy palm dissolve, or seem to melt."
[ll. 142-44]

While love is, as she tells us, all fire (l. 149), the excess of burning passion will "set the heart on fire" (l. 388) and must be cooled with tears. The hot and dry of fire opposes the cold and moist of water, so that between the two elements can be either chaotic strife or creative union. In the balance of these elements, as Adonis points out, lies the distinction between sweet love and sour lust:

"Love comforteth like sunshine after rain,
But lust's effect is tempest after sun:
Love's gentle spring doth always fresh remain,
Lust's winter comes ere summer half be done."
[ll. 799-802]

The union of Mars and Venus is precisely the harmonious blending of heat and moisture.[34] Venus seeks such a union

[32] "At gravissimus & suavissimus scriptor Euripedes multò etiam clarius demonstravit rerum omnium procreationem ex elementorum esse symmetria; atque vim illam sive divinam quem nascitur è motu coelestium corporum, sive naturalem vocemus, quae facit ut in hanc commistionem elementa ipsa deducantur, vel potius deducit, Venerem appellavit" (Conti, *Mythologia*, p. 125a).

[33] Giraldi, *De Deis Gentium*, p. 372.

[34] Sabinus, *Metamorphoses*, p. 143.

with Adonis, but he is cold and dry, with his eyes and passions fixed on earth (ll. 118, 340), and he can only intermittently supply either heat or moisture:

> Panting he lies and breatheth on her face.
> She feedeth on the steam as on a prey,
> And calls it heavenly moisture.
>                          [ll. 62–64]

> He sees her coming, and begins to glow,
> Even as a dying coal revives with wind.
>                          [ll. 337–38]

Adonis spoke sound doctrine concerning the elements, but refuses the act of temperance of which Shakespeare wrote in his Anacreontic sonnets (153, 154): to cool his torch in her fountain. The strife of elements with which Venus is left makes her subject to a chaos within, the very tempest which Adonis predicted. Her grief at his loss is an earthquake of wind struggling with earth (ll. 1046–47), and she threatens finally to consume herself in a reaction of air, earth, fire and water which seems like a reverse alchemy:

> "My sighs are blown away, my salt tears gone;
> Mine eyes have turn'd to fire, my heart to lead.
> Heavy heart's lead melt at mine eyes' red fire!
> So I shall die by drops of hot desire."
>                          [ll. 1071–74]

The struggle to harmonize the elements, as Pico believed, was the struggle for the *discordia concordans* which sustains love and beauty.[35] The inability of Venus to overcome that strife foreshadows the tragic ending of the poem. The debate structure, operating in individual lines and images as well as in the central action of the poem, becomes a syntactic prin-

---

[35] Pico, *A Platonic Discourse upon Love . . . in Explication of a Sonnet by Hieronimo Benivieni*, 2. 5.; trans. Thomas Stanley (1651; reprint ed., Boston: Merrymount Press, 1914), p. 26.

ciple which prepares us for a resolution, in which the unity of the poem would reside in the simultaneous closure of plot and argument. The ending of the poem, indeed, is cast as an aetiology, appropriate for the conclusion of a rationalized myth:

> "For he being dead, with him is beauty slain,
> And beauty dead, black Chaos comes again."
> [ll. 1019-20]

> "Since thou art dead, lo here I prophesy,
> Sorrow on love hereafter shall attend:
> It shall be waited on with jealousy,
> Find sweet beginning, but unsavoury end."
> [ll. 1135-38]

Precisely at the point where we expect logical conclusion, though, the syntax of plot and argument breaks down, for the aetiology is false. Black Chaos is already loose in the world in Cynthia's jealousy, in the bristling boar, and in Venus's own passions, which were from their sweet beginning full of gluttony, jealousy, wrath, and anguish. Shakespeare has stretched the sinews of prolepsis, for the action of the poem is as much a result as a cause of its conclusion. As if that were not enough, Shakespeare adds a second conclusion, which demonstrates the opposite point about love. From the blood of Adonis springs a flower, which Venus plucks: so Venus remains faithful to Adonis and the two are, finally, fruitful:

> "Here was thy father's bed, here in my breast:
> Thou art the next of blood, and 'tis thy right.
> Lo in this hollow cradle take thy rest;
> My throbbing heart shall rock thee day and night:
> There shall not be one minute in an hour
> Wherein I will not kiss my sweet love's flower."
> [ll. 1183-88]

As in Titian's painting, Shakespeare's debate between Venus and Adonis is never resolved. A series of metaphors mediates between them, each of which generates the same antithesis. Love is life and death, harmony and chaos, bliss and agony, beauty and horror—the paradoxes teeter out of sight on the even feet of oxymoron:

"Ne'er settled equally, but high or low,
   That all love's pleasure shall not match his woe."
                                                          [ll. 1139-40]

The tension of paradox, though, is constantly released by the shifting structures of the poem: by its proleptic narrative, by its double ending. The terms of the debate slide from one set of images to another, joined at innumerable points. The conflict moves from syllogisms to proverbs, to goddesses, to horses and rabbits, to colors and elements. With each set of terms, an abstract dualism is momentarily balanced in a sensible image, generating a kind of "insight," or brief resolution, for, as E. H. Gombrich observes, "the sense of sight provides an analogue to the non-discursive mode of apprehension which must travel from multiplicity to unity."[36] In that pattern of tension and release, of the recurrent dualism momentarily resolved in an image, lies the experience of cohesion which gives unity to the poem.

Shakespeare's sophisticated reworking of a literary myth comes surprisingly close to recovering the function that Lévi-Strauss suggests for primary myth: to bridge the gap between conflicting values through "a series of mediating devices, each of which generates the next one by a process of opposition and correlation. . . . The kind of logic in mythic thought is as rigorous as that of modern science: . . . the difference lies, not in the quality of the intellectual proc-

---

[36] Gombrich, "*Icones Symbolicae*: Philosophies of Symbolism and Their Bearing on Art," in *Symbolic Images*, p. 170.

ess, but in the nature of the things to which it is applied."[37] Just as primary myth may be an alternative form of logical reasoning indulged in by whole societies, Shakespeare's manner of paradox-making has the characteristics of a persistent personal syntax. Indeed, if we think of myth as a conceptual form rather than as a content, we might call it Shakespeare's personal myth, a way of perceiving and reconciling the paradoxes of experience.

*Venus and Adonis* has been compared to the sonnets, the early comedies, even the tragedies. In its handling of paradox, it most closely resembles the mature comedies, or even a problem comedy. What makes a problem comedy problematic is the realization that the tension between opposed values is a permanent condition of life.[38] In *Measure for Measure*, Angelo and Escalus enter into a formal debate between Justice and Mercy in Act 2, but the conflict disappears in the final sentencing of all the characters to marriage. High comedy conceals similar difficulties, for its argument, as Northrop Frye tells us, is individual fulfillment and social harmony—admirable values both, but perhaps less easily reconciled than Frye's formula would admit.[39] *As You Like It* is obviously a play working toward both values, and its ending brings them into a *theatrical* balance through the simple technique of a double ending. First Hymen, the embodiment of social harmony, links each couple; then Jaques, the soul of humorous individualism, repeats Hymen's action and nearly his very words, giving to each the fulfillment of his ambition.

Two insightful critics of Shakespeare, Norman Rabkin

---

[37] Claude Lévi-Strauss, *Structural Anthropology*, trans. Claire Jacobson and Brooke G. Schoepf (New York: Basic Books, 1963), pp. 213-23.

[38] A. P. Rossiter, *Angel with Horns and Other Shakespeare Lectures*, ed. Graham Storey (New York: Theatre Arts, 1961), pp. 116-17.

[39] Northrop Frye, "The Argument of Comedy," in *English Institute Essays, 1948*, ed. D. A. Robertson (New York: Columbia University Press, 1949), pp. 60-61.

and Stephen Booth, have examined this obsessive paradox-making. In *Hamlet*, Rabkin finds, "Shakespeare tends to structure his imitations in terms of a pair of polar opposites," between which we must, but cannot, choose.[40] Examining the sonnets, Booth finds the reverse—that one set of opposites is incommensurate with another—that syntactic paradox leads us one way, imagistic paradox another, prosodic a third, with no release of the tension created.[41] *Venus and Adonis* offers us, I think, something between the two models: by shifting, in the manner described by Booth, from one set of terms—one whole structure—to another, a release from paradox is achieved. The style of *Venus and Adonis* might best be epitomized in the metaphors of red and white: a constant shifting of the significance of the images and of the syntactic structures linking them, which are held together as a series simply by the repetition of the image itself.

As Rabkin observes, though, the reconciliation "cannot be reduced to prose paraphrase or statements of theme because the kind of 'statement' a given play makes cannot respectably be made in the logical language of prose."[42] For a work like *Venus and Adonis*, where the serial form of narrative encourages the serial form of logical discourse, the achievement of a purely aesthetic resolution is particularly fine. It is done by shifting out of the dialogue of argument into a discourse of images—literally, iconography—thus opening the possibility of an iconic resolution of the same sort that Shakespeare habitually achieved on the stage through the visual image of coupling. Paradox, then, is too neat a word; it suggests a final, balanced position, the *seeming* opposition overcome. Shakespearean paradox, in *Venus and Adonis* at least, is a problem not of seeing or seeming, but of being. Erotic experience can be described only by combining two ways of

[40] Rabkin, *Shakespeare and the Commom Understanding*, p. 12.

[41] Stephen Booth, *An Essay on Shakespeare's Sonnets* (New Haven: Yale University Press, 1969), especially pp. 59-60, 104-7.

[42] Rabkin, *Shakespeare and the Common Understanding*, p. 12.

thinking, the discursive and the iconic, and shuttling from one to the other. The variety of that experience can be described in no other words and the unity recalled in no other way.

## The Skillful Painting of *Lucrece*

In 1593 Shakespeare promised Southampton "some graver labour" to follow *Venus and Adonis*. Indeed, Muriel Bradbrook has persuasively argued that *Venus* itself was an attempt by Shakespeare to silence the slanders uttered by Greene in 1592 and to establish himself as a respectable poet.[43] *Lucrece*, which appeared on 1594, fulfills the promise made in *Venus*, for it is a "minor epic" in the sense that Ariosto and Spenser are epic, concerned with "Knights and Ladies gentle deeds, . . . Fierce warres and faithfull loves." In the progress from *Venus and Adonis* to *Lucrece*, Shakespeare travels the Vergilian path, beginning in a middle style akin to sonnet, pastoral, and comedy, and ending in the regions of epic and tragedy. The erotic and the heroic are mingled in Tarquin's siege of the fort of Lucrece's chastity, until the moment when he is able to "make the breach and enter this sweet city."

In her agony after the rape, Lucrece calls to mind a vast tapestry or painting of the fall of Troy that decorates her villa and uses it to form an extended comparison between bedroom and battlefield:

"For even as subtle Sinon here is painted,
So sober sad, so weary and so mild,—
As if with grief or travail he had fainted, —
To me came Tarquin armed to beguild
With outward honesty, but yet defil'd

---

[43] Muriel Bradbrook, "Beasts and Gods: Greene's *Groats-Worth of Witte* and the Social Purpose of *Venus and Adonis*," *Shakespeare Survey* 15 (1962):62-72.

With inward vice. As Priam did him cherish,
So did I Tarquin,—so my Troy did perish."
                                                    [ll. 1541-47]

When he describes the response of Lucrece to this "well-painted piece," Shakespeare defines her stature as a woman and as the hero of his poem—but more than that. Whereas the iconography of *Venus* was an art that concealed art, operating on an invisible and even unconscious level, the *ekphrasis* of *Lucrece* is a self-reflective art that calls attention to its own artifice. In his elaborate description of this "piece of skillful painting," Shakespeare draws on Vergil and classical art theorists to create for his poem a proper epic *ekphrasis* comparable to the shield of Achilles, to the bronze doors at Carthage where Aeneas sees written the fate of his people, or to the "clothes of *Arras* and of *Toure*" which decorate Malecasta's castle in the *Faerie Queene*. By describing the painter's wondrous skill, Shakespeare invokes the ancient *paragone* of poet and painter, asserting his own mastery of his craft and his equality to the ancient masters of the art.

The Troy passage is set into the poem as an extended simile or icon. Originally the term 'icon' meant 'statue' or 'image' before becoming a technical term of rhetoric.[44] The *Rhetorica ad Herennium* defines it as a comparison between two things, used either for praise or blame.[45] Aristotle notes that icon is best suited to poetry and Erasmus praises it for vividness.[46] Some confusion may arise here from the different terminology used by Jean Hagstrum in *The Sister Arts*. He calls 'iconic' any poetry which describes a work of the visual arts, and reserves *ekphrasis* for the rhetorical figure in which the work of art is made to speak (like Keats's urn).[47] I shall

[44] Marsh H. McCall Jr., *Ancient Rhetorical Theories of Simile and Comparison* (Cambridge: Harvard University Press, 1969), p. ix.

[45] *Rhetorica ad Herennium*, 4. 49. 62.

[46] Aristotle, *Rhetoric*, 3. 4. 1; Erasmus, *De Utraque Verborum ac Rerum Copia* (Cologne, 1566), p. 366.

[47] Jean Hagstrum, *The Sister Arts* (Chicago: University of Chicago Press, 1958), p. 18, n. 34.

stay with the broader usage of classical and Renaissance rhet-
oricians, who call any vivid, sensuous image 'iconic'; define
*ekphrasis* as an extended description of something, such as a
person, place, battle or work of art; and use *prosopopoeia* for
the lending of voice to an inanimate object.[48] This usage has
the advantage of emphasizing the comparative nature of
iconic imagery and defining more closely for us the function
of such imagery in a long poem. Once we have established
how the Troy passage fits into the poem, we can examine it
in detail to see just what kind of artifact it describes and what
it reveals about the poet and his heroine.

Shakespeare's icon sums up a comparison which has been
carefully developed from the opening line of the poem.
"From the besieged Ardea all in post" comes Tarquin, from
battle to bed and, one may wonder, from Ardea to ardor. In
a system of "moral heraldry," as Bradbrook calls it, Shake-
speare transforms the faces of both protagonists into the
shields of opposing warriors.[49] In Tarquin's face and coat of
arms are written the signs of his dishonor:

"Then my digression is so vile, so base,
    That it will live engraven in my face.

"Yea, though I die the scandal will survive
    And be an eye-sore in my golden coat;
Some loathsome dash the herald will contrive,
    To cipher me how fondly I did dote."
                                    [ll. 202-7]

While the foul intent of Tarquin is immediately visible to
Shakespeare, to the reader and to Tarquin himself, it is hid-
den from Lucrece, who

[48] Cf. *Ad Herennium*, 4. 53. 66; Quintilian, *Institutio Oratoria*, 8. 3. 61-71;
Erasmus, *Copia*, pp. 288-94.
[49] Muriel Bradbrook, *Shakespeare and Elizabethan Poetry* (London: Chatto,
1951), pp. 110-16.

Could pick no meaning from their parling looks,
Nor read the subtle shining secrecies
Writ in the glassy margents of such books.
                                        [ll. 100–102]

For all her simplicity, the face of Lucrece is painted with equal subtlety:

When beauty boasted blushes, in despite
Virtue would stain that o'er with silver white.

But beauty in that white entituled
From Venus' doves, doth challenge that fair field;
Then virtue claims from beauty beauty's red,
Which virtue gave the golden age to gild
Their silver cheeks, and call'd it then their shield;
    Teaching them thus to use it in the fight,
    When shame assail'd, the red should fence the white.

This heraldry in Lucrece's face was seen,
Argu'd by beauty's red and virtue's white;
Of either's colour was the other queen.
                                        [ll. 55–66]

First virtue is white and beauty blushing red; then beauty is white, like Venus's doves, and virtue red by association with the golden age. The very slipperiness of the image suggests there is an ambiguity about moral heraldry. It is hard to tell from the crest just what is under the visor. If Lucrece had trouble reading Tarquin's face, her own features, however clear and honest, are no less a puzzle for the poet, and in that puzzle is something of an ambivalence toward the epic tradition. Tarquin is decidedly villainous, a perfect antihero, whose own soul is desecrated by his crime.[50] But Lucrece, as his opponent, is not at first clearly heroic either in understanding or in action.

[50] Sam Hynes, "The Rape of Tarquin," *Shakespeare Quarterly* 10 (1959): 451-53.

Is she, after all, sufficiently noble to be the heroine of a little epic? As Saint Augustine asked, if she was chaste, why did she kill herself, and if guilty, why worthy of praise?[51] The question has been repeated at some length by two modern Augustinians, Don Cameron Allen and Roy Battenhouse.[52] We might—should—be tempted to dismiss this out of hand as shallow misogyny, confusing the victim with the criminal, except that Lucrece repeatedly asks the same question of herself. In her first words after the rape she speaks of her "offences," "disgrace," "unseen sin," "guilt," and "shame" (ll. 746-56). The misogyny is enough part of the poem that we must deal with it.

Livy and Ovid clearly say that Lucrece consented to her rape under duress. Chaucer is evasive. He takes Ovid's verb "succubuit," "she yielded," to mean that she sank away or fainted, eliminating the nagging question of her state of mind:

> She loste bothe at ones wit and breth,
> And in a swogh she lay, and wex so ded,
> Men myghte smyten of hire arm or hed;
> She feleth no thing, neyther foul ne fayr.[53]

Shakespeare takes a third way, having Tarquin use force throughout. Even so, Lucrece spends the night examining herself and the other potential culprits, Night, Opportunity, Time, and, incidentally, Tarquin. So the unstable identity of the opening lines is still unfixed as she comes to the "well-painted piece." Its function as *comparatio* is all the more important for this reason. In viewing the work, Lucrece may be able to view herself, to successfully "read" it and her own

---

[51] Augustine, *City of God*, 1. 19.

[52] Don Cameron Allen, "Some Observations on *The Rape of Lucrece*," *Shakespeare Survey* 15 (1962):89-98; Roy Battenhouse, *Shakespearean Tragedy: Its Art and Its Christian Premises* (Bloomington: University of Indiana Press, 1969), pp. 14-17.

[53] *The Legend of Good Women*, ll. 1815-18, in *The Works of Geoffrey Chaucer*, ed. F. N. Robinson, 2nd ed. (Boston: Houghton Mifflin, 1957), p. 509.

character as neither she nor Shakespeare could do at the outset.

In seeing how Lucrece "reads" the Troy-piece, we may first ask just what it is she is looking at. Shakespeare describes at least six different scenes: the Greek army arrayed before the walls, Nestor addressing the troops, Hector issuing forth from the gates, the battle on "Simois' reedy banks," the final sack of the citadel, and (out of chronological order) Sinon deluding Priam. He praises the painter's realism and his "art of physiognomy," which is not the description of features, but the rendering of the emotions in each face. What could depict so many scenes, with such a technique? Is it a tapestry or a painting? Even to think about Elizabethan painting is to encounter next to nothing which could evoke such a description. Sidney Colvin, convinced by the detail of the passage that Shakespeare had an actual work in mind, suggested a tapestry of fifteenth-century France.[54] Margaret Thorp in 1931 thought it was a panel painting.[55] A.H.R. Fairchild suggested that Shakespeare was combining the composition of fifteenth-century French tapestries with the "physiognomy" of sixteenth-century works.[56]

Personally, I vote for a tapestry. The only real objection to a tapestry is the term "painted," which, as Fairchild points out, Elizabethans, and Shakespeare, used with great looseness as a synonym for "colored" or "portrayed."[57] Indeed, for humanist painters, "pinxit" is regularly interchanged with "finxit."[58] But there seems little point to all this argu-

[54] Sidney Colvin, "The Sack of Troy in Shakespeare's 'Lucrece' and in Some Fifteenth-Century Drawings and Tapestries," in *A Book of Homage to Shakespeare,* ed. Israel Gollancz (Oxford: Clarendon Press, 1916), pp. 88-99.

[55] Margaret Thorp, "Shakespeare and the Fine Arts," *PMLA* 46 (1931): 687-88.

[56] A.H.R. Fairchild, *Shakespeare and the Arts of Design,* University of Missouri Studies, vol. 12 (Columbia, 1937), pp. 139-43.

[57] *Ibid.,* pp. 110, 144.

[58] Anne-Marie Lecoq, " 'Finxit.' Le Peintre Comme 'Fictor' au XVIᵉ Siècle," *Bibliothèque d'Humanisme et Renaissance* 37 (1975):225-43.

ment since we have no evidence of what Shakespeare might have actually seen. The only painter he mentions by name is the notorious Giulio Romano, waxworker, of the *Winter's Tale*. Richard Burbage was a painter, but the two works attributed to him (at Dulwich College) are small portrait heads, hardly helpful with the vast historical piece Shakespeare describes.[59] W. S. Heckscher, having surveyed Shakespeare's few references to art, concludes that he is never so vague as when he is describing what he has actually seen and never so detailed as when constructing from the imagination.[60] The passage really tells us less about the actual object than about the illusion it creates. It is sufficiently incomplete that we may see what we please as long as we see *something*.

The incompleteness of the description on such a crucial point is a sign that it is essentially a verbal, not a visual formulation. The opening of the passage stresses the painter's skill in imitation: "In scorn of nature, art gave lifeless life" (l. 1374). The conceit is a tired one which Shakespeare repeats in various guises in *Timon, Pericles, Venus and Adonis* and the *Winter's Tale*.[61] Fairchild has protested that Shakespeare was too refined aesthetically to be interested in mere imitation of nature and *trompe l'oeil*, but a fair look at his words suggests that he, like most of his contemporaries, demands it.[62] The expressiveness for which Vasari praises painters is achieved through some particularly vivid physical detail, and Carel van Mander, the "Vasari of the North,"

[59] Sir Edward Cook, ed., *A Description and Historical Catalogue of the Pictures in the Gallery of Alleyn's College of God's Gift at Dulwich* (London: n.p., 1914), nos. 380, 395.

[60] W. S. Heckscher, "Shakespeare in His Relationship to the Visual Arts: A Study in Paradox," *Research Opportunities in Renaissance Drama* 13-14 (1970-71):57-58.

[61] *Timon*, 1. 1. 35-38; *Pericles*, 5. Chorus, 5-7; *Venus*, 1. 291; *Winter's Tale*, 4. 4. 86-88 and 5. 3. 19-20, 67-68.

[62] Fairchild, *Shakespeare and the Arts of Design*, p. 137. W. Moelwyn Merchant points out Shakespeare's concern and sophistication with the visual arts in *Shakespeare and the Artist* (London, Oxford University Press, 1959), pp. 9-12.

hails Pieter Aertsen for deceiving the eye and making the
dead seem alive.[63]

Shakespeare's *ekphrasis* begins with praise for the perfect
imitation of the visible (ll. 1366-86), then praise for the per-
fect rendering of expression (ll. 1387-1407), and finally praise
for the artist's ability to suggest the parts of the figure invis-
ible to the eye (ll. 1408-28). These are the criteria by which
Pliny measures the perfection of painting. First Zeuxis was
able to render exactly what the eye could see. Then Parrha-
sios "added vivacity to the features," and learned "to give
assurance of the parts behind, thus clearly suggesting even
what it conceals." At last Apelles excells all others, not in
any particular technique but through a certain grace which
combines the excellences of others.[64] If Shakespeare had any
intention of constructing a proper Roman decoration for Lu-
crece's house, Pliny would have been the likely place to start.

The adherence of Shakespeare's *ekphrasis* to classical aes-
thetics is underscored by a parallel, first noted by E. H.
Gombrich, between Shakespeare's description of Nestor ha-
ranguing the troops with the account by Philostratus of a
painting of the siege of Thebes.[65] It is worth quoting in full.
"Some are seen in full figure, others with the legs hidden,
others from the waist up, then only the busts of some, heads
only, helmets only, and finally just spear-points. This, my
boy, is perspective; since the problem is to deceive the eyes
as they travel back along with the proper receding planes of
the picture."[66]

[63] Svetlana Leontief Alpers, "*Ekphrasis* and Aesthetic Attitudes in Vasari's
*Lives,*" *Journal of the Warburg and Courtauld Institutes* 23 (1960):193; Carel van
Mander, *Grondt der Schilder-Const*, bk. 7, chap. 55, in *Northern Renaissance
Art, 1400-1600*, ed. Wolfgang Stechow (Englewood Cliffs, N.J.: Prentice-
Hall, 1966), p. 63.

[64] *Historia Naturalis*, 35. 61-96, in *The Elder Pliny's Chapters on the History
of Art*, trans. K. Jex-Blake (London, 1896), pp. 107-33.

[65] Gombrich, *Art and Illusion*, rev. ed. (Princeton: Princeton University
Press, 1969), p. 211.

[66] Philostratus, *Eikones*, 1, 4, trans. Arthur Fairbanks, Loeb ed. (London,
Heinemann, 1931), p. 17. While Fairbanks notes that the phrase translated

For much imaginary work was there,—
Conceit deceitful, so compact, so kind,
That for Achilles' image stood his spear
Gripp'd in an armed hand; himself behind
Was left unseen, save to the eye of mind:
A hand, a foot, a face, a leg, a head
Stood for the whole to be imagined.
[ll. 1422-28]

Even in translation, the parallel strikes me as sufficiently full and detailed to be an actual borrowing. Both stress the painter's cheating skill, and linger over the spear. If Shakespeare's "lesse Greeke" were inadequate to the task, he could have read Philostratus in any of the five Latin editions between 1517 and 1550, or in the 1578 French translation of Blaise de Vigenère.

Whether we accept Philostratus as a source or not, his *ekphrasis* establishes a rhetorical pattern for describing a visual artifact which was so widely diffused that it would have been virtually impossible for any serious poet to be ignorant of it. Philostratus does not so much describe as suggest, concentrating not on the object itself, but on how it would appear to a viewer. In a sense he practices, as does Shakespeare, exactly the kind of rhetoric and the kind of art to which Plato objected.[67] The representation, either in word, paint or marble, is not true to life, much less to an objective ideal. It is distorted to accommodate the process of perception, and those very distortions are Shakespeare's main interest.

The remainder of the passage, describing the fall of Troy, is largely modeled on two *ekphraseis* in the *Aeneid*: the description of the bronze doors of the temple of Venus at Carthage in Book 1, and Aeneas's account of the battle in Book

---

as "perspective" means literally "the principle of proportion," Blaise de Vigenère's widely read French translation of 1578 also renders it as "perspective" (Paris, 1615, p. 26).
[67] Gombrich, *Art and Illusion*, pp. 126-27.

2.[68] Vergil departs from the bronze doors to describe the original event itself, which his viewer, Aeneas, of course witnessed:

ter circum Iliacos raptaverat Hectora muros
exanimumque auro corpus vendebat Achilles.
tum vero ingentem gemitum dat pectore ab imo,
ut spolia, ut currus, utque ipsum corpus amici
tendentemque manus Priamum conspexit inermis.

(Thrice had Achilles dragged Hector round the walls of Troy and was selling the lifeless body for gold. Then indeed from the bottom of his heart he heaves a deep groan, as the spoils, as the chariot, as the very corpse of his friend met his gaze, and Priam outstretching weaponless hands.)[69]

The striking thing is Vergil's simultaneous use of telescopic and microscopic vision, picking out small details amid a scene crowded with events and passions, violating the supposed temporal boundaries of the visual arts. Quintilian had this or similar style in mind in his discussion of the ornate, which Erasmus would quote in the *Copia*:

So, too, we may move our hearers to tears by the picture of a captured town. For the mere statement that the town was stormed . . . fails to penetrate the emotions of the hearer. But if we expand all that the one word "stormed" includes, we shall see the flames pouring

[68] Sources for *Lucrece* are examined by Rollins in the New Variorum Edition, pp. 416-26; and by Bullough, *Narrative and Dramatic Sources*, 1:179-83. In " 'Nothing Undervalued to Cato's Daughter': Plutarch's Porcia in the Shakespeare Canon," *Comparative Drama* 11 (1978):307-9, John W. Velz makes a convincing case that Shakespeare also draws on Plutarch's description of the sorrowing response of Brutus's wife Portia to a painting of the fall of Troy.

[69] *Aeneid*, 1. 483-87, trans. H. Rushton Fairclough, Loeb ed. (London: Heinemann, 1932).

from house and temple, and hear the crash of falling roofs and one confused clamour blent of many cries.[70]

The pattern Shakespeare is following, one established by Vergil, Philostratus, Quintilian, and of course Homer, was codified in the *Progymnasmata* of Hermogenes, the rhetorician of the second sophistic. *Ekphrasis* he defines as:

> an account in detail, visible, as they say, bringing before one's eyes what is to be shown. . . . Ekphrasis of actions will proceed from what went before, from what happened at that time, and from what followed. Thus if we make an ekphrasis on war, first we shall tell what happened before the war, the levy, the expenditures, the fears; then the engagements, the slaughter, the deaths; then the monument of victory; then the paeans of the victors and, of the others, the tears, the slavery.[71]

The poet, departing from the literal limits of the scene to what came before and after, strives to make it as vivid as possible for the audience by rendering the emotions of the participants. To Quintilian this was the highest of all oratorical achievement, though not the most difficult to attain.[72]

The achievement of this vividness is a common goal for both poetry and painting in the ekphrastic tradition. Plutarch, after quoting the aphorism of Simonides that painting is silent poetry and poetry is a speaking picture, observes that the two arts differ only in the materials by which they seek the same end.[73] As the humanist theorists of each art dwelt on that material difference, they defined the limits of

---

[70] Quintilian, *Institutio Oratoria*, 8. 3. 67-68, trans. H. E. Butler, Loeb ed. (London: Heinemann, 1921). Cf. Erasmus, *Copia*, pp. 288-89.

[71] C. S. Baldwin, *Medieval Rhetoric and Poetic* (1928; reprint ed., Gloucester, Mass.: Peter Smith, 1959), pp. 35-36.

[72] Quintilian, *Institutio Oratoria*, 8. 3. 70-71.

[73] Plutarch, *Moralia*, 346, trans. Frank Cole Babbitt, Loeb ed., 15 vols. (London: Heinemann, 1936), 4:501.

each art by the capacities of the other. Castelvetro, for example, says that painting can only show bodies, not the soul, while poetry can never equal the visual immediacy of painting.[74] So Shakespeare concludes in Sonnet 24 that his eyes, like painters, "draw but what they see, know not the heart."

The highest form of skill, then, is to surpass the limits of your material and achieve the perfection of the rival art. Pliny sums up Apelles' gift, which made him the paragon of artists, in that he could paint the unpaintable.[75] Likewise Ortelius lauds Bruegel and Erasmus praises Dürer:

Nay, he even depicts that which cannot be depicted: fire, rays of light, thunder, sheet lightning, lightning, or, as they say, the "clouds on a wall": in fine, the whole mind of man as it reflects itself in the behavior of the body, and almost the voice itself.[76]

The *topos* appears in an entertainment for the queen at Mitcham in 1598 attributed to John Lyly and Shakespeare knows it when he writes Act 1 of *Timon*.[77]

The *paragone* of the arts could be developed into a comparison of artists. Pliny likens Apelles to Homer, and Titian, the modern Apelles, was rival to Ariosto, the modern Homer.[78] The painter may take his themes from literature, as did Titian in the mythological canvases he called "poesie," while the poet may decorate his verse with *ekphraseis*. Shakespeare perfectly fulfills the goal of the *paragone* in his Troy-

[74] H. B. Charlton, *Castelvetro's Theory of Poetry* (Manchester: Manchester University Press, 1913), p. 63.

[75] Pliny the Elder, *Historia Naturalis*, 35. 96.

[76] Erasmus, *De Recta Latini Graecique Sermonis Pronuntiatione*, in Stechow, *Northern Renaissance Art*, p. 123.

[77] *Queen Elizabeth's Entertainment at Mitcham: Poet, Painter, and Musician*, ed. Leslie Hotson (New Haven: Yale University Press, 1953), p. 20; *Timon* 1. 1. 30-94. Cf. Anthony Blunt, "An Echo of the 'Paragone' in Shakespeare," *Journal of the Warburg and Courtauld Institutes* 2 (1938-39):260-62; Merchant, *Shakespeare and the Artist*, pp. 171-74.

[78] Rosand, "*Ut Pictor Poeta*," pp. 529-32.

piece with the variety of its action and vividness of emotion. He stresses how the painter has shown the things impossible to depict—the concealed parts of the body, the sounds of the scenes, the feelings of the participants. Since this impossible painting is so perfect, he may well praise the artist for rivalling nature. Since it is possible only in the medium of poetry, and is measured by the standard of Vergil, he is also subtly praising himself.

The Vergilian model defines not just the task of the artist, but also the response of the audience to the artist's skill. Vergil lingers over Aeneas's reaction to the scene of Troy:

> constitit et lacrimans, "quis iam locus," inquit, "Achate,
> quae regio in terris nostri non plena laboris?
> en Priamus! sunt hic etiam sua praemia laudi,
> sunt lacrimae rerum et mentem mortalia tangunt."

> (He stopped and weeping cried: "What land, Achates, what tract on earth is now not full of our sorrow? Lo, Priam! Here, too, virtue has its due rewards; here, too, are tears for misfortune and mortal sorrows touch the heart.")

> [*Aeneid*, 1. 459-62]

His close identification with the emotions portrayed move Aeneas to a fresh lament over his own fate. Lucrece, too, overcome with the sorrow of Hecuba, laments that the painter gave her "so much grief, and not a tongue":

> "Poor instrument," quoth she, "without a sound,
> I'll tune thy woes with my lamenting tongue,
> And drop sweet balm in Priam's painted wound,
> And rail on Pyrrhus that hath done him wrong,
> And with my tears quench Troy that burns so long,
>   And with my knife scratch out the angry eyes
>   Of all the Greeks that are thine enemies."

> [ll. 1464-70]

As she moves through the tapestry naming and sorrowing with each figure, she comes finally to Sinon, whose smooth face conceals his inner treachery. Confronting him, she must finally penetrate surfaces, and in doing so, recognize just how similar her own story is:

> "It cannot be," quoth she, "that so much guile,"—
> She would have said,—"can lurk in such a look."
> But Tarquin's shape came in her mind the while,
> And from her tongue "can lurk" from "cannot" took.
> [ll. 1534-37]

Shakespeare's one violation of chronological order, leaving Sinon for last, is thus dictated by his rhetorical order, moving from the tapestry itself, to Lucrece's vocal response, to her recognition of the similarity to her own fate: from *ekphrasis* to *prosopopoeia* to icon.

We may think of Shakespeare as recapitulating the instructions for looking at a painting which Philostratus gave in sections 1-4 of the *Eikones* (concluding with the siege of Thebes). First, he tells us, the mere physical illusion of the paint creates wonder, but to interpret it properly we must look away from the painting to the events which are depicted. As we enter the illusion, we expand the scene with our own imagination, hearing its sounds, seeing what is only suggested, until our identification with it is so close that we are actors in it: "Let us catch the blood, my boy, holding under it a fold of our garments."[79] This expressive view of aesthetic experience was shared as well by Renaissance art theorists. Dependent on Philostratus, Pliny, and the poets for their knowledge of classical painting, they were influenced by *ekphrasis* perhaps as deeply as their literary colleagues.[80] Alberti echoes Horace to explain how we look at

---

[79] Philostratus, *Eikones*, 1, 4.
[80] Cf. Alpers, "*Ekphrasis* and Aesthetic Attitudes"; and Baxandall, *Giotto and the Orators*, pp. 85-96.

paintings: "We weep with the weeping, laugh with the laughing, and grieve with the grieving."[81] Lucrece's response is exactly to seek out the "face where all distress is stell'd" (l. 1444) as the analogue to her own grief. This is not an act of simple empathy but of judgment. As Lomazzo explains in his *Tract of Painting*:

> The picture mooveth the eye, and that committeth the species and formes of the things seene to the memory, all which it representeth to the understanding, which considereth of the truth and falshood of those things, which being perfectly understood it representeth them to the will, which if the thing be evill, it abandoneth and forsaketh, if good, it loveth, and naturally embraceth the same.[82]

Lucrece does not empathize equally with all the figures in the painting. She must penetrate the appearance of each to weigh properly the gullibility of Priam with the duplicity of Sinon. It is in looking at the painting, in examining by comparison the woes of Hecuba, that Lucrece is finally able to face the full diabolism of Tarquin and her own lack of responsibility for what has occurred. This is no easy lesson, for Hamlet needed supernatural prompting to discover that "one may smile and smile, and be a villain" (1. 5. 108). In that moment of recognition Lucrece reaches her fullest heroic stature.

I have claimed at this point that Lucrece bears no responsibility for what has happened. Why, then, does she kill herself? The reasoning for the final act returns us to Shake-

---

[81] Alberti, *On Painting*, trans. John R. Spencer (New Haven: Yale University Press, 1956), p. 77 and note. Cf. Horace, *Ars Poetica*, 101-3, and Cicero, *De Amicitia*, 14. 50. Lomazzo, arguing the same point, quotes Horace in *A Tracte Containing the Artes of Curious Paintinge Carvinge & Buildinge*, trans. Richard Haydocke (London, 1598), sig. Aa1$^{r-v}$.

[82] Lomazzo, *Artes of Curious Paintinge*, sig. A2$^v$.

speare's misogyny, for while Lucrece is not to blame, she is clearly guilty.[83] As Collatine and Lucretius say in lines 1709–10, her mind is pure though her body is soiled. Lucrece is dwelling with the most severe mind-body split conceivable, and only by suicide can she make this fully clear so that others can read her as she has read the Troy tapestry, and revenge her as she has sought to revenge Hecuba by tearing at Sinon with her nails.

For Lucrece has herself become an emblem, and she fears the interpretations which others may make of her. Immediately after her apostrophe to Night she laments:

> "Yea, the illiterate that know not how
>   To cipher what is writ in learned books,
>   Will quote my loathsome trespass in my looks."
>                                         [ll. 810-12]

She fears that she and Collatine have become an example of cuckoldry, "And Tarquin's eye may read the mot afar" (l. 830) she adds in the technical language of devices. Yet the inability of others to interpret this way suggests that Lucrece at first misunderstands her own symbolism. When Lucrece's maid enters, she weeps at the sight of the face of her mistress without knowing the reason. She has empathy without judgment. When the groom enters to receive the message to Collatine, he blushes from sheer nervousness, which Lucrece takes to mean that he has seen her shame.

The blushing servants, who are the first audience of the ravished Lucrece, are imperfect prototypes for her own response to Hecuba. Indeed, the maid's response, like that of

---

[83] Several of Shakespeare's heroines, especially in the comedies, are of course remarkable women, especially by comparison with those in the works of his contemporaries. I use the term "misogyny" not to make a relative judgment about Shakespeare, but simply to refer to the portrayal of women as inferior to men in mental capacity and range of activity. For a fine analysis of the significance Shakespeare gives to the rape of a married woman in a patriarchal society see Coppélia Kahn, "The Rape in Shakespeare's *Lucrece*," *Shakespeare Studies* 9 (1976):45-72.

Lucrece to the tapestry, is one of like to like. As Lucrece will be "impressed" by the emotions of the tapestry, so the maid is "impressed" by the countenance of her mistress:

> For men have marble, women waxen, minds,
> And therefore are they form'd as marble will;
> The weak oppress'd, th'impression of strange kinds
> Is form'd in them by force, by fraud, or skill.
> Then call them not the authors of their ill,
>   No more than wax shall be accounted evil,
>   Wherein is stamp'd the semblance of a devil.
>                                    [ll. 1240-46]

"By force, by fraud, or skill": Tarquin, Sinon and the painter. The metaphor of wax has undergone an interesting displacement, beginning as an explanation of the behavior of the maid, but ending with what men do to women. Is it too much to speculate that the process of "impressing" which is worked out in Lucrece's initial reaction to the Troy-piece can be a model for the rape itself: that is, that Tarquin, who is elsewhere called a devil, stamps his evil in the wax that is Lucrece?

Though Lucrece will desperately claim that "I am the mistress of my fate" (l. 1069), she is at the outset pliant and without anything that might be called a free will. Isabella will say to Angelo in *Measure for Measure*:

> For we are soft as our complexions are,
> And credulous to false prints.
>                    [2. 4. 129-30]

Shakespeare indeed stresses the point in *Lucrece* by likening the moral condition of women to the beautiful but passive flower:

> No man inveigh against the withered flower,
> But chide rough winter that the flower hath kill'd;

Not that devour'd, but that which doth devour
Is worthy blame; O let it not be hild
Poor women's faults, that they are so fulfill'd
    With men's abuses! those proud lords to blame
    Make weak-made women tenants to their shame.
                                                    [ll. 1254-60]

Her inability to control her own body limits the actions of
the heroic self which Lucrece defines while standing before
the Troy-piece. Only at the end of the passage does she rise
beyond external impressions to judge, define, and act. And
even then she is, paradoxically, Hecuba the sufferer, not
Aeneas the rebuilder. In Hecuba,

    . . . the painter had anatomiz'd
Time's ruin, beauty's wrack, and grim care's reign.
                                                    [ll. 1450-51]

Lucrece bears

The face, that map which deep impression bears
Of hard misfortune, carv'd in it with tears.
                                                    [ll. 1712-13]

The world crowds in on her, shaping her body and mind,
while she has little scope to push back and control events. If
she were a man, she could of course avenge herself. "O God,
that I were a man!" cries Beatrice in *Much Ado*, "I would eat
his heart in the market-place" (4. 1. 306-7). But they are
women, and must employ men to wield their swords. The
only women in all of Shakespeare's plays who successfully
use weapons on stage are the villains: La Pucelle, Queen
Margaret, and Regan. There are no Jaels and no Judiths.
    The only power left to Lucrece is in the realm of art. As
audience, she can enter into the epic action of Troy. As art-
ist, she can move her own audience by the vivid portrayal of
the significance of her figures. Immediately after the rape,

Lucrece was plagued with misreadings, seeing herself as Adultery, an image which her servants found unintelligible. After her confrontation with the Troy-piece, she is prepared to present herself as the image of woe and suffering and to demand from Collatine and Lucretius the revenge she offered to Hecuba. Her suicide is nothing more or less than the *energeia* or forcibleness which gives the tableau its impact. It releases her blood, which separates into two rivers, one of pure red, the other black and foul. She shows what could not be seen, the inner self which signifies visually what all have insisted verbally:

"Though my gross blood be stain'd with this abuse,
    Immaculate and spotless is my mind."
                    [ll. 1655-56]

The *ekphrasis* or detailed description of the blood is followed by *apostrophe*, in which Lucretius and Collatine each address Lucrece, pour out their sorrows, and proclaim their own impending deaths. Only Brutus seems fully to understand her meaning, and chides the others:

"Why Collatine, is woe the cure for woe?
Do wounds help wounds, or grief help grievous deeds?
Is it revenge to give thyself a blow
For his foul act by whom thy fair wife bleeds?
Such childish humour from weak minds proceeds;
    Thy wretched wife mistook the matter so,
    To slay herself that should have slain her foe."
                    [ll. 1821-27]

Is this really a condemnation of her suicide? I do not think so. What Brutus scorns is the mere empathy of answering woe with woe; he is calling for the men to perform the same vengeance on Tarquin which Lucrece herself sought to inflict on Sinon. He reprimands the men for considering suicide, calls them childish, and speaks of "weak minds," much like the phrases Shakespeare has earlier used for all women. Her mistake, then, is that she is a woman, blocked from full heroic action in the public realm, condemned instead to constantly proving her sexual honor.

Brutus stands as a marker for the ultimate failure of Lucrece in heroic terms but her success in artistic terms. We may compare him to that figure which Alberti recommended that the artist place at the margin of the picture:

> In an *istoria* I like to see someone who admonishes and points out to us what is happening there; or beckons with his hand to see; or menaces with an angry face and with flashing eyes, so that no one should come near; or shows some danger or marvelous thing there; or invites us to weep or to laugh together with them.[84]

It is Brutus who directs the response of the audience to the story of Lucrece, pointing out to the Romans their proper course of action, and pointing out to Southampton the artistry of his servant Shakespeare.

[84] Alberti, *On Painting*, p. 78.

# Chapter 5

# Chronicle, History, Legend

The oblivion into which Samuel Daniel and Michael Drayton have sunk masks the fate of historical poetry generally. While writers have in practice always mixed invention and fact to make fiction, literature and history came to be thought of in the late sixteenth century as opposite in their goals, one dedicated to imaginative truth, the other to factual truth, and only recently have the theorists of the two disciplines dared to think otherwise. The revolution in historical and poetic theory in the sixteenth century produced for the poets of the Elizabethan minor epic a peculiar crisis of identity. Daniel and Drayton were born in the world of Holinshed's *Chronicles* and died in the world of Selden's *History of Tithes*. Each entered on the career of the poetic historian by employing that mixture of Petrarch and old chronicles that characterized the minor epic in the first half of the 1590s. Each progressed on the Vergilian path to write full-dress historical epics stuffed with dynastic propaganda and glances at contemporary politics. But for each, the struggle to reconcile chronicle to minor epic ended in doubts about the nature of historical fiction and the validity of his personal achievement. This thwarting of the poet's normal course of development is symptomatic of a deeper problem with which both grappled: at stake were nothing less than the definitions and uses of both poetry and history. Was poetry just lies or could the humanist dream of literature as a social force prove itself true? Was history just a chronological record of what happened or was it a narrative designed or even invented by the historian?

The concepts of poetic and historical truth in the Renaissance follow courses of development rather like the discussions of inspiration and *ut pictura poesis* examined in the last two chapters. Each begins with a collection of epithets and commonplaces gathered out of classical authors which humanist poets sprinkled over the surface of their verse. Chief among such commonplaces were those Cicero applied to history: "testis temporum, lux veritatis, vita memoriae, magistra vitae, nuntia vetustatis."[1] What begins as a style, though, becomes in time a theoretical system with an increasingly deep impact on actual practice. In the case of historical theory, this process might be described in four stages. The Florentine chancellors of the early quattrocento, Coluccio Salutati, Leonardo Bruni, and Poggio Bracciolini, developed a new style of history inspired by Cicero and the recently restored text of Livy. They emphasized the moral and encomiastic purposes of history and valued those techniques, notably the invented speech, that best vivified and beautified the record of the past. In the first decades of the cinquecento, two more Florentines, Niccolò Machiavelli and Francesco Guicciardini, pioneered a new analytical history of contemporary politics, inspired now by Thucydides and Tacitus. It is important to note, though, that Machiavelli and Guicciardini achieved their goals while observing the rules of the humanist style, especially by using sequential narrative and invented speeches. The great revolution in the theory of history does not come until the middle of the century, with the dialogues of Francesco Patrizi (1560) and especially with the "new history" of the Frenchmen François Baudouin (1561), Jean Bodin (1566), and Louis Le Roy (1575).[2] While

---

[1] "The witness of the times, the light of truth, the life of memory, the master of life, the spokesman of past times" (Cicero, *De Oratore*, 2. 9. 36).

[2] For rhetorical dimensions of early Florentine humanist history see Nancy S. Struever, *The Language of History in the Renaissance* (Princeton: Princeton University Press, 1970); for political dimensions see Hans Baron, *The Crisis of the Early Italian Renaissance*, rev. ed. (Princeton: Princeton University Press, 1966). Felix Gilbert examines late fifteenth-century humanist history and early sixteenth-century political history in *Machiavelli and Guicciardini* (Princeton: Princeton University Press, 1965). Italian historical theory of the cinquecento is surveyed by Giorgio Spini in "Historiography: The Art of History in the Italian Counter Reformation," in *The Late Italian*

I will later need to distinguish among these writers more carefully, I might note now what they shared: a desire to broaden the subject matter of history to include laws, institutions, and economics; a strong sense of anachronism; a skeptical attitude toward source materials; and a conviction that the historian must avoid rhetorical embellishments, notably the set speech. In the course of the seventeenth century, as more and more historians began to practice what the Frenchmen preached, the writing of history gradually came to be an exercise in the collection and analysis of documents, recognizably akin to the modern discipline that now bears the same name.

This slow evolution in Continental historiography took place rather more quickly among English historians and with something like revolutionary speed among the English poetic historians.[3] Just as English connoisseurs of art learned

---

*Renaissance, 1525-1630,* ed. Eric Cochrane (New York: Harper, 1970), pp. 91-133; and by Eric Cochrane in the last chapter of *Historians and Historiography in the Italian Renaissance* (Chicago: University of Chicago Press, forthcoming). Sixteenth-century French historical theory is surveyed by J.G.A. Pocock, *The Ancient Constitution and the Feudal Law* (Cambridge: Cambridge University Press, 1957), chap. 1; and by Julian H. Franklin, *Jean Bodin and the Sixteenth Century Revolution in the Methodology of Law and History* (New York: Columbia University Press, 1963); it is examined in detail by George Huppert, *The Idea of Perfect History: Historical Erudition and Historical Philosophy in Renaissance France* (Urbana: University of Illinois Press, 1970); and by Donald R. Kelley in his magisterial study, *Foundations of Modern Historical Scholarship: Language, Law, and History in the French Renaissance* (New York: Columbia University Press, 1970).

[3] The best overview of sixteenth-century historiography in England is F. J. Levy, *Tudor Historical Thought* (San Marino, Ca.: Huntington Library, 1967). The late Tudor historians, notably Camden and Stow, are the subject of F. Smith Fussner's *The Historical Revolution: English Historical Writing and Thought, 1580-1640* (New York: Columbia University Press, 1962). A thorough examination of one aspect of the chronicle tradition is provided by Henry Angsar Kelly, *Divine Providence in the England of Shakespeare's Histories* (Cambridge: Harvard University Press, 1970). Among the few works discussing the impact of French theory is Leonard F. Dean, "Bodin's *Methodus* in England before 1625," *Studies in Philology* 39 (1942):160-66; see also his *Tudor Theories of History Writing,* University of Michigan Contributions in Modern Philology, no. 1 (Ann Arbor: University of Michigan Press, 1947).

about Alberti at about the same time as they did Zuccaro, so English knowledge of quattrocento Italian history did not much precede an awareness of mid-sixteenth-century French trends. The interval from the publication of Caxton's *Chronicle* to Polydore Vergil's humanist *Anglica Historia* is half a century, from Holinshed to Camden's *Brittania* just nine years. This process of acceleration (rather like Lenin's idea that the bourgeois stage of Russian history might be compressed into a matter of weeks) was partly, though not entirely, the result of English insularity. Part was the result of historical accident. For instance, Guicciardini's *History of Italy*, though begun in 1537, was not printed until 1561, long after his death, while Patrizi's *Dialoghi* were available in English translation as early as 1574 because a follower of his, Jacopo Aconcio, happened to be exiled in England. Part was also the result of the persistence of earlier traditions. A good illustration is the *Artis Historicae Penus*, edited by Johann Wolf at Basel in 1576, which was the standard anthology of historical theory in the last quarter of the sixteenth century. In it one could find Patrizi, Baudouin, and Bodin alongside *On Thucydides* by Dionysius of Halicarnassus and *How to Write History* by Lucian, both favorite sources for the quattrocento humanists, as well as the *De Historica Facultate* of Francesco Robortello, who "did nothing more than repeat point by point . . . Aristotle, Lucian, and Cicero."[4] The English poet with a taste for Continental novelties who picked up the *Penus* would encounter writings that extolled the alliance between poetry and history side by side with others that would shortly make historical verse a problematic if not impossible notion.

### DANIEL AND LUCAN

The revolution in English historical verse was in large part fought out in the back alleys of the minor epic, for the simple

---

[4] Spini, "Historiography," p. 98.

reason that vast poems like Daniel's *Civil Wars* or Drayton's *Barons Warres* take years to write and the brevity of the minor epic made it a natural arena for experiment. Perhaps the point is best illustrated by the case of Samuel Daniel, whose minor epic poem *The Complaint of Rosamond* marked the first step in his attempt to fashion himself into the English Lucan and to make his *Civil Wars* into a vernacular *Pharsalia*. Drayton complained that Daniel was "too much *Historian* in verse," and Jonson lamented that he "wrott civill warres & yett hath not one batle in all his Book," concluding that Daniel was "a good honest Man . . . but no poet."[5] As with Greene's attacks on Marlowe, Drayton and Jonson were merely hitting the poet with his own club, for Renaissance literary theorists haggled ceaselessly over whether Lucan was poet or historian, whether he had acted honorably in his dealings with the tyrannical Nero, and whether the overblown rhetoric of the *Pharsalia* could be endured. Scaliger, Mazzoni, and the Englishman William Webbe lined up for Lucan; Minturno, Castelvetro, and Sidney against; Tasso wandered indecisively between the trenches.[6] The whole

[5] Michael Drayton, "To My Most Dearely-Loved Friend Henery Reynolds Esquire, of Poets and Poesy," l. 126 (Hebel, 3:229). Ben Jonson, "Conversations with William Drummond of Hawthornden," in *Works*, ed. C. H. Herford and Percy Simpson, 11 vols. (Oxford: Clarendon Press, 1925), 1:132, 138. Cf. Everard Guilpin: "Daniel (as some holds) might mount if he list, / But others say that he's a Lucanist," *Skialetheia* (1598), Satyre 6. 77-78, ed. D. Allen Carroll (Chapel Hill: University of North Carolina Press, 1974), p. 90.

[6] J. C. Scaliger, *Poetices* (Heidelberg, 1594), bk. 1, chap. 2; Jacopo Mazzoni, *Della difesa della comedia di Dante* (Cesena, 1688), bk. 4, chap. 32; William Webbe, *A Discourse of English Poetrie*, in G. Gregory Smith, *Elizabethan Critical Essays*, 2 vols. (Oxford: Oxford University Press, 1904), 1:238. Antonio Minturno, *L'arte poetica* (Venice, 1563), p. 34; Lodovico Castelvetro, *Poetica d'Aristotele vulgarizzata et sposta* (Vienna, 1570), pt. 1, sec. 8.; Sir Philip Sidney, *A Defence of Poetry*, in *Miscellaneous Prose of Sir Philip Sidney*, ed. Katherine Duncan-Jones and Jan van Dorsten (Oxford: Clarendon Press, 1973), p. 80. In the first of his *Discourses on the Art of Poetry* (1587), Tasso condemns Lucan for choosing a subject so vast as to leave no room for his own invention. In the *Discourses on the Heroic Poem* (1594), trans. Mariella

question got so stale that Thomas Nashe could only hold his nose and jeer: "I can but pittie their folly, who are so curious in fables and excruciate themselves about impertinent questions, as about *Homers* Countrey, [or] parentage, . . . [or] whether *Lucan* is to be reckoned amongst the Poets or Historiographers."[7]

Nashe's impatience doubtlessly reflects his awareness that the squabble over Lucan was part of a far older and wider debate, for the humanists were at their favorite game of rehashing arguments from classical authors. Every Renaissance attack on Lucan quoted Quintilian (*Institutio Oratoria*, 10. 1. 90), who had thought Lucan's style better suited to the orator than to the poet, and Aristotle, who declared that poetry was distinct from history (*Poetics*, 9). The defenders could cite Cicero, who treated both poetry and history as branches of oratory, and point to a different passage in the *Institutio Oratoria* where Quintilian calls history "a kind of prose poem," since it strives to preserve the memory of its subject and win glory for its author (10. 1. 31). Dionysius of Halicarnassus, who is almost unknown today but was a great authority to the humanists, claimed that history must be

Cavalchini and Irene Samuel (Oxford: Clarendon Press, 1973), he praises the poems of Homer, Statius, and Lucan for their noble action (p. 49) and dismisses the charge that Lucan is not a poet because he portrays what actually happened. Instead he reasons that "if Lucan is not a poet, it is because he binds himself to the truth of particulars with little regard to the universal" (p. 61). Ben Jonson was also of two minds, depending on the occasion. In his railings against all poets, dead or alive, to Drummond of Hawthornden, he asserted that Lucan was fine in patches, but the whole of the *Pharsalia* showed he was no true poet. Yet in a commendatory verse to Thomas May's translation of Lucan (London, 1627), he asks: "What Muse, or rather God of harmony / Taught *Lucan* these true moodes! / replyes my sence / What godds but those of arts, and eloquence? / *Phoebus*, and *Hermes*?" (sig. a7ʳ).

  [7] Thomas Nashe, *The Anatomie of Absurditie*, in Smith, *Elizabethan Critical Essays*, 1:336; cf. Sir John Harıngton's Preface to *Orlando furioso* two years later: "Least of all do I purpose to bestow any long time to argue . . . whether *Lucan* writing a story in verse be an historiographer" (Smith, *Elizabethan Critical Essays*, 2:196).

lofty in character, which makes it sound rather like epic. He denounced Thucydides for a breach of decorum in portraying the Athenians in a bad light, not because his accusations were untrue, but because they were ignoble.[8]

The historical poets were hard pressed to choose between their friends and their enemies, for the defense mounted by Cicero, Quintilian, and Dionysius pacified the frontier between poetry and history at the cost of threatening their capitals. By reducing both disciplines to forms of panegyric or epideictic rhetoric, they deprived poetry and history of their deeper claims to moral and factual truth. Now the claim to truth is one thing to make in theory, and quite another to perform in practice, when the things men say might win them the wrath of princes. Dionysius of Halicarnassus, who placed such value on praise, was librarian to Augustus Caesar. The candid Thucydides was an exiled Athenian general. If to Dionysius Thucydides appeared to be moved by malice in his portrayal of the Athenians, Dionysius himself looks to us like the trepidous timeserver.

The style of Lucan's *Pharsalia* is more in the epideictic than the deliberative vein and the poem has some flattering references to Nero clustered near the beginning that sound a bit sycophantic. From Tacitus, though, the humanists knew the full story of Lucan's relations with Nero. When the jealous emperor forbad him to recite his verses in public, Lucan joined the conspiracy of Piso which, when discovered, brought death both to the poet and to his uncle, Lucius Annaeus Seneca. The standard life of Lucan appended to most sixteenth-century editions recounts these episodes in terms

[8] Dionysius of Halicarnassus, *On Thucydides*, trans. W. Kendrick Pritchett (Berkeley: University of California Press, 1975), chap. 39-40. Dionysius praises the excellence of Herodotus, who "made his prose utterance resemble the best kind of poetry" (chap. 23). Lucian waffles in *How to Write History*, decrying the contamination of history by poetic embellishment but allowing invented speeches, occasional panegyric, and sublimity in the description of battles. But the historian's language must never be vehement, intricate or clever—which would let Lucan out. See Lucian, *Works*, 8 vols., trans. K. Kilburn, Loeb ed. (London: Heinemann, 1959), 6:13, 59, 71.

generally laudatory to Lucan, adding only that he denounced his innocent mother as one of the conspirators in a futile attempt to win pardon from Nero. Still, in Sir Arthur Gorges's translation (published in 1614 but perhaps written earlier), one "W. R." praises Lucan for not hiding the truth "to please the time" (sig. A4ᵛ), and the marginal glosses explain away the flattery of Nero in the early lines of the poem:

> It should seem that this was written in the beginning of *Neroes* reigne, which was most excellently governed for the first 5 yeares, with singular Justice & temperance [i.e., during the period when Seneca was tutor to Nero].
>
> [1. 33-37]

> This is meere Ironicall flattery.
>
> [1. 53-59]

> In this he teacheth *Nero* how he should governe, by an Imagination of what is.[9]
>
> [1. 60-62]

The elevation of Lucan as an epic truth-teller inevitably invited comparison with Homer and Vergil. Homer of course was a notorious liar, and Vergil might, like Dionysius of Halicarnassus, be suspected of creeping too close to the emperor's bosom. On the title page of his translation of 1627, Thomas May showed Lucan bleeding to death in his bath [fig. 11] and addressed Vergil:

---

[9] *Lucans Pharsalia: containing the Civill Warres betweene Caesar and Pompey*, trans. Sir Arthur Gorges (London, 1614), p. 4. Lucan's tactful allusion in line 57 to the "onus" of the emperor's divinity is rudely translated by Gorges as "thy ponderous heft." It is worth noting that in his recent monograph, *Lucan: An Introduction* (Ithaca: Cornell University Press, 1976), Frederick M. Ahl has proposed similar ironic readings of the same passages (pp. 17-61). The standard fifteenth-century commentaries of Sulpizio and Omnibono recognize the figure *ironia* in lines 37-38, but perhaps only in the rhetorical sense that Lucan pretends to praise war.

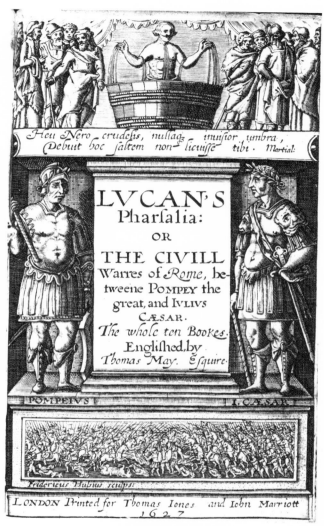

*Heu Nero crudelis, nullaq immisior umbra,*
*Debuit hoc saltem non licuisse tibi. Martial:*

LVCAN'S
Pharſalia:
OR
THE CIVILL
Warres of Rome, be-
tweene POMPEY the
great, and IVLIVS
CÆSAR.
*The whole ten Bookes.*
Engliſhed, by
*Thomas May. Eſquire*

POMPEIVS. I. CÆSAR

*Fridericus Hulſius ſculpſ:*

LONDON *Printed for Thomas Iones and Iohn Marriott*
1627

11. *The Death of Lucan.* Title page, Lucan, *Pharsalia*, trans. Thomas May
(London, 1627). Newberry Library, Chicago.

Thou gott'st *Augustus* love, he *Nero's* hate;
But twas an act more great, and high to moove
A Princes envy, then a Princes love.

The difference between them lies in points of style. As
"S. S." explained in commendatory verses to the Gorges
translation, Homer and Vergil turned their poetic invention
to both matter and manner, while Lucan lavished his inven-
tion on the manner only (sig. A5ʳ). Thus his style is more
ornate and obscure than that of Vergil without lessening its
truth. The late-fifteenth-century rhetorician Giovanni Sulpi-
zio compared the two Romans in a widely reprinted com-
mentary: "Dives est: & magnificus Maro: hic [Lucanus]
sumptuosus: & splendidus. Ille maturus: sublimis: abundans:
hic vehemens: Canorus: effusus. . . . Virgilius nitidus beatus:
compositus: Lucanus varius: floridus: aptus."[10]

The stylistic difference between Vergil and Lucan was at
heart political. It was a commonplace derived from Tacitus
that Ciceronian rhetoric declined with the withering of Ro-
man republicanism and was replaced with a florid rhetoric
that would be out of place in a court of law, where one must
reach men's minds, but was perfectly suited to the court of
a prince, where the will of one man is supreme. Augustus,
who ruled with justice and kept the veneer of republican in-
stitutions, represents the midpoint in this decline. As em-
peror he demands flattery, but Vergil can be his propagandist
without too great a moral peril. With Nero the situation is
obviously different. Even under a bad prince it is possible to
live a good life, Tacitus reminds us, but it is not done easily.

---

[10] Giovanni Sulpizio, ed. *Annei Lucani Bellorum Civilium scriptoris accuratis-
simi Pharsalia* (Venice Augustino de Zani, 1511), sig. Aa3ʳ. The subjective
nature of poetic epithets makes them very difficult to translate. Cognates
are probably best, since Renaissance critics tended to use cognate forms
when transferring to vernacular writers the conventional epithets of classical
writers. Hence Vergil is "rich, magnificent, mature, sublime, abundant,
brilliant, felicitous, and composed." Lucan is "sumptuous, splendid, vehe-
ment, sonorous, effusive, varied, florid, and pointed."

What Lucan represents is the tension inherent in such an attempt. His style reflects the Asiatic decadence of imperial taste (particularly in the deification of the emperor), while his loyalty to the *fides historiae* embodies the ideals of his uncle Seneca. The words are decorated but the matter is true.

Lucan was born, Lucanists are made. Daniel grew slowly to his role in distant but stoical England. His first piece of historical verse, the minor epic *Complaint of Rosamond*, has, as we have seen, more of Petrarch in it than of the chronicles. The chronicle accounts of Rosamond barely mention her among the other domestic troubles that Henry II experienced with his wife, his sons, and his nobles. Typical is Caxton's *Chronicle* (i.e., Ranulf Higden's *Polychronicon*, translated by John of Trevisa and edited by Caxton):

> And he [Henry II] that hadde prysonned his wyf Elyanor the quene and was pryvely a spouchebreker / and lyved now openly in spousebrekyng and is not ashamed to mysuse the wenche Rosamund / To this fayre wenche the kyng made at Wodestoke a chambre of wonder crafte slyly made by dedalus werke / leste the Quene sholde fynde and take Rosamund / but the wenche dyed soone and is beryed in the chapyter hows at Godestow . . . This wenche had a lytel Coffre scarcely of twey fote longe made by a wonder crafte that is yet seen there. / Therein it semyth that geauntes fyghtyn / beestes startlyn / foules fleyn / and fysshes leepe withoute ony mannes moevynge /[11]

Higden/Trevisa/Caxton are hardly bothered by the confusions in their account of Rosamond whereby Henry, having imprisoned his wife Eleanor and lived openly in adultery, seeks to conceal from her his affair with Rosamond. On one hand, they focus on remarkable objects and events that are

---

[11] [The Chronicles of England], bk. 7, chap. 22 (Westminster: Caxton, 1482), fol. 357r.

worthy of everlasting fame (or infamy), while on the other, they observe a providential scheme of six monarchies for the work as a whole. But there is little attempt to show this providence at work in the reward or punishment of individual deeds. They are concerned to preserve truth in both divine and human terms without much communication between the two. They ponder the obscure way that history in the gross drifts into conformity with God's will, or rather, comes to reveal a divine plan that is scarcely visible in any given particular.

To Daniel, it is precisely the area between the particular and the universal that is of interest. He focuses on the character of Rosamond rather than on marvelous events, makes the labyrinthine architecture of Woodstock and the Ovidian casket into emblems of her mental state, and turns her sudden death into a murder at the hands of Eleanor. The result is to articulate a material and psychological level as the internal principle of organization for his poetic history. The chronicle disintegrates events into facts: "this year a sow with two heads was born in Surrey" or accumulates them into schemes: "the troublesome reign of Henry IV" or "the sixth age of man." Humanist history finds its truth in the middle scale where fact becomes scheme and scheme can be seen breaking down into its component events.

By inventing much of his *res* as well as his *verba* in *Rosamond*, Daniel has set out to vivify the past and make it present. The middle scale of truth frees him from the timeless perspective of providence without binding him to the particle of past time occupied by the single event. Hence he has neither the wonder of the chroniclers that the remote past can be known at all nor the despair of the French historiographers at the paucity of good documentary evidence. To Daniel the remoteness of the past is something to be overcome by the force of rhetorical elaboration, giving an order to words that reflects the material and psychological orders of time. Like Petrarch, Boccaccio, and the authors of the *Mirror for Magistrates*, Daniel imposes a poetic scheme, the rise and fall of tragedy, onto a single episode from the chronicles while expanding that episode into a "life" of its protagonists. He then makes the tension between this orderly scheme and the flux of events the subject of long commentary by his two main characters, Henry II and Rosamond. The invented speeches shift Daniel's historical focus from the providential pattern used by universalist historians from Eusebius to Ranulf Higden, to the theatrical patterns of a political historian like Thucydides or Guicciardini.

To compare Daniel to Thucydides or Guicciardini may seem perverse, but his amorous verse and their practical prose stand at the opposite poles of humanist history and between them its nature and scope is defined. In the opening debates at Athens and Sparta in which the two states decide to embark on their fatal war, Thucydides shows men calculating the weight that chance and human cunning will have in its outcome. In the Melian dialogue, which so raised the ire of Dionysius of Halicarnassus, he breaks openly into a dramatic mode, assigning speeches not to particular individuals but to two choruses labeled "Athenians" and "Melians." In this passage F. M. Cornford found the proof that the *Peloponnesian War* is Aeschylan in its conception.[12] Whether or not one accepts Cornford's arguments that the "real" causes of the war lay in imperialist economics, he is clearly right that Thucydides wants to show the fall of Athens through a combination of chance (the death of Pericles), passion (the wrath of Cleon), and misdirected reason (the disastrous expedition to Syracuse).

Similarly, Guicciardini shows men struggling to master the chaos of events in the tragedy that was Italian history after the death of Lorenzo the Magnificent. The Emperor Charles V is shown listening with unusual prudence to the debates of his counselors, but more often Guicciardini finds that the decisions of princes are based on ambition and greed.

---

[12] F. M. Cornford, *Thucydides Mythistoricus* (London: Arnold, 1907), chap. 8, 10.

Neither cunning nor virtue is a guarantee of success, however, and Guicciardini points to the fortunate career of the monstrous Roderigo Borgia to confound those who think themselves able to sift the secrets of providence. Indeed, Felix Gilbert finds much of the difference between Machiavelli and Guicciardini in the extent to which Machiavelli still clung to the idea that Fortune would sometimes yield to *virtú*.[13]

Daniel's Rosamond operates in a humbler sphere, but in her long speeches reflecting on how she came to sin and imminent death she confronts the same inscrutable confusion of providence, chance, will, and misguided calculation. A long debate with a cunning old crone leads her to yield to Henry's advances for two reasons, the calculated desire to keep the favor of her ruler, and the promptings of her own erotic nature, which has been roused by the lascivious scenes on the casket Henry has sent her. Once fallen and facing death, she acknowledges her responsibility for what she has done, but sees herself to be, at least in part, the scapegoat of a decadent society and the victim of a capricious fate.

Still, there are important and obvious differences between Daniel and the political historians. They are dealing with public deeds in their own lifetimes or the lifetimes of their fathers. He is telling of private actions in the distant past. Thucydides and Guicciardini both are interested in eyewitnesses more than in documents. For them the past is alive in the memory of their informants and their purpose is summarized by the "rule of Polybius": history aims at political and military instruction and is best written by those with political and military experience.[14] Like them, Daniel cannot

---

[13] Gilbert, *Machiavelli and Guicciardini*, pp. 288-301.

[14] The focus of classical historiography on contemporary politics is emphasized by Arnaldo Momigliano in a number of essays, including "Ancient History and the Antiquarian," and "The Place of Herodotus in the History of Historiography," in *Studies in Historiography* (London: Weidenfeld and Nicolson, 1966); "The Historian's Skin," "Polybius' Reappearance in Western Europe," and "Tradition and the Classical Historian," in *Essays in An-*

tell exactly what happened. He must shape his material according to the information available and make plausible conjectures when it is not, as in the invented speeches recording what was likely to have been said by the actual participants. Armed not with memory but with old chronicles and a humanist-historical poetics of presence, Daniel must in *Rosamond* use far more violent rhetorical elaboration to overcome the greater obscurity of his subject. And whereas a Thucydides or a Guicciardini could assume the unparalleled importance of his subject matter, Daniel faces the further problem of giving public meaning to private actions. This he does by elaborating his speeches for emotional as well as analytical point. His desire to impress the human significance of his subject matter on his audience is witnessed by the incessant contemporary references to the sheer pathos of the poem.[15]

If the histories of Thucydides and Guicciardini are self-conscious verbal imitations of a lost reality, then Daniel's extreme elaboration of his subject in *Rosamond* clearly makes his work not history, but a poetic imitation of history. It is fiction in the most perfect tradition of Plato's cave, an imitation of an imitation of a dubious reality. Such a mode is possible precisely because of the obscurity of his subject. He need not fear that any records will turn up to contradict him, or that any living soul recalls the matter differently, so he can freely invent his matter without telling lies.[16] Poetic truth consists not of what can be proven true but of what has not been (or even cannot be) proven false. It colors in the blank spots in our knowledge of the past.

---

*cient and Modern Historiography* (Middletown: Wesleyan University Press, 1977); and "Greek Historiography," *History and Theory* 17 (1978):1-28.

[15] Cf. Francis Meres, *Palladis Thamia*, in Smith, *Elizabethan Critical Essays*, 2:316; Thomas Churchyard, *Churchyards Challenge* (London, 1593), p. 126 [136]; Michael Drayton, *Matilda*, ll. 29-35; Giles Fletcher the Elder, *The Rising to the Crowne of Richard the Third* (1593), ll. 13-14, in *Licia* (Cambridge, 1593), and William Covell, *Polimanteia* (Cambridge, 1595), sig. R2ᵛ-R3ᵛ.

[16] Cf. William Nelson, *Fact or Fiction: The Dilemma of the Renaissance Storyteller* (Cambridge: Harvard University Press, 1973), pp. 43-49.

For just that reason, *Rosamond* is not a work that would elevate Daniel to his coveted position as the English Lucan; if it is not false, neither can it claim to be true. If Daniel is to show the profit of his experiment with the minor epic, he must do so by displaying it in the more public form of the epic. Like the political historians, Lucan takes as his subject contemporary or near-contemporary politics, the civil wars that began when Julius Caesar crossed the Rubicon and that ended with the defeat of Marc Antony at Actium. He digs in the ground on which his prince is standing. Daniel finds a similar subject for his *Civil Wars* (imitating the variant title of Lucan's work, *De Bello Civili*) in the English Wars of the Roses, which were slightly more distant from his own time, but which ended similarly with the establishment of the ruling dynasty and which also reflected divisions still present within the poet's society. We know from the Hayward affair and the Essex rebellion just how touchy Elizabeth could be about references to the deposition of Richard II. To desire to be Lucan is nothing less than to join a dangerous cabal of political poets, to move from the bower to the forum, and to make poetic truth a force in a real world.

The danger of such ambitions is manifest in Daniel's historical tragedy *Philotas*, begun in 1601 and printed in 1605. When the envy of lesser men leads Alexander the Great to suspect his loyalty, the noble Philotas foolishly conceals a real conspiracy. When it is discovered, he is destroyed. Inevitably, the play was taken to refer to the earl of Essex and Daniel could only beg his patron Mountjoy (who was similarly hard pressed to cover his tracks) to forgive "mine indiscreation, & misunderstanding of the tyme," and disingenuously object that by "taking a subject that lay (as I thought) so farre from the time, and so remote a stranger from the climate of our present courses, I could not imagine that Envy or ignorance could possibly have made it, to take any particular acquaintance with us" (Michel, *Philotas*, pp. 39, 156).

The appeal of Essex may well have been great to a man who above all feared civil disunity and who may have suspected, as many did, that chaos would follow the death of the childless Elizabeth. The *Civil Wars* (the first four books of which were published in 1595) echo Lucan in their invocation of *furor*:

> What furie, ô what madnes held thee so,
> Deare *England* (too too prodigall of blood)
> To waste so much, and warre without a foe,
> Whilst *Fraunce*, to see thy spoyles, at pleasure stood!
> [1. 2. 1–4]

In his Apology for *Philotas*, Daniel argues quite logically that his admiration for Essex did not extend to the earl's final acts of disloyalty, and there is no hint in the *Civil Wars* that he considers Elizabeth herself the source of England's past or present woes. His flattery of her is worth comparing to that offered by Lucan to Nero:

> Yet now what reason have we to complaine?
> Since hereby came the calme we did injoy;
> The blisse of thee *Eliza*; happie gaine
> For all our losse: when-as no other way
> The heavens could finde, but to unite againe
> The fatall sev'red Families, that they
> Might bring foorth thee: that in thy peace might growe
> That glorie, which few Times could ever showe.
> [Daniel, 1. 3]

> Quod si non aliam venturo fata Neroni
> Invenere viam . . .
> Iam nihil, o superi, querimur; scelera ista nefasque
> Hac mercede placent; diros Pharsalia campos
> Inpleat et Poeni saturentur sanguine manes;
> Ultima funesta concurrant proelia Munda;
> His, Caesar, Perusina fames Mutinaeque labores
> Accedant fatis et quas premit aspera classes
> Leucas et ardenti servilia bella sub Aetna:

Multum Roma tamen debet civilibus armis,
Quod tibi res acta est. Te, cum statione peracta
Astra petes serus, praelati regia caeli
Excipiet gaudente polo; . . .
Tum genus humanum positis sibi consulat armis,
Inque vicem gens omnis amet; pax missa per orbem
Ferrea belligeri conpescat limina Iani.
Sed mihi iam numen.

    (But if no other way to *Neroes* raigne
The Fates could finde . . .
Now we complaine not, gods, mischeife, and warre
Pleasing to us, since so rewarded are;
Let dire *Pharsalia* grone with armed Hoasts,
And glut with blood the Carthaginian Ghosts:
With these let *Munda's* fatall Battle goe,
*Mutina's* Siedge, *Perusias* famine too:
To these add Actiums bloody Navall fight,
And neere Sicilia *Sextus* slavish Fleete.
Yet much owes Rome to civill enmity
For making thee our Prince; when thou the sky
Though late, shal clime, & change thine earthly reigne,
Heaven, as much grac'd, with joy shall entertaine,
And welcome thee . . .
Then let Mankinde forget all warre and strife,
And every Nation love a peacefull life.
Let peace through all the world in this blest state
Once more shut warre like *Janus* Iron gate.
O be my god. . . .)[17]
      [Lucan]

Daniel bases his praise of Elizabeth on quite specific deeds that she has indisputably performed. Lucan admires Nero strictly for his divinity, and perhaps wishes too heartily for

---

[17] Lucan, *Pharsalia*, 1. 33-63. Latin text from Loeb ed., ed. J. D. Duff (London: Heinemann, 1928). English translation by Thomas May (London, 1627).

his departure to the heavens and stresses too strongly that peace will be attained *after* Nero is gone.

The differences extend past the content of the praise to its manner. In his piling up of the horrible wars Rome has seen and in the strenuous "Te" of his address to the emperor, Lucan shows that florid style which, as we have seen, has imperial overtones. Daniel adopts instead a poetic style closely allied to Attic prose, a style not suited to the flattery of tyrants.[18] Daniel's Elizabeth is more like Vergil's Augustus than like Lucan's Nero. In his Atticism, Daniel resembles the French *politiques*, among them the historians he was now reading, like Jean du Tillet, Louis Le Roy, and François Baudouin. Cicero had represented Roman republican traditions to quattrocento Florentine humanists facing an invasion from the north, but in the sixteenth century the Italian city governments were replaced by princely courts, and a humanist could argue even in Florence that liberty was best assured by the rule of a grand duke, if that grand duke was paying him.[19] England and France, in any event, had no native republican traditions and looked to monarchy as the alternative to baronial strife and dismemberment. To sixteenth-century Gallicans facing political pressure from the south, "Ciceronianism" becomes the sign of ultramontane usurpation, Jesuitical sophistry, and civil disruption.[20] Daniel constantly al-

[18] See Anthony LaBranche, "Samuel Daniel: A Voice of Thoughtfulness," in *The Rhetoric of Renaissance Poetry*, ed. Thomas O. Sloan and Raymond B. Waddington (Berkeley: University of California Press, 1974), pp. 123-39; Cecil C. Seronsy, "Well-Languaged Daniel: A Reconsideration," *Modern Language Review* 52 (1957):481-97; and Morris W. Croll, " 'Attic Prose' in the Seventeenth Century," ed. John M. Wallace, in *Style, Rhetoric, and Rhythm: Essays by Morris W. Croll*, ed. J. Max Patrick et al. (Princeton: Princeton University Press, 1966), pp. 51-101.

[19] Baron, *Crisis of Early Italian Renaissance*, p. 71.

[20] Marc Fumaroli, "Aux Origines de la Connaissance Historique du Moyen Age: Humanisme, Réforme et Gallicanisme au XVIᵉ Siècle," *XVIIᵉ Siècle Revue*, no. 115 (1977):5-29, and "Rhetorical Trends in France in the Renaissance" (Paper delivered at the Newberry Library Conference on Rhetoric in the Renaissance, Chicago, 20 April 1979). Cf. Kelley, *Foundations of Modern Historical Scholarship*, p. 303.

luded to the French wars of religion as what he feared for England. To Daniel, as to the *politiques*, the power of the monarchy was the instrument best suited to prevent further national self-destruction, and, like the *politiques*, he adopted a style that declared his allegiance.

In the *Civil Wars*, Daniel has acted the role of Lucan more vigorously than Lucan did, pursuing truth to the exclusion of poetic invention, to the point where Jonson's and Drayton's attacks on him are inevitable. His epic stands in stark contrast with a work like Ronsard's *Franciade* (except that neither was completed), in that Ronsard chose a subject out of the legendary past precisely so that there would be no confusion of poetry and history, and elevates this legendary past as part of a conscious program of flattery to the nation and the king who paid him.[21] Daniel's commitment to truth has brought him from minor epic to epic to the limit of prose, and there is really nowhere left to go except further into prose. The contrast is underscored by Daniel's last project, the *Collection of the History of England* (1612), where he examines periods as ancient and legendary as those treated by Ronsard, but with wholly different purposes and techniques.

The *Collection* is, in Daniel's own claim, merely the "contexture" or weaving together of the fragmentary and confused accounts available in the chronicles. This self-effacement elevates the sources rather than the historian's own narrative as the locus of truth, but it is in a sense a subterfuge to conceal the remarkable change Daniel has wrought in those sources in the process of making them orderly and comprehensible. First, he has selected his sources carefully. Among them are the familiar names, William of Malmesbury, Henry of Huntington, Matthew Paris, Froissart, Polydore Vergil, Grafton, Halle, et al. Conspicuously absent is

---

[21] See Ronsard's Third Preface to the *Franciade* (1587) in *Critical Prefaces of the French Renaissance*, ed. Bernard Weinberg (Evanston: Northwestern University Press, 1950), pp. 258-69; and David Maskell, *The Historical Epic in France, 1500-1700* (London: Oxford University Press, 1973), pp. 69-71.

Geoffrey of Monmouth. By omitting Britain's most famous liar, Daniel can treat the rest of his sources as if they were public documents or official annals of past times (as indeed Halle's *Chronicle* was), accurate in the main but unlikely to record anything unflattering to the state.

Just what this means for Daniel can be seen by a comparison with Livy, the supreme model for the humanist poetic historian, and favorite author of Daniel's earlier years, who drew on similar quasi-official annals for the early history of Rome. Recounting the descent of the Romans from the gods, Livy reflected:

> As for such things as are reported, either before, or at the foundation of the citie, more beautified and set out with Poets fables, than grounded upon pure and faithfull records, I meane neither to averre nor disprove. This leave and priviledge hath antiquitie, by interlacing the acts of gods and men together, to make the first rising of cities more sacred and venerable. And if it may be lawful for anie people under heaven to consecrate and ascribe unto the gods, their Original: certes, such is the renowmed martiall prowes of the Romans, that all nations of the world may as well abide them [the Romans] to report Mars above the rest, to be the stockefather both of themselves and of their first founders, as they [other nations] can bee content to live in subjection under them.[22]

Livy's exquisite irony is visible in the hundreds of pages that follow, recording the actual beginnings of Rome in a band of fugitives and outlaws, and the bitter opposition of every crossroads town in Italy to Roman domination. For Livy, the writing of ancient history is an act of bad faith offering as possibly true something you know is not but should be

[22] Livy, *The Romane Historie*, trans. Philemon Holland (London, 1600), p. 2.

true; this seems to be his definition of poetry as well. The
value of both lies not in truth or falsehood but in utility,
their power to correct morals and to allow the historian to
escape from the troubles of a decadent modern society.
Daniel's purpose in the *Collection* is the more narrowly de-
fined goal of the political historian, to educate policymakers.
The first edition of the *Collection* is dedicated to Robert Carr,
Viscount Rochester, in his role as privy councilor. Like Livy,
Daniel considers early history essentially unknowable, but
for that very reason thinks it best not to lend one's authority
to legendary accounts:

> How the beginnings of all people and States were as
> uncertaine, as the heads of great Rivers; and could not
> adde to our vertue, and peradventure little to our repu-
> tation to know them [he need not point out]. Consid-
> ering, how commonly they rise from the springs of
> poverty, pyracie, robbery and violence, howsoever fab-
> ulous Writers (to glorifie their nations) strive to abuse
> the credulity of after ages with heroycall, or miraculous
> beginnings.
>
> [Grosart, 4: 86]

Daniel's desire to include all that is useful to the policy-
maker moves him to a new principle for the treatment of his
sources. Christian universalist historians from Eusebius to
Higden would record all of time from the Creation to the
present, while the sixteenth-century chroniclers, such as
Grafton, sought a kind of universality by including every
reported incident of English history. Having lopped off the
distant past, Daniel proceeds to exclude from his narrative
everything not pertinent to affairs of state and government.
Within these limits, he subdivides his material in a new way,
scrapping the providential scheme of Ages or Monarchies.
He retains the divisions into individual reigns established by
England's first humanist historian, Polydore Vergil, and
groups the reigns into three sections inductively, "according
to the Periods of those Ages that brought forth the most

remarkable Changes." His division points are those a modern historian might pick: the coming of William the Conquerer; the ascent of Henry II after the turmoil of King Stephen's reign; the advent of the Tudors.

With this systematic alteration of the chronicles, Daniel has moved in force from the camp of humanist literary history to that of the French "new history," especially as it was articulated by François Baudouin in his *De Institutione Historiae Universae*, and by its most distinguished English practitioner, William Camden. Daniel, Camden, and Baudouin all continue to give voice to the humanist epithets about the goals of history, but substitute a new, systematic "method" for the old humanist "art" of history. Daniel's comparison of the origins of states to the heads of great rivers echoes Camden's opinion in the preface to the *Britannia*, and the style of Daniel's *Collection* suggests the imprint of Camden's *Annales of Elizabeth*, still in manuscript, but which Daniel was likely to have seen. Both drop the set speech as an unwarranted type of invention, both use the annalistic principle of organization, and both adopt an extreme terseness in prose, based, as Camden points out, on the *Annales* of Tacitus.[23]

From Baudouin and Camden also may come Daniel's awareness that the credibility of the historian lies in his treatment of source documents. Like Camden, Daniel quotes or paraphrases continuously from letters, proclamations, treaties, and other public monuments, and considers the comparison of sources to be an essential method for establishing their reliability. Baudouin advocated such "copying," so offensive to the inventive instincts of the literary historian, arguing that "we ought rather to be reciters than new creators."[24] Baudouin and Daniel both realized, though, that in dealing with earlier periods, the historian confronts unrelia-

[23] William Camden, "The Author to the Reader," *The History of the Most Renowned and Victorious Princess Elizabeth*, ed. Wallace T. MacCaffrey (Chicago: University of Chicago Press, 1970), p. 7.

[24] François Baudouin, *De Institutione Universae Historiae*, in *Artis Historicae Penus*, ed. Johann Wolf (Basel, 1579), pp. 637-38.

ble documents and finds many factual details to be unverifiable, especially exact numbers and dates. But what difference does it make, Daniel asks, if such-and-such a battle occurred a year earlier or later? Again his Pyrrhonism produces a self-effacement before the records:

> [He is] desirous to deliver things done, in as even and quiet an Order, as such an heape will permit, without quarrelling with the *Beleefe* of Antiquity, depraving the Actions of other Nations to advance our owne, or keeping backe those Reasons of State they had, for what they did in those times: holding it fittest and best agreeing with Integrity (the chiefest duty of a Writer) to leave things to their owne Fame, and the Censure thereof to the Reader, as being his part rather then mine, who am onely to recite things done, not to rule them.
>
> [Grosart, 4: 83]

Again this self-effacement is only apparent, for Daniel is still interested in the uses of history, and its utility lies not in knowledge of facts but in a knowledge of the principles and causes of historical change. Why do men rebel, make war or peace? Why do arts flourish here or the powers of the state decline there? For all his pruning of the chronicles, Daniel, like Baudouin, is reaching toward a new kind of universalist history, based not on the accumulation of facts nor on the intuition of a divine plan. Daniel is still looking for the generalities of history, the material and psychological principles of human behavior which may be collectively described as Nature. English history is a branch of the universal history of human nature, and human history a branch of natural history. Once grasped, the principles of such a history will make an orderly story out of any materials and make any time inform the wise prince.

In this goal, Daniel's *Collection* associates itself with that particular strand of the new historiography, of which Baudouin and Bodin were a part, sometimes called Neo-Bartolism. The philological purists, most eminently Guillaume Budé and Jacques Cujas, had concluded their historical studies of the Justinian Code with a position of extreme relativism, rejecting any attempt to relate Roman law to the radically different circumstances of modern France. To men such as Baudouin and Bodin, the fine points of philology could be ignored to extract those general principles of law which the Justinian Code shared with all law everywhere. From the basis of universal legal history, one can project a new, comparative, cultural history which will "recall the humanist doctrine that the utility of history in general was that it could provide moral and practical examples to be imitated or avoided in the present."[25] Daniel's "new history" in the *Collection* is universalist not in time or place but in scope, accumulating the sands of *res gestae* into the mountain of human nature as it manifests itself in every aspect of society. Exemplary is Daniel's proposed account (never written) of the Tudor dynasty, wherein he intends to describe the discovery of the New World, the consequent alteration of the Old by an increase in the money supply and subsequent inflation, the rise of banking and its involvement in international politics, the evolution of a state-system based on a balance of power, a change from military solutions in international crises to a politics of statecraft and espionage, and "strange alterations in the State Ecclesiasticall: Religion brought forth to bee an Actor in the greatest Designes of Ambition and Faction."

For all its disclaimers of poetry and avoidance of anything stylish even in the language of prose, the *Collection* is as fully

---

[25] Pocock, *The Ancient Constitution*, p. 23. In the *Defense of Ryme*, Daniel lifts material from Louis Le Roy's *De la vicissitude des choses en l'universe*. Le Roy was a disciple and biographer of Budé and the *Vicissitude* is largely a popularization of the ideas of the master (see Kelley, *Foundations of Modern Historical Scholarship*, pp. 80–85). However, Daniel significantly altered the material derived from Le Roy, and those changes are consistent with the "neo-Bartolism" I have ascribed to him here. See my article, "Samuel Daniel: The Poet as Literary Historian," *Studies in English Literature* 19 (1979):55–69, which complements the present discussion at other points as well.

a creation of the imagination as was *Rosamond*. In all of his works, the historian's truth is an order of words, not a certain knowledge of the past; amid the revolution of European historiography, that much of the humanist vision remained constant for Daniel. But where in *Rosamond* it was Daniel's rhetoric that bore truth, in the *Civil Wars* he subjugates the truth of words to the truth of things done. In the *Collection* he further denies the truth of his own words and defers to the words of others, his "sources," for his initial access to knowledge of the past. Yet even the sources are imperfect, for they rarely record accurately or without contradiction what actually happened. The truthfulness of both *res* and *verba* (so laboriously sought in the *Civil Wars*) is exposed as another poetic fantasy. What Daniel puts in their place is his new construction of the principles of historical action, that middle level of being, suspended between raw facts and transcendental schemes, that he had sought to inhabit from the beginning. The remarkable creativity of the *Collection* is played out as an editorial act in which Daniel arranges and comments upon the texts written by others, texts which are in turn bad copies of the text of human nature. The changes in the form of Daniel's poetical historiography proceed through changes in the form of language itself. *Rosamond* begins by predicating the creative power of language in order to make the dead past as densely and opaquely present as a living body. The *Collection* claims a living power to guide men of state by denying the creativity of all language, and striving to make it a transparent lens.

## DRAYTON'S LEGENDS

Daniel's move from *Rosamond* to the *Civil Wars* and the *Collection* involves complex changes from minor epic to epic, from poetry to prose, and from humanist to "new" historiography. Like Daniel, Michael Drayton began his career as a historical poet with minor epic. He went on to dynastic epic with his *Mortimeriados* (1596) and *The Barons Warres*

(1603). And in the end he abandoned narrative history for the chorographic form of *Poly-Olbion* (1612), which was annotated by no less than the great historian John Selden.

Whereas Daniel used each form just once, Drayton experimented with several poems in almost every genre and revised his work obsessively. Rather than retrace for Drayton the development that led Daniel from the minor epic to other genres, it seems more fruitful to exploit his obsession and examine in some detail the development of his work within the genre of minor epic. The rapid succession of Drayton's first three short historical poems, *Peirs Gaveston* (1593), *Matilda* (1594), and *Robert Duke of Normandy* (1596) allows us to eliminate several of the factors that complicated Daniel's history and to focus more narrowly on the interaction between historiography and the form of the minor epic. While Daniel reacted to the split between history and poetry by abandoning first the minor epic and then all historical poetry, Drayton accepted the fictionality of the form and experimented with new ways of finding poetic truth in historical materials.

Less sensitive than Daniel to Continental developments, Drayton nonetheless introduced a new complication when he decided to call his poems "legends," thereby enmeshing them in the language of Reformation politics. The medieval saint's life or "legend" was a conscious mixture of divine truth and poetic invention that came under sharp correction as a historical and literary form at the hands of John Foxe in his *Actes and Monuments* and to a lesser extent in Spenser's *Faerie Queene*. By recollecting the Reformation battle over the legend, Drayton's poems expose and reorder the balance between verisimilitude and the marvelous that underlies both poetic and historical narrative. The tendency of humanist history to attain verisimilitude by ascribing human or natural causes to all events was, if anything, amplified by the political historians and the "new" historians. In his earliest poetic history, Drayton adopted this historical causality in his search for poetic verisimilitude. But as he developed the form of the "legend" in his later poems, he reintroduced the marvelous into his verse as a sign of a new, transcendent, and un-historical causality that defines the fictional nature of his work and ratifies the split between poetry and history.

Drayton's first chronicle poem, *Peirs Gaveston*, is an attempt to "overdo" Daniel's *Rosamond* at the new game of humanist historical verse. If Daniel invents speeches for his characters, Drayton writes orations. If Daniel uses an Ovidian image or two to analyze his narrative, Drayton uses five or six. And if Daniel shapes Rosamond's life into the rise and fall of tragedy, Drayton turns Gaveston into something like a human yo-yo as he is exiled to France by Edward I, recalled to England when Edward II becomes king, exiled to Ireland by the jealous nobles, restored and raised to new titles, banished to Belgium, secretly recalled, captured by the barons, executed, and finally inscribed on the roll of fame by the obsequies ordained by the king.

Daniel and Drayton both use rhetorical amplification to lift the lives of their protagonists to the level of "wonders," making them subjects for Fame and hence suitable as the material of history. But Daniel had been careful to make the rhetorical splendors of *Rosamond*—its set speeches, its tragic scheme, the wondrous casket described in the chronicles— part of a middle level of material and psychological coherence capable of acting as a natural cause in his narrative. By contrast, Drayton's rhetorical wonders in *Peirs Gaveston* form external paradigms controlling the fatal actions of his characters. Gaveston is described over and over again as a comet rushing through the heavens in brief splendor, or he and Edward II are figured as Castor and Pollux, signifying their constancy as lovers. Simultaneously, the rotation of the sign of the Gemini in the heavens represents Gaveston's fortune as he rises from obscurity to the pomp of a royal favorite and descends again to the executioner's block. Reinforcing the astrological imagery is Drayton's reiterated metaphor of history as a tragic stage on which the main actors ascend and fall at the beck of Fortune. To be sure, Fortune and stellar influence appear often enough as causes in the work of the historians. One has only to recall Guicciardini's meditations on Fortune or Bodin's long excursus in his *Methodus ad Facilem Cognitionem Historiae* on the role of the stars in human history. Both are perceived as natural forces, and the underlying ideology of the historians does not yet separate off human history from natural history. Still, Fortune and the stars mark the boundaries of natural process by Renaissance or modern ideology, and in appealing to them Drayton has dismembered the delicate balance between individual will and transpersonal forces that engenders the individual act in *Rosamond*. This is most apparent on the level of plot, where Daniel's microscopic analysis of a single cycle of rise and fall is supplanted by the repetitive cycles of *Peirs Gaveston*. The effect is to change the scale of causality to one so large that the will of the individual is scarcely visible.

As a tragedian whose eyes are fixed on the polestar rather than on the pit, Drayton casts himself in the role of the prophetic poet, reading in the heavens the course of history. It is a role he has played in his earlier poems as well. After a fling as a modern David in his youthful translation of the Psalms, he takes up those doctrines that passed in Elizabethan England for Neoplatonism in his pastoral *Idea the Shepheards Garland* (1593) and his sonnet sequence *Ideas Mirror* (1594). His mythological poem *Endimion and Phoebe* (1595) is a Chapmanesque piece of mystical-Platonical-astrological Ovidianism that breaks off as a fragment amid a vision of cosmic order based on the numbers three and nine. Poetic form in these poems can be called "mythic" in the sense that Raymond Waddington uses the term for Chapman's poetry: "Mythic form . . . both describes the structure of the narrative within the conventional mold of genre and points to a transcendent form, the realm of ideas or truth which Chapman believed to be inherent in the myth."[26] Drayton treats the stellar patterns of *Gaveston* as omens or portents, reveal-

---

[26] Raymond Waddington, *The Mind's Empire* (Baltimore: Johns Hopkins University Press, 1974), p. 15.

ing to his characters what awaits them in the narrative and
to his readers the significance of what befalls them. The stars
are transcendent signs, poised on the brink of another, time-
less world which is figured in the reduplication inherent in
the revolutions of the heavens, and reiterated by the poem's
theatrical images, which imply an inherent reproducibility
that belies the apparent uniqueness of Gaveston's life.

It is startling after this mythic amplification to encounter
Drayton's end note to *Peirs Gaveston*, where he laments the
vagueness and inconsistency of sixteenth-century chroniclers
and records his own diligent researches among the collec-
tions of John Stow. He claims to have relied on "those Writ-
ers who lyved in the tyme of *Edward* the second, wherein he
[Gaveston] onely florisht, or immediately after, in the golden
raign of *Edward* the third, when as yet his memory was fresh
in every mans mouth: whose authorities (in myne opinion)
can hardlie be reproved of any, the same beeing within the
compasse of possibility, and the Authors names extant,
avouching what they have written." To Drayton, historical
truth is principally a matter of getting the details right, such
as the number of times Gaveston was banished, and the
gauge of accuracy is the age and credibility of the sources
from which he has drawn his facts. Drayton's modern edi-
tors have demonstrated that his boasts are not altogether hol-
low, since he indeed consulted the fourteenth-century *An-
nales Londoniensis*, kept by a city merchant, and the *Annales
Paulini*, kept at the Cathedral of St. Paul's.[27] Although the
chronicles are both anonymous, their age itself establishes
their good faith, and Drayton has only to copy out what his
"authorities" have written, so long as what they say is not
overtly miraculous or impossible.

The note reveals how much *Peirs Gaveston* is left straddling
two unconnected notions of truth, both narrative, but one
particular, historical, and based on the authority of others,

---

[27] Commentary on *Works*, ed. Kathleen Tillotson and Bernard H. New-
digate, 5:24–25.

the other mythic, poetical, and based on Drayton's own insight. The key to his reconciliation of the two lies in his intent to navigate through the shoals of fact by the compass of possibility, thereby suggesting a notion of verisimilitude as the proper channel for poetic history. Aristotle differentiated history from poetry on the grounds that the historian narrates what actually occurred, while the poet narrates what might possibly occur, in accordance with probability or necessity (*Poetics*, 9). To Aristotle, inevitably, history was what Thucydides and Herodotus did, the investigation of contemporary war and politics, based on the eyewitness reports of reliable men. Seeing was believing. The skeptical approach to first-hand reports that characterizes modern historiography is a later development, derived from the critical methods applied to documents. Drayton has no living eyewitnesses, and so the referent of his narrative is not a thing, an event that really, certifiably happened; it is what fourteenth-century men of good faith *think* occurred, as constrained by the judgment of modern men of good faith. Historical narrative as well as poetic narrative is governed by verisimilitude. Drayton, however, is sliding between two different notions of verisimilitude, neither of which is quite the same as Aristotle's.[28] On the one hand, the verisimilar is a matter of opinion, what men think happened. On the other, it is what is prescribed by the general principle of probability or necessity, principles that are in turn opinions, what men think is probable or necessary.

Tasso recognized this *rapprochement* of poetry and history when he reasoned in his *Discourses on the Heroic Poem* (1594) that the poet must eliminate from a historical epic events that actually happened if men would regard them as impossible, and include events that didn't happen if they seem more probable. By invoking the rule of opinion, Tasso reduced the verisimilar from an absolute to a relative quality

[28] I am indebted to Tzvetan Todorov's "Introduction to Verisimilitude," in *The Poetics of Prose*, trans. Richard Howard (Ithaca: Cornell University Press, 1977), pp. 80-88.

and, paradoxically, made room for the marvelous. Whereas the verisimilar is defined by its ability to have a cause ascribed to it from among those things that men recognize as the agents of nature, the marvelous and the merely factual alike seem to lack cause, to exist in isolation from the web of nature. Just as the historian must connect his facts to the laws of probability to make them verisimilar, so the poet must somehow make probable the impossible or marvelous. Tasso has only to invoke the axiom that to God all things are possible; then the verisimilar is seen to be merely that which finds a visible cause, while a thing that is marvelous "when regarded in itself and confined within natural limits, [can be] verisimilar when considered apart from these limits in terms of its cause, which is a powerful supernatural force accustomed to performing such marvels."[29]

Tasso makes the marvelous a mere optical illusion that appears only to the extent that its causes are invisible. He redeems the place of the marvelous in narrative by making God himself the author of the narrative of history, and the poet an imitator or borrower from that divinely inscribed, and most authoritative source. Hence causation, divine and natural, is elevated as the ordering principle of truthful narrative, and noncausative narrative, like Ariosto's *Orlando furioso*, appears by contrast to be merely fabulous. Drayton's bridge across the gaps between history and poetry and the factual and the marvelous in *Peirs Gaveston* is a replica of Tasso's. His chronicle material must be verisimilar in itself, but then must be teased up to the level of the marvelous by poetic amplification in order to be worthy of the fame bestowed on its subject by the historian. He then synthesizes the marvelous and the verisimilar, and the causal and the factual, by making the marvelous (his stellar omens) the cause of the verisimilar (his random, reported facts) to produce a poetic narrative inscribed with truth.

---

[29] Tasso, *Discourses on the Heroic Poem*, p. 38. This argument is already worked out in his earlier *Discourses on the Art of Poetry*.

The theological implications of their poetical-historical courses were soon apparent to both Tasso and Drayton. Concerned by criticism of his use of the marvelous in the early drafts of the *Gerusalemme Liberata*, Tasso strove in his "Prose Allegory" and *Discourses* to establish the truth of the poem in all its aspects. In areas where he concedes historical falsehood, he claims poetic truth through allegory.[30] If the marvelous appears only when its causes are invisible, it ceases to be marvelous and disappears at the moment when its poetic power has so enraptured the reader with wonderment as to make the supernatural itself visible to him. Drayton acknowledges this pull of the marvelous toward divine truth in his *Matilda*, published in the same year as Tasso's *Discorsi*, when he adopts for the first time the generic designation "legend," for the term has immediate resonance as a form of sacred history.

Drayton introduces the term "legend" by way of rebuking Daniel's *Rosamond* for the false devotional language that was an aspect of the poem's Petrarchism:

> Faire *Rosamond*, of all so highly graced,
> Recorded in the lasting Booke of Fame,
> And in our Sainted Legendarie placed,
> By him who strives to stellifie her name,
> Yet will some Matrons say she was to blame.
>   Though all the world bewitched with his ryme,
>   Yet all his skill cannot excuse her cryme.
>                                         [ll. 29-35]

Rosamond had prayed to Daniel to write an encomiastic history that would simultaneously restore her fame and convey her soul to Elysian rest by means of the prayerful sighs wrung from the pitiful heart of Delia. The poem borders on a double blasphemy, since Rosamond's credentials for sal-

---

[30] The growth of Tasso's conception of the allegory of *Gerusalemme Liberata* is traced by Michael Murrin in *The Allegorical Epic: Essays in its Rise and Decline* (Chicago: University of Chicago Press, 1980), pp. 92-107.

vation are dubious and her prayer suggests doctrines of pur-
gatory and saintly intercession that are anathema to the re-
formed church. (This borderline blasphemy is of course very
much in keeping with the moral ambivalence of the Petrar-
chanized minor epic.) Drayton's subject, Matilda, has a
somewhat better claim to the title of a virgin-martyr, having
been murdered at the order of King John when she refused
to submit to his lust. Having corrected Daniel in his choice
of subject matter, Drayton then invokes a more perfect lit-
erary model and mythic referent, Edmund Spenser's celebra-
tion of Elizabeth in his "Legend of Chastity," Book 3 of the
*Faerie Queene.*

If Drayton's poem is both a correction and a sacred parody
of Daniel's *Rosamond*, it also corrects and parodies (as does
Spenser) that which Daniel has parodied, the saint's lives ac-
cumulated in the *Golden Legend*. Begun by a thirteenth-cen-
tury Dominican, Jacobus da Voragine, the *Golden Legend* was
a populist work, written as a group of stories to be inserted
into the divine office on the appropriate saints' days for the
edification of a lay audience.[31] Hence the title "legend" is
drawn from the Latin gerund "legendum," meaning some-
thing to be read. Tied to the ecclesiastical calendar, the
*Golden Legend* has something of the shape of a universal his-
tory, recording the acts of the Church through a series of
biographies capable of infinite repetition and expansion into
the future.

As a sacred history, a legend is essentially a record of the
marvelous, as the account of England's first martyr, St. Al-
ban, bears witness. As he is led across a river to the place of
his martyrdom, many of the spectators attempt to swim
across and are drowned, so the martyr dries up the river and
restores to life the bodies found in the muddy bottom.

And then one of the knyghtes that drewe saynt Albon
towarde his martyrdome sawe these myracles that god

---

[31] Helen White, *Tudor Books of Saints and Martyrs* (Madison: University of
Wisconsin Press, 1963), pp. 25-34.

shewed for hym / & anone threwe away his swerde & fell downe at the feet of saynt Albon sayenge / I knowlege to god myn error & demaunde forgyvenes. . . . Then at the last they came to a hyll where this holy Albon shold fynysshe & ende his lyf / In whiche place laye a grete multytude of people nygh deed for hete of the sonne & for thurst. . . . And then anone the wynde blewe a fresshe cole / & also at the feet of this holy man Albon sprange up a fayre well / wherof all the people mervayled to see the cold water sprynge up in the hote sondy grounde / & so hygh on the toppe of an hyll. . . . [Then they] toke this holy man & bounde hym fyrst to a stake / & after henge hym on a bough by the heere of his heed / & sought amonge the people one to smyte of his heed / and than a cruell man was redy / & in an angre toke his swerde and smote of the heed of this holy man at one stroke / that the body fell to the grounde / and the heed henge styll on the bough / & the turmentour as he had smytten of his heed / bothe his eyen stert out of his heed and the wretche myght in no wyse be restored agayne to his syght. . . . And the nyght after was seen a fayre beme comynge downe fro heven to the sepulcre of saint Albon by whiche aungels descended and ascended all the nyght durynge / syngynge hevenly songes.[32]

Though it always recapitulates the whole life of its subject from birth to death, the legend has only one essential element, the fact that its subject suffers for his faith. Suffering requires no sequence of events, merely a duration of time, and hence the narrative of St. Alban is built only superficially as a causal sequence. It is a repetition, potentially endless, in which the tormentors, unchanging in their malice, heap torture upon torture on the saint (here directed as well at his surrogate, the converted soldier, who is mutilated by the

[32] *The Golden Legende* (London: Wynken de Worde, 1527), fol. 137ᵛ -138ᵛ.

heathen mob). The saint, in return, performs miracle after miracle, any one of which would suffice to show his godliness. Their repetition punctuates the otherwise trivial events of life (crossing rivers, climbing hills, and so on) with a continuous manifestation of divine grace. With the protagonists fixed into their opposed attitudes of hate and love, the only peripeteia can occur among the spectators in the narrative or the auditors of the narrative, who are moved to wonder and devotion. The pedagogical aim of the *Golden Legend* demands that the marvelous be its informing principle, as the window to the contemplation of divine things.

It is precisely this use of the marvelous in sacred history that John Foxe set out to discredit as he composed his *Actes and Monuments* from his place of exile at Basel during the reign of Mary Tudor. At stake was nothing less than the credibility of reformation as a principle, for the intellectual defense of Protestantism largely turned on a historical argument, that the Apostolic church was the earthly model of the true church, that the Roman church had grown corrupt, abusive, and worldly in the epoch from Constantine to Luther, and that the reformed churches more perfectly reflected the liturgy, government, and ethics of the Apostolic church. The heavenly armies rushed to the armory of secular historiography: the French "new historians," for instance, were in many cases Huguenot activists, and Anglo-Saxon studies in England received their impetus from Archbishop Parker's desire to establish the nature of the primitive English church. On the other side, the Spanish Jesuit Melchior Cano made crucial contributions to the theory of historical evidence, and Foxe's reformation of historiography was quickly matched by the researches of the Bollandist Fathers in Catholic Belgium.

Foxe assaulted the *Golden Legend* on two fronts, which resemble the grounds whereon Drayton established the credibility of his fourteenth-century chronicles. First Foxe impugns the general credibility of the narrative by questioning the good faith of the authors and of their pedagogical intent.

The stories are "Monkish miracles and grosse fables, where-
with these Abbey monkes were wont in time past to de-
ceave the Church and God, and to beguile the whole world
for their owne advantage."[33] By reinterpreting the intent of
the authors, Foxe makes their marvelous narrative signify
not God's omnipotence but the universal falsehood of the
Roman church. "Thus out of this fountayne have gushed out
so many prodigious lyes in Church Legendes, in Saintes
lives, in monkish fictions, in fabulous miracles, in false and
forged Reliques," and so forth (p. 584). In his recounting of
individual saint's lives, Foxe analyzes the received narrative
for antiquity of sources, internal consistency, and probabil-
ity, rejecting the tale of St. Alban on all three grounds:

> The rest that foloweth of this story in the narration of
> *Bede*, as of drying up the River, as *Alban* went to the
> place of his execution: then of making a welspring in
> the top of the hill, and of the falling out of the eyes of
> him that did behead him (with such other prodigious
> miracles mentioned in his story) because they seeme
> more legendlike, then truthlike: againe, because I see no
> great profit, nor necessitie in the relation thereof, I leave
> them to the free judgement of the Reader, to thinke of
> them, as cause shall move him.
>   The like estimation I have of the long story, wherein
> is written at large a fabulous discourse of all the doings
> & miracles of *S. Alban* taken out of the Librarie of *S.
> Albans*, compiled (as there is saide) by a certaine Pagan
> who (as he sayth) afterwarde went to Rome, there to be
> Baptised. But because in the beginning or Prologue of
> the Booke, the sayde writer maketh mention of the
> ruinous walles of the towne of *Verolamium*, containing
> the storye of *Albanus*, and of his bitter punishments:
> which walles were then falling downe for age, at the
> wryting of the sayde booke, as he saith: Therby it see-

---

[33] John Foxe, *Actes and Monuments* (London, 1583), p. 89.

meth this story to be written a great while after the mar-
tyrdome of Alban, either by a Britaine [Celt], or by an
English [Anglo-Saxon] man. If he were a Britaine, how
then did the Latin translation take it out of the [Old]
English tounge, as in the Prologue hee him self doeth
testifie. If hee were an Englishman, how then did he go
up to Rome for baptisme, being a Pagan, when he
myght have bene baptised among the Christian Brit-
aines more neare at home.

But among al other evidences and declarations suffi-
cient to disprove this Legendary story of S. Alban, noth-
ing maketh more against it, then the very storie it selfe.

[pp. 88-89]

Foxe has changed the meaning of the word "legend" from
its root meaning to its present one. By differentiating be-
tween a saint's acts and saintly legends, he demands the
sharpest possible rejection of the marvelous on behalf of the
verisimilar, on the grounds that the marvelous is both untrue
and, more surprisingly, not useful. The latter contention is
possible only by reference to Foxe's belief that unreflective
devotion is what he does *not* want to arouse among the faith-
ful precisely because of its blind and irrational basis. If, on
the other hand, he is to escape the charge of denying the
supremacy of God's providence over the laws of nature and
of logic, it is because his book is a providential history of a
different sort from the *Golden Legend*. Fox has no trouble
seeing the hand of God in the general shape of time, which
is clearly proclaimed in the prophetic passages of Scripture.
It is the presumption of modern man attempting to divine
God's purpose in individual instances that he doubts. Thus
while Foxe is absolutely certain that Thomas Cromwell was
raised up by God to suppress the monasteries, in fulfillment
of Psalm 113:

He raiseth the nedie out of the dust & lifteth up the
poore out of the dung,

That he maie set him with the princes, *even* with the
princes of his people.

[ "Geneva Bible," 1560]

he does not describe any specific miracles as signs of Crom-
well's calling. God is powerful enough to bring about his
will within the laws of nature.

By making sacred history the account of the workings of
the Holy Spirit within the human soul, Foxe has quarantined
the "legend" as a genre infected by the marvelous. If the
legend in this sense is practiced only by popish monks with
the deceitful intent of passing off their work as exemplary
history, it may conversely be practiced in a reformed manner
by Protestant poets of good faith like Spenser and Drayton
who openly proclaim their works as exemplary fiction. In
his legend of *Matilda*, Drayton gives us no footnote about
historical accuracy and has drawn his story from what is in
his own and Foxe's terms the worst possible kind of source,
a sixteenth-century chronicle kept at the Augustinian mon-
astery of Dunmow, whose account of the incident in ques-
tion is not corroborated by others.[34] Though it resembles the
material of history, the story of Matilda is clearly a "legend"
in the pejorative sense and is to be treated as poetry. Where
Spenser manifests the supernatural allegorically in his poetic
legend of chastity through a series of fabulous beasts, strange
metamorphoses, and miraculous visions, Drayton does it in-
visibly through the implicit causes of the events he narrates.
*Matilda*, like *Peirs Gaveston*, adopts as its first level of narra-
tive order the "natural" and hence verisimilar sequence of
the birth, fortunes, and death of its main character. Narrative
and heroine find a common origin at her birth; her attrac-
tiveness to the king embroils the realm in war between king
and nobles, and her death seals up all strife. But Drayton
subjugates this pattern to the spiritual sequence whereby the
secular saint transforms the lives of those who witness her

[34] Tillotson and Newdigate, "Commentary," 5:32.

passion. This pattern makes her death the center of the narrative and elongates it into a sequence of three epiphanies, as Matilda accepts her martyrdom, as her father Lord Robert Fitzwalter accepts God's will and forswears further vengeance, and as King John repents and undertakes a monthly pilgrimage to her grave.

Just how remarkable these conversions are is made apparent by a comparison with the treatment of the same story two years earlier by Drayton's friend John Stow. In his *Annales* Stow describes an ongoing political crisis between King John and his barons that is projected onto the sexual plane by John's violent appetites:

> [He] reprehended sometimes one, and sometimes another of his nobilitie as traitors, calling them jealous, whose beds (as he bragged) he had defiled and defloured their daughters.
>
> The *Chronicle* of *Dunmow* sayth, this discord arose betwixt the king and his barons, because of Mawd [Matilda] called the Faire, daughter to Robert fitz Walter, whome the king loved, but her father would not consent, and thereupon ensued warre throughout England. The king spoyled especially the Castell of Baynard in London and other holdes and houses of the barons. Robert fitz Walter, Roger fitz Robert, and Richard Mount Fichet passed over into France, some also went into Wales, and some into Scotland, and did great domage to the king. While Mawd the faire remayned at Dunmow, there came a messenger unto her from king John about his suite in love, but because she would not agree, the messenger poysoned a boyled or potched egge against she was hungrie, whereof she died, and was buried in the quier at Dunmow.[35]

Without declaring whether or not he thinks the Dunmow account is true, Stow establishes its verisimilitude by subor-

[35] John Stowe, *The Annales of England* (London, 1592), p. 247.

dinating it as effect and illustration of the general principles governing the king's behavior. He goes on to record how John is unexpectedly reconciled to Baron Fitzwalter because he needs good fighting men, and then miraculously repents his wicked ways. There is little of conscience in John's contrition, though, for he sees himself threatened simultaneously by papal interdiction, a French invasion, and rebellion at home. By acknowledging the pope as his secular overlord, he converts one adversary into an ally and even wins a papal interdiction against the barons who force his submission to Magna Carta at Runnymede.

Had Drayton wanted merely to rid the form of the legend of its miracles, he could have adopted Stow's political reading of the story of Mawd/Matilda. Had he wished merely to create Protestant poetic history, he might have rejected the whole incident as a monkish slander against the memory of a staunch defender of royal prerogatives. King John was, after all, one of John Foxe's and Bishop Bale's favorite monarchs precisely because of his struggles with the pope. Instead, Drayton disavows Stow's political verisimilitude in order to subordinate his poem to the rule of the marvelous, though not in the sense of the *Golden Legend*. No prodigies appear in the heavens to mark her death; no unseasonable rose grows from her grave; no pestilent scrofula afflicts the king for his crime (though the inelegant poached egg mercifully disappears). The miracles occur at the level of psychological coherence, in the contagious spiritual experience that infects the characters in the poem as it infected the knight who converted upon witnessing the miracles wrought by St. Alban. Upon his banishment, Baron Fitzwalter (like Gaveston or Edward II) had railed against the blindness of Fortune that left the person he loved prey to his enemies. The news of her death leads him rather quickly and incomprehensibly to the realization that providence rules all and vengeance must be left to God.

Like the conversion of the king (which follows hard upon), this peripeteia forms a gap in the narrative that is explicable only if one assumes a cause that lies outside both the "natural" level of the narrative and the natural world it imitates. The gaps are challenges to the reader's assumptions about the "general principles of probability or necessity" that constitute the verisimilar. Drayton's God, to whom all things are possible, will fill in the gaps one way; a modern reader might fill them with an argument about the violent and patriarchal nature of sexuality in a society where the king and his earls can make war over Matilda's chastity as if it were a disputed fief. To a Machiavelli or a Guicciardini (or a Stow), the narrative would quite simply be inaccurate, incoherent, and improbable as history.

   While abandoning its claim to historic truth, the legend of *Matilda* maintains its claim to verisimilitude by its naturalistic narrative sequence and by its appeal to a transcendent truth that is necessary if the marvelous events that punctuate the narrative are to *seem* natural in any way. With little of the rhetorical heightening of *Peirs Gaveston*, Drayton has maintained the "mythic" form of *Matilda*, giving it a claim to poetic truth of which John Foxe might approve: the exemplification of the universal principles by which divine grace acts in the individual soul. Two years later, in *Robert Duke of Normandy*, Drayton joins the "tragic" form of *Peirs Gaveston* to the "legendary" form of *Matilda* to produce a poem that marks a more radical departure from the norms of history toward those of poetry. By juxtaposing two different forms of historical narrative and subordinating both to a third, marvelous narrative, Drayton drives the quarry of transcendent truth so far from his rhetorical nets as to suggest that neither poetry nor history can capture it.

   The subject of *Robert* is again from the chronicles (this time Holinshed's).[36] When William the Conqueror chose his second son, William Rufus, as his heir, his eldest son Robert Curthose seized Normandy by force. Joining Godfrey of

[36] Tillotson and Newdigate, "Commentary," 5:38-39.

Bouillon on the First Crusade, Robert entrusted Normandy
to his youngest brother, Henry Beauclerc, who used his op-
portunity to take the English crown upon the death of Wil-
liam Rufus, to usurp Normandy, and to imprison and blind
Robert upon his return. The story has more than enough ups
and downs for a Fortune tragedy in the manner of *Peirs Ga-
veston*, while the matter of the Crusades is ideal for a secular
saint's life in the manner of *Matilda*. So Drayton does both,
giving us two chronological narratives side by side, told in
different manners. The political tale is related by the goddess
Fortune herself as a string of incidents without any internal
connections, just "one damn thing after another." As nar-
rated by the goddess Fame, however, Robert's life is an il-
lustration of character, a study of the lineaments of the
Christian warrior. Where Fortune had ticked off the years of
Robert's life like a metronome, Fame speeds through the
early and late times of Robert's misfortune, and slows down,
dilates, expatiates on his glorious years in the Holy Land.

By juxtaposing the two narratives of Fortune and Fame,
Drayton brings into conflict two sharply different ideas of
poetic history. The history of *res gestae* set forth by Fortune
illustrates the essentially random meaninglessness of human
actions. The heaps of events are reduced to a simple pattern
of alternation that dominates nature as well as man:

> The flood of mischiefe thus comes in againe,
> What *Fortune* works, not alwaies seems pretended,
> The wind thus turn'd, blows back the fire amaine,
> Where first mischance began, she will be ended,
>    And he defend him, from those he offended:
> For this we find, the course of fatall things,
> Is best discern'd in states of Realms & Kings.
>
>               [ll. 722-28]

Fame's history, by contrast, is encomiastic, and Robert's
goodness is celebrated, indeed, openly exaggerated:

Truth in his life, bright Poesie uphold,
His life in truth adorning Poesie:
Which casting life in a more purer mold,
Preserves that life to immortalitie,
  Both truly working, eyther glorifie;
Truth by her power, Arts power to justifie,
Truth in Arts roabs, adorn'd by Poesie.
[ll. 911-17]

Fortune analyzes history in something like the manner of
a linguist. She accumulates a large body of historical occur-
rences and redistributes them according to a recurrent pat-
tern, a diachronic "figure." In this case the figure is a per-
sistent pattern in which the action of one character is
thwarted by the action of another. This pattern of reversal
becomes the signature of Fortune, like an author addicted to
oxymoron. Fame by contrast signs her history with the con-
trary figure, *accumulatio*, in which potentially contradictory
terms (Truth/Art, life/immortality) are reconciled and made
to reinforce one another. The poem's two opposite methods
of plotting juxtapose two contrasting figures of thought,
which are reinforced again at the syntactic level by their use
of rhetorical schemes:

[Fortune]:  The conquest *William* made upon this Ile,
            With Norman blood be-peopling Brittany,
            Even now as Brittons made within a while
            Turne with revenge to conquer Normandy,
              Thus victory goes back to victory:
            That his own blood, wins what before he won,
            His conquering son, subdu'd his conquering son.
                                        [ll. 708-14]
 [Fame]:  Eternall sparks of honors purest fire,
          Vertue of vertues, Angels angeld mind,
          Where admiration may it selfe admire,

Where mans divinest thoughts are more divin'd,
Saint sainted spirit, in heavens own shrine
enshrind,
Endeared dearest thing, for ever living,
Receiving most of *Fame*, to *Fame* more giving.
[ll. 869-75]

Both Fortune and Fame bury their subjects under a soft snow
of *ploces* and *polyptotons* through the incessant repetition of a
few words in shifting senses and parts of speech. Fortune is
particularly enamored of *ploce* and *epanalepsis*: "Thus *victory*
goes back to *victory* . . ."; "His *conquering son*, subdu'd his
*conquering son*." By beginning each clause with the triumph
of one Norman prince and ending with the triumph of an-
other, Fortune displays in microscopic form the tragic plot
of vicissitude that she finds in history as a whole. Fame by
contrast is addicted to combining *polyptoton* with *epanalepsis*.
By the quick repetition of terms ("Angels angeld," "saint
sainted," "shrine enshrind," "of Fame, to Fame") she em-
phasizes and elevates Robert's virtues to figure forth her con-
ception of history as encomium and divine comedy.

Beneath the stylistic twinning of the two narratives is a
level of structural similarity. Fortune's narrative is admoni-
tory, allowing no defense against the vicissitudes of history
except philosophical resignation from history. Fame claims
to bring immortality to her subject and to inspire her audi-
ence in their quest for transcendent virtue. Each is a chrono-
logical sequence appealing to values that lie outside of time.
The effect of each singly is doubled by their juxtaposition,
which calls into question whether any one temporal sequence
can include all the elements of truth. This subjugation of
history to the ahistorical is redoubled by the fact that the two
narratives are embedded in a third narrative that is openly
fantastic, a dream-vision in an overtly archaic, late medieval
style. The poem has opened with the poet strolling out from
London into an enchanted realm, like Spenser's Faerieland,

in which Thames meets Medway in a lover's embrace. When the poet has been lulled to sleep by the songs of birds, the two goddesses appear as in a dream, leading Robert of Normandy himself, and begin their debate over the significance of his life.

In *Rosamond* and *Gaveston*, the complaint framework had been a simple device to measure the obscurity of the past and overleap it with the rhetorical presence of a living voice. The hypermarvelous nature of the frame in *Robert* would seem to have the opposite effect of placing his history at a distance from our own experience. This effect is reaffirmed as each of the goddesses makes a point of exposing her rival as a mere fiction. Thus Fortune notes that Fame is nothing but words:

> First, in opinion had'st thou thy creation,
> Form'd with conceit, the needy Poets frend,
> And like opinion, keep'st no certaine fashion,
> Yet in a circle still thy course doth end:
>     And but a Post which all base rumors send,
> An needles burden of an idle song,
> The prophane accent of each witles tongue.
>                 [ll. 141-47]

Fame, in return, reduces Fortune to an optical illusion, appearing only as the shadow of man's ignorance of the true causes of events:

> Those ignorant which made a God of Nature,
> And Natures God divinely never knew,
> Were those which first erected *Fortunes* stature,
> From whence this vile idolatry first grew,
>     Which times defect into mens eares still blew:
> Grounding their usurpations foolish lawes,
> On the opinion of so poore a cause.
>                 [ll. 281-87]

By embedding his historical narrative in a poetic narrative, Drayton makes the verisimilitude of history disappear and the marvelous itself dissolve in self-conscious rhetoric to reveal a blank space beyond. He has laid bare the structures of both historical and poetic narrative and left no ground of truth except by appeal beyond them to the divine and irrelevant tautology that God is truth itself. Drayton's incessant revisions of the poems between 1596 and 1619 change their verbal details but do not alter their fundamental narrative structure. His epigrammatic summary of the meaning of *Robert* in the 1619 *Works* says as much as he knew in 1596: "to shew the World, that Events are not the measure of Counsels, Gods pleasure over-swaying in all, for hidden Causes." What history call you this, Faustus might ask, *che sera sera*? Drayton has abandoned the historian's project of constructing a web of human and natural causes that holds all that happens in a delicate set of mutual relations. Through the power of the marvelous, he glimpses the possibility of stirring his audience to contemplation of higher truths, only to see the divine remain untouched and his rhetoric reach only to a realm of fiction somewhere between this world and that. While Daniel abandoned the minor epic to search for new notions of historical truth, Drayton clung to the form as he clung to the fictive power of its language. But like Daniel, Drayton saw that the Renaissance discovery of fiction was the reef on which poetry and history broke asunder.

# Chapter 6

## Spenser's Ovidian Epics

Of all the elements that contributed to the Elizabethan minor epic, Ovid's *Metamorphoses* is the most important. As the minor epic stands somewhere between the sonnet and the epic in the Renaissance hierarchy of genres, so the *Metamorphoses* is loftier and more resonant than the elegiac love poetry of Ovid's early years, even as it emulates and parodies the Vergilian epic, against which it is inevitably measured. In its fluid nature, the *Metamorphoses* can fragment into episodes of satire, pastoral, and elegy, or it can raise itself to a heroic vein and collect itself into a continuous epic poem. As such, it is the ultimate model for the minor epic as a mixed genre.

It is the Ovid of erotic fragments, not the Ovid of epic, that one most often encounters in discussions of his impact on Renaissance literature.[1] Ovid's poetry was regarded in the sixteenth century as a school of love, a storehouse of myths, and a textbook of rhetorical elegance. Many Elizabethan poets—one thinks especially of Marlowe, Shakespeare, and Beaumont—caught the peculiar mixture of desire, violence, comedy, and self-conscious brilliance of language that characterizes the more familiar episodes of the *Metamorphoses*. But these episodes make up only a fraction of the poem, which makes an epic claim to tell the history of the world in a "perpetual song" that runs from the creation of the uni-

[1] Notable exceptions are Muriel Bradbrook's discussion of metamorphosis as a theme in *Shakespeare and Elizabethan Poetry* (London: Chatto, 1951), chap. 4; and Richard Lanham's analysis of Ovid as archrhetorician in *The Motives of Eloquence: Literary Rhetoric in the Renaissance* (Berkeley: University of California Press, 1976), pp. 48-64.

verse out of Chaos down to the apotheosis of Caesar in Ovid's own lifetime.

The quintessential Ovidian poet of Elizabethan England is the great epic poet of the age, Edmund Spenser, for Spenser perhaps alone considers the nature of the whole of the *Metamorphoses* in his own Ovidian verse. Spenser's great theme is flux, from the early *Shepheards Calendar* and *Complaints* to the "Mutabilitie Cantos" that have come to stand as the conclusion of the *Faerie Queene*. In virtually everything he wrote, Spenser borrowed episodes or glanced at figures from Ovid, but in two poems especially he confronted the formal problem presented by metamorphic verse: in his minor epic poem *Muiopotmos: or the Fate of the Butterflie*, and in Book 3 of the *Faerie Queene*.

In *Muiopotmos*, Spenser takes episodes from the *Metamorphoses* and reshapes and combines them into a unified narrative that emulates the form of Vergil's *Aeneid*. But by the simple trick of portraying less-than-heroic characters, a butterfly and a spider, he retains the comedy, skepticism, and pathos of Ovid's *Metamorphoses*. While *Muiopotmos* reflects the minor epic's parodic aspiration toward the elevation of epic, Book 3 of the *Faerie Queene* suggests a dissolution of epic form into the mixed and unstable state of the minor epic. In what is ironically called the "Legend of Chastity," Spenser ransacks the *Metamorphoses* for his materials. From them he makes a discontinuous and polyvalent narrative mingling history and myth, moving between earthly marvels and arcane revelations, and drawing on the poetic manners of pastoral, satire, the Petrarchan sonnet, the minor epic, and the heroic. In short, from its fragments Spenser recreates the Ovidian "perpetual song."

## OVID'S PERPETUAL SONG

The struggle to define the genre of the *Metamorphoses* brings into conflict two ways of reading that have dominated the interpretation of the poem for at least six centuries, and still dominate it today.[2] One way of reading makes the *Metamorphoses* an epic poem, a vast and systematic examination of universal flux. Such readings focus on the "Creation Epic" of Ovid's opening, the philosophical discourse of Pythagoras in Book 15, and the celebration of the Caesars with which the poem closes. In their impulse toward order, they are inevitably ideological—though the exact content of the ideology changes with the times—for they read through and past the poem to bring it into contact with other poems (starting with the *Aeneid*) and with the theological and political systems around it. The other impulse is to fragment the *Metamorphoses* into an episodic poem and accept as absolute the fictional boundaries of its artifice. Such readings may find some useful morality in it—if indeed they find any meaning at all—but they focus on its human pathos in Ovid's tales of love and hate, and on the ingenuity and variety of the poet's invention. These two radically different ways of reading appear throughout the Middle Ages and the Renaissance, and they shall appear in the interpretation of Spenser's Ovidian epics as well.

One might consider in this light the theological readings of the *Metamorphoses* that arose in the early fourteenth century with the commentary of Giovanni del Virgilio, the *Metamorphosis Ovidiana Moraliter Explanata* of Pierre Bersuire, and the anonymous *Ovide Moralisé*. While they show no particular concern with poetic form, their efforts to apply the techniques of contemporary Biblical exegesis to the *Metamorphoses* are attempts to take seriously Ovid's claim to have written a continuous history of the world from the Creation

---

[2] See especially Brooks Otis, *Ovid as an Epic Poet*, 2nd ed. (Cambridge: Cambridge University Press, 1970); and the attacks on Otis by G. Karl Galinsky in *Ovid's Metamorphoses: An Introduction to the Basic Aspects* (Oxford: Basil Blackwell, 1975). Otis finds in the *Metamorphoses* an anti-Augustan, anti-epic plan (pp. 366-67). Galinsky feels that if one can pin any generic label on the poem "one must call the genre of the *Metamorphoses* a mixed one" (p. 41).

down to the apotheosis of Caesar in his own day. Their attempts yield an Ovid who is orthodox in his general outline, since his opening account of Creation and the Flood is to them clearly based on Moses. Where he is heterodox, a wise reader can nonetheless pluck wisdom from his error. The doctrine of metempsychosis expounded by Pythagoras in Book 15, for instance, is squarely in conflict with the Christian doctrine of resurrection. But to Giovanni del Virgilio, Ovid's erroneous teaching can still remind us of the transience of all things under the heavens and admonish us to rely on the eternal God.[3]

Such interpretation gives unity to the *Metamorphoses* at the expense of its verbal surface. Its nature is aptly revealed by an illumination in William Caxton's manuscript of the *Metamorphoses* (actually a translation combining Bersuire and the *Ovide moralisé*) showing the poet, his head wreathed in laurel, kneeling to receive a vision of the Almighty [fig. 12]. Were it not for the laurel wreath, one would suppose from the appearance of the lovely Gothic chapel, the manuscripts scattered on the floor, the monk-like clothing, and the sword, that the kneeling figure is Caxton or the author of the *Ovide moralisé*, not Ovid. Theological interpretation confers on the pagan poet the gift of divine inspiration but it is apt to treat his text as only a launching pad to the beyond. The exegete is forever tempted to spend his time explicating the extrapoetic system toward which the poet is thought to refer, and pay only occasional regard to the poem itself.

In the early sixteenth century there appeared a humanist *Metamorphoses* based on a poetic appreciation of Ovid's text. This new Ovid is most visible in the edition by Raphael Regius (1493), who prizes Ovid as the most "elegant" and "ingenious" of poets. Regius points out Ovid's rhetorical colors and Hellenistic diction and constantly admires the clever way that he connects story to story and book to book. Regius is

<hr>

[3] Giovanni del Virgilio, *Allegorie Librorum Ovidii Metamorphoseos*, 15. 3, in Fausto Ghisalberti, "Giovanni del Virgilio espositore delle 'Metamorfosi,' " *Il Giornale Dantesco* 34 (1933):104.

12. *Ovid.* Ovid, *Metamorphoses*, trans. William Caxton. 1480. Pepys Library, Magdalene College, Cambridge.

not opposed to allegory; indeed, he offers quite a bit of Ovidian moral advice in his prefatory epistle to Francesco Gonzaga and even suggests that Ovid's battle scenes will prove instructive to the soldier. He is opposed specifically to theological allegory because of its inappropriateness to a Roman poet. To Regius, Ovid's account of the Creation smacks of Hesiod, Plato, and the Stoics.[4] Similar is his treatment of Ovid's claim that Caesar was transformed into a star. In the twelfth century, Arnulf of Orleans had recounted the story of how the new star appeared during the funeral games of Caesar and Augustus proclaimed it to be none other than the

[4] Raphael Regius, ed., *Metamorphoseis* (Milan, 1510), p. 1$^{r-v}$.

soul of his deified father. Arnulf reasons with a fine disregard for chronology that the star must in fact be that which led the Magi to the infant Christ.[5] To Regius the whole thing is strictly a bit of flattery tossed in by Ovid to please Augustus, and not very dignified flattery at that.[6]

Regius has "re-poeticized" Ovid at the cost of the poem's unity, for he disintegrates it into an encyclopaedia of classical culture and a series of elegant rhetorical figures. As poetic theory itself became more systematic in the sixteenth century, the reinterpretation of the *Metamorphoses* in poetic terms led inevitably to a reconsideration of its unity. Initially such attempts were rather awkward and tentative. The Aldine edition of 1502 spoke loudly by silence: it has no commentary of any sort and prints the text of the *Metamorphoses* uninterrupted by arguments ("fabulae") for each episode. In his revision of the Regius edition (1543), Jacobus Micyllus recognizes that the title of the *Metamorphoses* "contains the general proposition of the whole argument. . . . Indeed Ovid describes in these books many transformations both of things and of persons which even now are reported to have occurred from the beginning of the world up to his own day."[7] Arthur Golding goes a step further in 1567 in seeing one episode as a microcosm of the whole. He recognizes the "Sermon of Pythagoras" as "a sum of all the former woorke," and traces through the fifteen books a "dark Philosophie of turned shapes" that operates on all levels of being.[8]

---

[5] Arnulf of Orleans, *Allegoriae super Ovidii Metamorphosin*, 15. 9, in Fausto Ghisalberti, *Arnolfo d'Orléans, un cultore di Ovidio nel secolo XII*, Memorie del Reale Instituto Lombardo di Scienze e Lettere, vol 24 (Milan: Hoepli, 1932), p. 229.

[6] Regius, *Metamorphoseis*, p. 162ᵛ.

[7] "Epigraphe est, sive Titulus operis, continens generalem propositionem totius argumenti. . . . Describit enim in his libris Ovidius, plerasque transformationes cum rerum, tum personarum, quae iam inde ab initio mundi usque ad ipsius tempora accidisse fabulis traduntur." *Metamorphoseos*, ed. Raphael Regius and Jacobus Micyllus (Basel, 1543), p. 1.

[8] Arthur Golding, trans., *Ovid's Metamorphoses*, ed. John Frederick Nims (New York: Macmillan, 1965), pp. 405, 413.

Still, Golding is elsewhere the child of the fourteenth-century commentators, relying on moral and physical allegory to elucidate Ovid's "dark" sayings and finding the imprint of Moses in Ovid's "Creation Epic." The great champion of the poetic Ovid in the sixteenth century is the Italian theorist Giambattista Giraldi Cinthio, who in his treatise *Dei romanzi* (1554) comes to a startling and insightful understanding of the unity of the *Metamorphoses* in purely formal terms. Theoretical discussion of epic form was based mainly on Aristotle and applied mainly to Vergil, and so was singularly unsuited to a poem like the *Metamorphoses*. Giraldi Cinthio pursued more rigorously than others the humanist principle of historical relativity and recognized that Aristotle's discussion of epic applied only to classical poems with unified plots. To Giraldi Cinthio the vernacular romances of Ariosto and Boiardo are as fully heroic as the *Iliad* or the *Aeneid*. If they use multiple plots and mix high matter with low, this is merely the change necessary to adapt to a new language and a new civilization. In all other respects they observe the norms of epic, most importantly in their use of a unified narrative voice and a single proposition for the work.

By his subtle reconciliation of Aristotelian theory with the form of the romance, Giraldi Cinthio was able to see Ovid anew in the features of his descendants. Ovid was a "modern" among the ancients, and hence the most suitable for imitation:

> We see that Ovid, ingenious poet, laid aside in his *Metamorphoses* the laws of Vergil and Homer and did not follow the laws of Aristotle given us in his *Poetics*; nevertheless, he emerged as a beautifully artistic poet, with such benefit to the Latin language that he became a wonder. He was not reprehended nonetheless because he did not follow in the footsteps of others. This happened because he devoted himself to the writings of matter for which rules and examples did not exist, just as there were no materials on our Romances. Just as he who would write a poem of one action would err if he

ignored his models and the laws derived from all the works of like composition, so he who would write Romances of more than one action would err if he did not follow those who are now recognized as great and excellent.[9]

Giraldi Cinthio finds Ovid most notable for the un-Vergilian way that he weaves together diverse materials into a sequence stretching from the beginning of the world to the present. He particularly admires Ovid's sense of the marvelous and his power of invention, as evidenced, for instance, in making Numa and Pythagoras contemporaries. His only reservation—one often applied to Ariosto as well—is that Ovid "allowed too much to nature and followed too much his own sweet will, so that his works are like fields of the greenest corn, overly soft and luxuriant. This has caused him to appear more [ingenious] than profound, more licentious than attentive to law, more copious than diligent."[10] Elegance of form is achieved at the cost of immorality in matter.

Giraldi Cinthio's frank avowal of the licentiousness of the *Metamorphoses* lets loose the genie that the fourteenth-century commentators had kept restrained in the bottle of allegory. Though un-Aristotelian in its results, Giraldi Cinthio's definition of the form of the romance is Aristotelian in its method. Since allegory is never discussed in the *Poetics*, Giraldi Cinthio does not consider it a part of the romance and indeed mocks the "ravings" of those who think that Homer "deals with mysteries, secrets of nature, and celestial things."[11] He does not begrudge the poet his claim to inspiration, but he does not allow it to distract him from the technical refinement that is the soul of art.

If Giraldi Cinthio prizes the *Metamorphoses* as an elegant

[9] Giovanni Battista Giraldi Cinthio, *On Romances*, trans. Henry L. Snuggs (Lexington: University of Kentucky Press, 1968), pp. 40-41.

[10] Giraldi Cinthio, *On Romances*, p. 121. Snuggs mistakenly translates "ingegnoso" as "ingenuous"; cf. *Scritti estetici di Giambattista Giraldi Cintio*, ed. G. B. Pigna. 2 vols. in 1 (Milan, 1864), 1:163.

[11] Giraldi Cinthio, *On Romances*, pp. 33-34; cf. pp. 25-27.

fantasy, no small number of his contemporaries were ill at ease with fiction for the sake of fiction. Theological allegory appears in the most unlikely places, as when an early edition of Regius adds a charming illustration showing Christ himself creating the world [fig. 13]. After Regius and Giraldi Cinthio, Ovid is celebrated in poetic terms but nonetheless often read as a dynastic historical allegory (like the romance of Ariosto, which celebrates the Estensi) and a moral and theological allegory (like the romance of Tasso). In short, Ovid threatens to become once again an inspired poet and a second-rank Vergil. Perhaps the epitome of an Ovid both poetical and allegorical is the translation of the *Metamorphoses* by Lodovico Dolce (1553), dedicated to the modern Caesar, Charles V. To Dolce the revolt of the Giants against Jove merely shows the futility of those who struggle against the universal sway of the emperor.[12] Ovid boasted at the end of the *Metamorphoses* that so long as Rome's dominion lasted his fame would live—something that would not have made Augustus very happy. But the first page of Dolce's translation [fig. 14] makes clear that the *translatio imperii* gives Ovid's claim a validity he never dreamed of, as he becomes the prophet of terrestrial and celestial princes alike. In the body of his translation, Dolce persistently is influenced by Ariosto in his rendering of Ovid,[13] so that the *Metamorphoses* is simultaneously made into a modern *romanzo* and an allegory of modern history, an epitome of "anticlassical" form and of political orthodoxy.

The shift from the medieval to the Renaissance Ovid is in only a minor way a shift in allegorical interpretation. What changes there are in such interpretation are more in degree than in kind. At no point does Ovid become wholly unallegorical and the period of the least-allegorical Ovid, that of the Aldine and Regius editions, is very brief. The lasting change in the sixteenth century is the rise of the poetic Ovid

---

[12] *Le trasformationi*, trans. Lodovico Dolce (Venice, 1555), pp. *ii^v-*iii^r.

[13] Daniel Javitch, "The Influence of the *Orlando Furioso* on Ovid's *Metamorphoses* in Italian," *Journal of Medieval and Renaissance Studies* 11 (1981).

13. *The Creation*. Ovid, *Metamorphoses*, ed. Raphael Regius (Milan, 1510). Newberry Library, Chicago.

whose *Metamorphoses* is a novel form of the heroic poem. Daniel Javitch has shown how after 1550 the "anticlassical" [that is, anti-Vergilian and heterodox] features of the *Metamorphoses* came to be perceived and appreciated.[14] This modern Ovid was nonetheless understood by late-sixteenth-century humanists as having a philosophical dimension which must be examined in the context of Graeco-Roman thought. So complex a poem is as likely to transform the orthodoxies of a Christian culture as it is to be transformed by them.

FORMS VARIABLE AND DECAYED

Calling Spenser an Ovidian poet is a bit polemical—unless one has Dolce's Ovid in mind—since Spenser is more famil-

[14] *Ibid.*

14. *The Creation.* Lodovico Dolce, *Le trasformationi* (Venice, 1555). New-berry Library, Chicago.

iar nowadays as England's Vergil. The opening of the *Faerie Queene* itself proclaims this allegiance:

> Lo I the man, whose Muse whilome did maske,
> As time her taught in lowly Shepheards weeds,
> Am now enforst a far unfitter taske,
> For trumpets sterne to chaunge mine Oaten reeds,
> And sing of Knights and Ladies gentle deeds.
> [1. Proem. 1]

By imitating the first lines of the *Aeneid*, Spenser marks himself as an emulator of Vergil's life as well as of his verse. Spenser is the celebrant of England's Augustus, the self-appointed propagandist for the Elizabethan *imperium*, the last defender of a harmonious and hierarchical world view, a soon-to-be-discarded image of the universe. But we must remember that the Vergil invoked in the first lines of the *Faerie Queene* was cancelled. Renaissance humanists knew as well as modern ones the story of how Varius set aside these lines when editing the text of the *Aeneid*.[15] Vergil's example like his text is made problematic, and doubly so when Spenser declares that his intent is to sing not of "arms and the man" but of "Knights and Ladies gentle deeds." Insofar as Ovid is the grandfather of the modern vernacular romance, he is the presiding genius of the *Faerie Queene*.

What Spenser does in his metamorphic poems is to Ovidianize Vergil and to Vergilianize Ovid. In his use of an Ovidian model in Book 3, Spenser poses for himself the problems of order and orthodoxy that confronted the commentators on the *Metamorphoses*. If the unity of the Vergilian epic and a systematic world vision are ideals to which Spenser aspires, the reality of his poetic achievement is a multiple and fluid conception of epic that occasionally rises to Vergilian heights but more often works in the mongrel

---

[15] The anecdote appears in the "Life of Vergil" by Suetonius and in the revision of Suetonius attributed to Donatus.

fashion of Ovid and the minor epic. What orthodoxy it pro-
claims is reached only through a ceaseless probing of the am-
biguities of the natural realm. *Muiopotmos* is by contrast
endowed with a perfect Vergilian form despite its less-than-
epic protagonists. It is a continuous, unified narration of the
exploits of a single set of characters and its Ovidian digres-
sions are carefully controlled and immediately relevant to the
main narrative. As it travesties the form of epic, so it calls in
question, however gently, the didactic use of poetry. The
Vergilianizing of *Muiopotmos*, like the Ovidianizing of the
*Faerie Queene*, shows how limited is the ability of any world
order, whether political or conceptual, ever to get the fluid
universe fully in its clutch.

  Probably written before the publication of Books 1-3 of
the *Faerie Queene*, *Muiopotmos* was printed in Spenser's 1591
volume of *Complaints. Containing sundrie small Poemes of the
Worlds Vanitie*. The title of the volume seems more a the-
matic than a generic designation (if indeed Spenser had any-
thing to do with it), for the contents range from animal fable
to vision and only a few of the poems show the characteris-
tics of the complaint form.[16] The Greek title of *Muiopotmos*
and the opening pattern of *narratio, invocatio*, and *propositio*
proclaim the norms of epic and its conclusion echoes the last
lines of the *Aeneid*:

> . . . the greisly tyrant . . .
> Under the left wing stroke his weapon slie
> Into his heart, that his deepe groning spright
> In bloodie streames foorth fled into the aire,
> His bodie left the spectacle of care.
>                    [*Muiopotmos*, ll. 433-40]

> . . . ferrum adverso sub pectore condit
> fervidus. ast illi solvuntur frigore membra
> vitaque cum gemitu fugit indignata sub umbras.

---

[16] For a review of modern interpretation of *Muiopotmos* and attempts to
define its genre, see Franklin E. Court, "The Theme and Structure of Spen-
ser's *Muiopotmos*," *Studies in English Literature* 10 (1970):1-4.

(. . . full in his breast he buries the sword with fiery
zeal. But the other's limbs grew slack and chill, and
with a moan life passed indignant to the Shades below).[17]

One might even be taken in by the epic pomp of Spenser's
*ottava rima* if the joke were not given away in the title. But
Spenser is concerned not to let his mock-epic turn into a
sophomoric gag and lets down his pretence in the third
stanza:

> Of all the race of silver-winged Flies
> Which doo possesse the Empire of the aire,
> Betwixt the centred earth, and azure skies,
> Was none more favorable, nor more faire,
> Whilst heaven did favour his felicities,
> Then *Clarion*.
>     [ll. 17-22]

As he reveals the true nature of his subject, Spenser sets up
a new guessing game by which he speaks in *periphrasis* and
begs his reader to decode his rhetoric. Hence the air becomes
an "Empire" which flies "possesse," such flies as can win the
favor of heaven.

This game works by enigma, as when Spenser masks un-
der the phrases "Phoebus arrowes" and "th'hayling darts of
heaven" the sun and rain that beat on Clarion's helmet. He
resorts to the comic letdown when the mighty forces which
Clarion tempts turn out to be no more than the "troublous
winde." He treasures the teasing revelation:

> Therein [his helmet] two deadly weapons fixt he bore,
> Strongly outlaunced towards either side,
> Like two sharpe speares, his enemies to gore:
> Like as a warlike Brigandine, applyde
> To fight, layes forth her threatfull pikes afore,

---

[17] *Aeneid*, 12. 950-52, trans. H. Rushton Fairclough, Loeb ed. (London:
Heinemann, 1918).

The engines which in them sad death doo hyde:
So did this flie outstretch his fearefull hornes.

[ll. 81-87]

Last is the mistaken identity, in which Spenser momentarily
thinks the fully armored Clarion is Hercules himself. Spen-
ser's word games exploit the charm of the literal made dif-
ficult as his language tricks and weaves around its object, his
art contending with, transforming, and excelling nature.[18]

Spenser's self-conscious display of art is repeated in the
poem's two mythic digressions. The first, spun out of the
merest hints in Ovid and in that other *Metamorphoses* by
Apuleius, tells how the butterfly got his wings. When the
nymphs of Venus gathered flowers one day, Astery excelled
the others, who then spitefully claimed that Cupid had aided
her. Fearing a new rival like Psyche, Venus breaks into a
jealous rage:

Eftsoones that Damzel by her heavenly might,
She turn'd into a winged Butterflie,
In the wide aire to make her wandring flight;
And all those flowres, with which so plenteouslie
Her lap she filled had, that bred her spight,
She placed in her wings, for memorie
Of her pretended crime, though crime none were:
Since which that flie them in her wings doth beare.

[ll. 137-44]

In the second digression, Spenser adapts Ovid's story of
Arachne to explain why spiders hate butterflies so much. In
Ovid's account, there is some question as to whether the
tapestry woven by Minerva is superior to that of Arachne.

[18] For a subtle reflection on the art/nature motif, see Judith Dundas,
"*Muiopotmos*: A World of Art," *Yearbook of English Studies* 5 (1975):30-38. I
am in essential agreement with Dundas's reading of the poem. See also John
B. Bender, *Spenser and Literary Pictorialism* (Princeton: Princeton University
Press, 1972), pp. 162-67.

But in Spenser's version, the victory of the goddess is be-
yond question:

> Emongst those leaves she made a Butterflie,
> With excellent device and wondrous slight,
> Fluttring among the Olives wantonly,
> That seem'd to live, so like it was in sight:
> The velvet nap which on his wings doth lie,
> The silken downe with which his backe is dight,
> His broad outstretched hornes, his hayrie thies,
> His glorious colours, and his glistering eies.
>
> [ll. 329-36]

Minerva's butterfly, like Spenser's, proclaims the supreme
artistry of the literal. Her skill is in attention to surface, the
nap of the wings and the downy back. In his digressions
Spenser looks to the poetic Ovid, the ingenious and elegant
Ovid. This is especially true in the cleverness with which he
links the digressions to the main narrative. Regius forever
marvelled at Ovid's way with such transitions, and both he
and Giraldi Cinthio admired the description of a tapestry or
a painting as a particularly fine way to weave in subsidiary
tales.[19] The story of Astery arises after Spenser describes the
wings of Clarion, then wonders if his master Cupid will be-
grudge the implicit denigration of his own splendid wings.
Then he recalls how the court ladies envied the wings of
Clarion too and sought to steal them, which brings him
quite naturally to his tale of Astery transformed because of
the jealousy of the nymphs.

The story of Astery subtly links all the realms of experi-
ence embraced by the poem, those of the gods, of humans,
and of insects. The butterfly of Minerva likewise stands at a
border. It leads on one hand to the epic realm within the
tapestry where Minerva strives with Neptune for the patron-
age of Athens. Across its other border it leads to her contest

---

[19] Regius, *Metamorphoseis*, p. 59a; Giraldi Cinthio, *On Romances*, p. 19.

with Arachne, and it glances outward to the butterfly and
spider of the main narrative. Arachne's tapestry too sets up
a hall of mirrors that reflects the structure of Spenser's poem.
She chooses for her subject the loves of the gods. In Ovid's
telling, her tapestry is a vast scene, depicting all the rapes
committed by Jove, by Neptune, by Apollo, by Bacchus,
and even by Saturn. In Spenser's poem, Arachne chooses a
single scene, the moment when Europa, mounted on Jove in
the shape of a bull, realizes her peril:

> She seem'd still backe unto the land to looke,
> And her play-fellowes aide to call, and feare
> The dashing of the waves, that up she tooke
> Her daintie feete, and garments gathered neare.
>                                              [ll. 281-84]

In the foreground Arachne places sporting Cupids and
nymphs, and around the whole she weaves a tendril of ivy.
She has reduced Ovid's multiple form to a unified one, just
as Spenser has done. She views with microscopic precision
a single scene, links the subsidiary figures closely to the nar-
rative, and encloses the whole within a decorative border.

So far I have read *Muiopotmos* as Regius and Giraldi Cin-
thio would read Ovid. But does not a poem from Spenser's
hand that forges links among the divine, the human, and the
natural realms demand to be read as Dolce or Golding would
read Ovid?[20] Must its formal unity not lead to a unity of
thought, or one episode within it emerge as the philosophical
center that raises the whole narrative from concrete fable to

[20] The most trenchant such attempt remains Don Cameron Allen's essay
on *Muiopotmos* in *Image and Meaning* (Baltimore: Johns Hopkins University
Press, 1960), pp. 20-41. For notable attempts to treat seriously the parallels
between humans and insects without violating the poem's comic surface,
see William Nelson, *The Poetry of Edmund Spenser* (New York: Columbia
University Press, 1963), pp. 71-74; and Judith H. Anderson, " 'Nat worth
a boterflye': *Muiopotmos* and *The Nun's Priest's Tale*," *Journal of Medieval and
Renaissance Studies* 1 (1971):89-106.

abstract signification? Such an episode stands precisely in the middle of the poem. It is Spenser's account of the garden where Clarion goes "to refresh his sprights." Gardens "in the middest" are especially to be watched, for Spenser's readers in 1591 would not be likely to have the Garden of Adonis far from their minds. The Vergilian dimension of *Muiopotmos*, however comic, also demands a philosophical center, a region set apart to explain the whole, like the underworld explored in Book 6 of the *Aeneid*.

The garden in *Muiopotmos* seems to fulfill such expectations, for as Clarion enters it, Spenser's voice immediately picks up a moral echo more appropriate to the affairs of men than of flies. Spenser finds in Clarion "a wavering wit," "unstaid desire," "glutton sense," and "riotous suffisaunce." The garden itself shows "riotous excesse," yet it is a paradise which Clarion doth "spoyle" with his play. On the other hand, Clarion exhibits "franke lustinesse" as he tastes the pleasures of the garden and not once does he "rudely . . . disorder" or "deface" its flowers. Spenser can only ask,

What more felicitie can fall to creature,
Than to enjoy delight with libertie?
[ll. 209-10]

Has Clarion sinned (if butterflies can sin)? Has he done anything to justify his death at the hands of the spider Aragnoll? The garden is an oracle with two mouths, or perhaps it is better compared to a Pythagorean riddle that twists and turns and tells us nothing. In the "Sermon of Pythagoras," in the great philosophical discourse that promises to unify the thought of the *Metamorphoses*, Ovid too arouses expectation only to disappoint it. Pythagoras tells of metempsychosis, of the changes of the seasons, of the shifting of the elements, and of the rise and fall of great empires. The climax of his vision is nothing less than an injunction against eating meat, and this in the midst of Ovid's great historical chronicle stretching from the fall of Troy to the apotheosis of Caesar. At his most Vergilian moment Ovid clowns.

And so does Spenser. His other explanatory devices are Ovidian, not Vergilian, digressions. The myths of Astery and Arachne invert their epic function. The introduction of a marvelous transformation into a narrative is a means of solving an impasse; it comes at the conclusion of the episode, as when Arachne is changed into a spider or when Vergil describes the Trojan ships turned into nymphs in Book 9 of the *Aeneid.* Spenser makes the transformations of Astery and Arachne antecedents of his narrative, not resolutions. They tell how the conflict of the spider and the fly came into being but they will not solve or explain it.

This is particularly visible in the case of Arachne, where Spenser has made a crucial alteration in Ovid's myth. In the *Metamorphoses* the tapestry of Arachne is described last, and when she finishes she is seemingly the winner:

Non illud Pallas, non illud carpere Livor possit opus.

(Not Pallas, nor Envy himself, could find a flaw in that work).[21]

But Pallas does envy it, tears the tapestry, and strikes Arachne viciously until the poor girl tries to hang herself. Medieval and Renaissance exegetes unanimously claim that this is no more than Arachne deserves, because of her wicked presumption and because the criminal subject matter of her tapestry makes it in fact inferior regardless of its art.[22] With

---

[21] Ovid, *Metamorphoses,* 6. 129-130, trans. Frank Justus Miller, Loeb ed. (London: Heinemann, 1916).

[22] Cf. Giovanni del Virgilio, 6. 27 (Ghisalberti, p. 72); Pierre Bersuire, *Metamorphosis Ovidiana moraliter . . . explanata* (Paris, 1515), p. 53$^r$; Regius, *Metamorphoseis,* pp. 58$^v$-59$^r$; Golding, *Ovid's Metamorphoses,* p. 408; and *Metamorphoseon,* ed. Johannes Raenerius (Lyons, 1588), pp. 184-90.

almost equal unanimity, modern critics find Ovid to be ex-posing once again the injustice of the gods. [23]

Each side has ignored half of what Ovid says, but Spenser does not. He too says that Arachne's tapestry is excellent, and in fact removes the impiety of her subject matter by limiting it to the one scene of Europa. It is

> Such as Dame *Pallas*, such as Envie pale,
> That al *good* things with venemous tooth devowres,
> Could not accuse.
>
> > [ll. 301–3; emphasis added]

But the superiority of Minerva's tapestry is self-evident in the lifelike splendor of the marginal butterfly. [24] The justice of her triumph acquits Spenser of portraying Clarion slain by the envy of unjust gods. But just as surely the self-in-duced metamorphosis of Arachne into the envious spider does not explain the death of Clarion as a punishment brought on by his own crimes. Clarion is everywhere the victim of envy, not the agent. Spenser does not begrudge the felicity of insects.

This is not to say that *Muiopotmos* utterly lacks a moral. Even Regius and Giraldi Cinthio readily assent that poetry must be edifying. If nothing else, *Muiopotmos* shows us that butterflies, like the other beautiful things of the earth, do not last forever. This is no less true, useful, and profound than Ovid's recommendation of a vegetable diet. By giving a Ver-

---

[23] See, for instance, L. P. Wilkinson, *Ovid Recalled* (Cambridge: Cambridge University Press, 1955), p. 199; Charles Segal, "Ovid's *Metamorphoses*: Greek Myth in Augustan Rome," *Studies in Philology* 68 (1971):384–86; Galinsky, *Ovid's Metamorphoses*, p. 67; and Court, "Spenser's *Muiopotmos*," p. 13. Interestingly, Otis finds the episode to be one of a series of "clear-cut theodicies in which obviously perverse pride is humbled by ob-viously just and noble goddesses" (*Ovid as Epic Poet*, p. 146).

[24] For a brief but useful piece of iconology demonstrating that marginal butterflies in late medieval manuscript illuminations signify nothing but themselves, see Andrew D. Weiner, "Spenser's *Muiopotmos* and the Fates of

gilian unity to his minor epic, Spenser removes those breaks and shifts in the multiple plot that the exegete longs to bridge with his abstractions.[25] Regardless of when *Muiopotmos* was written, this must be taken at the time of its publication in 1591 as Spenser's subtle bemusement with the high purpose of the *Faerie Queene*. At the same time, it makes *Muiopotmos* itself into more than an empty trifle. Spenser's desire to keep to the beautiful surface of things is reflected in the almost luxurious way that Clarion is ensnared in the web of Aragnoll:

> For striving more, the more in laces strong
> Himselfe he tide, and wrapt his winges twaine
> In lymie snares the subtill loupes among;
> That in the ende he breathelesse did remaine.
> [ll. 427-30]

It is the invitation to penetrate this rhetoric and see the literal butterfly at the moment of his death that gives pathos to the final Vergilian joke, as Clarion's "deepe groning spright . . . left the spectacle of care."

In *Muiopotmos* the minor epic form is Vergilianized, raised, and unified in order to tease us with the possibility of finding great significance in small events. Book 3 of the *Faerie Queene* is an Ovidianized epic whose form is lowered and divided and whose propositions are subjected to searching question. After two proper Vergilian books, Spenser lets loose in Book 3 an antic spirit that mimics and parodies Vergilian epic and Augustan orthodoxy. It is not enough that Spenser there

---

Butterflies and Men" (Paper delivered at Special Session on Renaissance Literature and Emblems, Modern Language Association, New York, 27 December 1976). Weiner argues on Calvinist grounds for the antiallegorical nature of the poem.

[25] Michael Murrin points out the dependence of allegory on the loose-knit or multiple plot in *The Veil of Allegory* (Chicago: University of Chicago Press, 1969), p. 73.

portrays an array of rapists, nymphomaniacs, sodomites, and sadists as his villains. Even his heroes act strangely under the impulse of love. The noble Arthur abandons his quest for Gloriana to chase after an unknown beauty, Sir Scudamour is utterly incapacitated by his frustrated passion, and Britomart rides around in men's clothing. Appropriately enough, the book ends in the 1590 edition with a luxurious if unheroic image of bisexuality in which Scudamour and Amoret embrace like

> . . . that faire *Hermaphrodite,*
> Which that rich *Romane* of white marble wrought,
> And in his costly Bath causd to bee site.
> [3. 12. 46]

I shall not attempt a complete description of Book 3 as an Ovidian epic here, much less of the whole of the *Faerie Queene.* That would lead far beyond the purposes of a book on the minor epic and merely repeat much that has already been said by Spenserians in recent years.[26] A few episodes will suffice to show how Spenser's Ovidian art brought the epic into contact with its lesser cousins, for Book 3 is a perfect example of the metamorphic continuous poem. It brings together satire, pastoral, and Petrarchism, history, prophecy, and the visual arts into a conceptual and artistic whole, and it does so only through a radical redefinition of the nature of the heroic poem.

Spenser adapts elements of the *Metamorphoses* to his romance according to Giraldi Cinthio's advice that the poet modernize the best classical models. Roman history gives way to British chronicle; the reincarnation of souls ("ani-

---

[26] I am thinking especially of Kathleen Williams, *Spenser's World of Glass* (Berkeley: University of California Press, 1966), chap. 3; also Donald Cheney, *Spenser's Images of Nature* (New Haven: Yale University Press, 1966), pp. 57-61; Angus Fletcher, *The Prophetic Moment* (Chicago: University of Chicago Press, 1971), pp. 90-106; and James Nohrnberg, *The Analogy of the Faerie Queene* (Princeton: Princeton University Press, 1976), *passim.*

mae") described by Pythagoras becomes a more acceptable reincarnation of forms; the tapestry of Arachne is replaced with "costly clothes of *Arras* and of *Toure*." Ovid describes in his *Amores* (2. 5. 17) how the crafty lover spills his wine at the table and writes the name of his beloved in the flowing liquor. Spenser makes the lover's game into a communication that travesties Communion:

> Now Bacchus fruit out of the silver plate
> He on the table dasht, as overthrowne,
> Or of the fruitfull liquor overflowne,
> And by the dauncing bubbles did divine,
> Or therein write to let his love be showne;
> Which well she red out of the learned line,
> A sacrament prophane in mistery of wine.
>
> [3. 9. 30]

Elsewhere the lovers in Book 3 act out the metaphors of Petrarchism, usually with comic results. When Florimel races on her palfrey across the path of Arthur, Guyon, and Britomart, her appearance is described in imitation of one of the most famous images in the *Canzoniere*:

> And her faire yellow locks behind her flew,
> Loosely disperst with puffe of every blast . . .
> [*Faerie Queene*, 3. 1. 16]

> Erano i capei d'oro a l'aura sparsi
> che'n mille dolci nodi gli avolgea . . .

> (Her golden hair was loosed to the breeze, which turned it in a thousand sweet knots).[27]

Petrarch's figure is itself a play on the moment in the *Aeneid* when Venus appears to her son on the shore near Carthage

---

[27] *Canzoniere*, 90, *Petrarch's Lyric Poems*, trans. Robert M. Durling (Cambridge: Harvard University Press, 1976).

(*Aeneid*, 1. 319-20). Venus has come to assist Aeneas on his epic mission and is prepared to use her erotic powers over Dido to that end. For Petrarch as for Vergil, eros and heroism are in conflict: he is tossed as if in the wind ("l'aura") by his contrary desires for Laura and for the laurel of poetic fame. Spenser picks up a heroic image that has been lyricized and reapplies it to epic. In the process he tests the heroic ideal against the erotic, and Sir Guyon and Arthur immediately fail as they rush off in mad pursuit of the lady.

Britomart is not immune for long, though. In Malecasta's castle she blunders into one of those Petrarchan encounters where eye beams dart, sighs heave, and the inward fire burns. When Malecasta creeps beneath the quilt and Britomart fears that her chastity is threatened, she responds with a killing rage that is a ludicrous exaggeration of the disdain felt by sonnet ladies. The erotic tinge to Britomart's violence takes an even more savage turn when she encounters Marinell. Passion isolates Britomart as she wanders to the shore in search of an appropriate setting for an amorous complaint. It makes her as solitary and inward as Marinell is in his flight from passion. Just as her feelings made Britomart blind to Malecasta's nature, so she is unaware and unconcerned to recognize this kinship with Marinell. Their encounter is inevitably violent as her amorous sorrow converts to "sudden wrath" and she leaves poor Marinell "tombled on an heape, and wallowed in his gore." The upshot is that each martial encounter is erotic at base and each is of questionable worth. The result is not so much to test the moral status of desire—that is questioned quite enough already—but to call in question the psychological roots of heroic action and to break down any simple claim of the military hero to nobility.

If the lyricization of epic tends to undercut the heroic ideal, the intervention of Ovid establishes a middle ground for the reconciliation of the erotic and the heroic. When the poet describes how Britomart fell in love with Artegall, he draws rather surprisingly on the story in the *Metamorphoses* of Myr-

rha's incestuous love for her father. "Imperious love" seizes
Britomart when she glimpses Artegall in the magic glass,
and she is divided between her fealty to love and her royal
birth until she is on the verge of madness or death. Love is
metamorphic, seizing the noblest hearts and transforming
them into monstrous versions of their heroic shapes.

Spenser's approach to the *Metamorphoses* is indirect here,
since his description of Britomart closely follows the pseudo-
Vergilian *Ciris*, accepted as authentic in the Renaissance. The
*Ciris* is set during an attack on Megara by the Cretan Minos.
Scylla, its heroine, is inflamed with desire for the besieger
when she glimpses him from the battlements, and presents
him with the magic lock of hair, cut from her father's head,
that protects his kingdom. Minos punishes her crime by
keelhauling her (without, of course, neglecting to sack the
city). The *Ciris* passes over the political themes inherent in
its story and concentrates instead on the operatic passion of
Scylla, elaborated in long duets with her nurse. The poem is
one of those most often mentioned as examples of the neo-
teric *epyllion*, and its language is densely ornamented in the
Alexandrian mode. In short, it is "Vergil" at his most Ovid-
ian.

There are two passages in Ovid's *Metamorphoses* analogous
to the *Ciris*, Ovid's own account of Scylla and the story of
Myrrha. In both, Ovid Vergilianizes the material of the *Ciris*
by weaving the episode into a larger framework to give it a
resonance beyond the erotic. Ovid's telling of the story of
Scylla takes on an epic symmetry and elevation derived from
the continuity of his narration and his sympathetic engage-
ment with Scylla's plight.[28] The tale of Myrrha inverts the
situation of Scylla since now the girl loves her father instead
of killing him, but it relies on the same narrative techniques.
Again the girl pines, has a long scene of confession and lam-
entation with her nurse, and at last goes in the night to enact

[28] Otis, *Ovid as Epic Poet*, pp. 62-65. If I cite Otis's interpretations of the
*Metamorphoses* frequently, it is because his "epic" and "ideological" mode of
reading is especially relevant to the *Faerie Queene*; cf. nn. 22-23 above.

her crime. When her father discovers her identity, she flees into the wilderness and is in time transformed into the myrrh tree. From the tree is born Adonis who, as we saw in Chapter 4, stands at the center of Ovid's antithesis between love and heroism. Passion destroys all bonds of nature or piety, or at best establishes ephemeral relationships based on chance, situation, and appearances, as shown in the brief love affair of Venus and Adonis. Yet its hold is far stronger than any claim of reason or sense of duty.

If Spenser takes the story itself from *Ciris*, he weaves it into the *Faerie Queene* after the model of the *Metamorphoses*.[29] That is, he uses Ovid to give an epyllionic episode by "Vergil" the elevation and continuity of epic. He begins with an intensely subjective identification with Britomart but breaks apart this privacy by introducing Merlin as an objective analyst. Under Merlin's tutelage Britomart throws off the "cloudy vele" in which her passion has wrapped her and resumes her true form. When, like Myrrha, Britomart flees into the wilderness, it is to seek out Artegall. By her union with him she joins together the warring ancestors of Britain, a far different peace than that which Scylla brought to Megara. While Myrrha's line ends with the death of Adonis, the long list of Britomart's descendants revealed by Merlin confers on Britomart an immortality. The monster passion is transformed in a union with heroism. By Ovidianizing the language and situation of erotic verse, Spenser has lifted it from the lyric to the heroic and from the private to the public.

The historical element of the *Faerie Queene* undergoes the opposite transformation, being changed from an impersonal mode into a dramatically subjective one. Book 3 contains two great chronicles, the prophecy of British history told by Merlin to Britomart and the story of the descendants of Troy

---

[29] That Spenser has Ovid in mind is made certain by verbal echoes of the *Metamorphoses*; compare *F.Q.* 3. 2. 41-49 with *Met.* 10. 311-12. Also, Spenser links Myrrha with Byblis (*F.Q.* 3. 2. 41. 1-2,), whose story is told by Ovid in Book 9 of the *Metamorphoses*.

recounted by Paridell. In neither case is Spenser much concerned with the veracity of his legends. They are embellishments on a noble facade whose value lies in their ability to incite wonder and emulation. Thus as Britomart hears Merlin's account of the fall of Britain, her response is partly patriotic and partly shaped by the highly theatrical situation in which it is delivered. This subjective use of history is even more visible in Paridell's recitation at Malbecco's castle. The situation is exactly parallel to that in Book 2 of the *Aeneid*: a stranger is washed up by the storm and tells his tale over dinner, in the course of which the hostess falls in love with him. The difference of course is that Paridell distorts the past freely for the purpose of seducing the lady and does not blush to describe his ancestor Paris as the "most famous worthy of the world."

If Paridell twists the Trojan past one way, Britomart changes it another, hearing echoes of her own ancestry everywhere. Twice she breaks in, so great is her enthusiasm, to ask him about the parts he has neglected and which concern only her of those listening. Each time Paridell recites them dutifully but with a notable lowering of his style. The apostrophes and long suspended sentences in which he described his own genealogy give way to a succession of declarative clauses:

> *Anchyses* sonne begot of *Venus* faire,
>   (Said he,) out of the flames for safegard fled,
>   And with a remnant did to sea repaire,
>   Where he through fatall errour long was led
>   Full many yeares, and weetlesse wandered
>   From shore to shore, emongst the Lybicke sands,
>   Ere rest he found. Much there he suffered,
>   And many perils past in forreine lands,
> To save his people sad from victours vengefull hands.
>                                                    [3. 9. 41]

Paridell's hyperbolic diction has been supplanted with the depressing language of "fled," "remnant," "weetlesse," and "sad." Aeneas's noble deeds are reduced to the blank generalities of "full many yeares," "from shore to shore," and "many perils past." When Britomart thrusts in again to ask about Brutus and Troynovaunt, Paridell can scarcely remember the matter and then speculates on what crimes Brutus must have committed to bring on his exile from Italy.

Nothing is allowed to divert attention from the noble Paris or his handsome descendant, and Hellenore, his intended audience, reads the narrative as she is supposed to do, "Fashioning worlds of fancies evermore / In her fraile wit." As Dido dreamed that Aeneas would share with her a Carthaginian empire, so Hellenore finds a false glory in a fantastic history. In each case the real fashioning of the world goes on, unobserved by the others, in the resolute consciousness of the hero. Spenser knows well the importance of the historical epic and the fabulous genealogy for the parvenu dynasties of Renaissance Europe, and he knows how much the invention of fabulous origins answers an inner human need. In emulating the dramatic recitation of history employed by Vergil in the *Aeneid*, Spenser has eroticized and trivialized the Troy-matter much as Ovid does in his brief retelling of it in Books 12 and 13 of the *Metamorphoses*. Like Ovid, he exposes the use of history for shallow flattery and self-glorification, even as he shows its genuine value to Britomart as a source of identity and inspiration to epic deeds.

At the same time, Spenser reopens the great problem of historical recurrence implicit in any comparison of the present with the past. Cantos 9 and 10 focus on two such recurrences. In the *Aeneid*, Anchises prophesied that from the fall of Troy a new Troy should arise on the Tiber. Britomart's Troynovant is the extension of that prophecy across another sea and another millennium. Against this heroic scheme Spenser places the reenactment by Hellenore and Paridell of the rape of Helen by Paris. In each case the motive is the same, whether it is the human jealousy of Menelaus that sets off the Trojan War or the divine jealousy of Juno as she hounds Aeneas from land to land. By giving history a primarily interior reference, Spenser has diminished its capacity

for epic. Instead he opens for himself the possibility of giving
his narrative a metamorphic resolution that reveals the true
springs of historical causality in the human heart. Spenser's
great "history" in Cantos 9 and 10 becomes a well-wrought
minor epic as he ends with the transformation of Malbecco,
who

> . . . through privy griefe, and horrour vaine,
>   Is woxen so deform'd, that he has quight
> Forgot he was a man, and *Gealosie* is hight.
>                                   [3. 10. 60]

Spenser's deflation of dynastic pomp is carried a step fur-
ther in the iconic passages of Book 3, in which he describes
two great cycles of art works, the "costly clothes of *Arras*
and of *Toure*" in Castle Joyeous (Canto 1) and the "goodly
arras of great majesty" in Busyrane's castle (Canto 11). The
first takes as its nominal subject the story of Venus and
Adonis; the second, like the tapestry of Arachne described
by Ovid, depicts the loves of all the gods. In each case their
true subject is the glory of their owners, so that they become
like a series of sketches for a court masque.

Inevitably both tapestry cycles are more narrative than pic-
torial. Those in Castle Joyeous record the dalliance of Venus
and Adonis in minute, almost oppressive detail. Spenser
praises the "rare device and wondrous wit" of the designs,
for the true artist must work with both mind and hand. But
Spenser's artist seems to succeed more by exhausting his au-
dience than anything else. Spenser's emphasis finally falls on
the tactile magnificence of the tapestries which makes them
a suitable part of the luxurious decorations of the room, no
different really from the richly furnished beds arranged about
it. The tapestry cycle in Busyrane's castle is even more ex-
haustive, showing the loves of all the gods and mortals too.
Again Spenser stresses the physical magnificence of the tap-
estries. And again he moves from the visual scene to a more
solid piece of decoration, in this case a gilt statue of Cupid.

In each case the movement from pictorial decoration to furniture is prelude to a third sight of courtly pomp. In Castle Joyeous that sight is Malecasta herself, enthroned "on a sumptuous bed, / That glistred all with gold and glorious shew." In Busyrane's castle it is the Masque of Cupid, in which the embodiments of erotic psychology march in procession before the Chariot of Cupid. Thomas Roche has pointed out that the masque is made up of so many Petrarchan conceits given physical dress.[30] As such, it is love language moved from the bower to the great hall, just as Malecasta has literally placed beds in her presence chamber. In each case there is a progression to the images, from the visual in narrative form (the tapestries) to the inanimate visual (the beds and the statue of Cupid) to the visual incarnate (Malecasta and Cupid himself). The progression fulfills the aspiration of poet and painter alike to set his idea before our very eyes as if it were alive. This is achieved by reducing eroticism to a visual tease, as when the artist shows how Venus "secretly would search each daintie lim" of Adonis as he bathes. But it is an exhausted love, a stupefaction that leads to idolatrous worship of an image, be it Malecasta who reigns "As the proud *Persian* Queenes" or Cupid:

And all the people in that ample hous
Did to that image bow their humble knee,
And oft committed fowle Idolatree.
[3. 11. 49]

Such art is simultaneously pornographic and propagandistic. Its physicality is at odds with its capacity to contain the "wondrous wit" that is the true goal of the painter. But there is in Book 3 another *ekphrasis* that offers an antidote to the other two. In the proem Spenser asks why he bothers to look to Faerieland for examples of Chastity when he could simply portray Elizabeth:

[30] Thomas P. Roche, Jr., *The Kindly Flame* (Princeton: Princeton University Press, 1964), pp. 74-79.

But living art may not least part expresse,
  Nor life-resembling pencill it can paint,
  All were it *Zeuxis* or *Praxiteles*:
  His daedale hand would faile, and greatly faint,
  And her perfections with his error taint:
  . . . But O dred Soveraine
  Thus farre forth pardon, sith that choicest wit
  Cannot your glorious pourtraict figure plaine
  That I in colourd showes may shadow it.
                                    [ 3. Proem. 2-3]

Beyond the flattery, Spenser realizes that the tendency of the
visual arts is to make concrete, to "colour" and to "show."
Poetry, he declares triumphantly—and in accordance with
the commonplaces of the age—is far closer to the realm of
"beautie daint" than the physical arts of painting and sculp-
ture. He makes good this boast in his verbal descriptions of
the tapestries, as in the famous stanza from the castle of Bu-
syrane:

For round about, the wals yclothed were
  With goodly arras of great majesty,
  Woven with gold and silke so close and nere,
  That the rich metall lurked privily,
  As faining to be hid from envious eye;
  Yet here, and there, and every where unawares
  It shewd it selfe, and shone unwillingly;
  Like a discolourd Snake, whose hidden snares
Through the greene gras his long bright burnisht backe
    declares.
                                    [3. 11. 28]

Spenser's verbal wit equals all the physical magnificence of
the tapestry, capturing the artistry with which gold and
silken threads are mingled. Simultaneously he pierces to the
essence that lies beneath this color and show to reveal how
it is morally "discolourd" and ugly.

But this is sifting the sands of good and evil; it is not the portrait of good itself. For that even Spenser's verbal art is inadequate. This is not simply humility; it is the price of Spencer's arresting vividness. Not that he abandons his attempt to eulogize Elizabeth—he is of course resolved to "shadow it" in "colourd showes" and "antique praises unto present persons fit." But he realizes the limits of that enterprise. What lies within his power is something closer to mock-praise, fit for mock-emperors like Malecasta and Cupid. The true justification for Elizabeth's reign, the non-physical portrait of inner perfection toward which the *Faerie Queene* gestures, must finally lie outside its limits.

Spenser's most forceful testing of those limits comes in the Garden of Adonis in Canto 6, where he gives his epic the philosophical center he denied to *Muiopotmos*. The center of that center is the vision of forms reincarnated:

All things from [Chaos] doe their first being fetch,
  And borrow matter, whereof they are made,
  Which when as forme and feature it does ketch,
  Becomes a bodie, and doth then invade
  The state of life, out of the griesly shade.
  That substance is eterne, and bideth so,
  Ne when the life decayes, and forme does fade,
  Doth it consume, and into nothing go,
But chaunged is, and often altred to and fro.

The substance is not chaunged, nor altered,
  But th' only forme and outward fashion;
  For every substance is conditioned
  To change her hew, and sundry formes to don,
  Meet for her temper and complexion:
  For formes are variable and decay,
  By course of kind, and by occasion;
  And that faire flowre of beautie fades away,
As doth the lilly fresh before the sunny ray.

[3. 6. 37-38]

As in *Muiopotmos*, a shift in diction tests how we wish to read the poem. Spenser's highly scientific language here invites the willing exegete to look outside the poem for a cosmic system that will interpret this vision. There have been many proposals, the most plausible of which is that Spenser's "formes" are like the "seminal reasons" described by Plotinus.[31] But the philosophical provenance of Spenser's "formes" does not reveal his artistic use of them as a center for the echoing motives within the poem. For that we are led once again to the *Aeneid* and the *Metamorphoses*, which are the two great exemplars in the use of a philosophical discourse to unify an epic narrative.

In Book 6 of the *Aeneid*, Anchises explains to his son how the "life-seeds" ("semines") are born into bodily shape and after death return to Elysium to be purified before being born again. This revelation comes as the climax in a progression through increasingly abstract understandings of the forces of life and death. Aeneas has begun his journey to the underworld with ritual actions when he visits the Sybil, undergoes a sacrificial purification, and searches for the Golden Bough. Crossing the Styx, he at first confronts an underworld of palpable forms. Then he witnesses a moral realm when he is shown the punishment of evil in Tartarus and the reward of virtue in Elysium. When at last he reaches Father Anchises, the anthropomorphic gods and physical underworld are left behind, and Anchises tells how "mens agitat molem," a world-spirit animates all things, and the individual soul moves in harmony with it. Anchises then returns to the world of history as he shows to Aeneas the

---

[31] The arguments are very intricate. See Josephine Waters Bennett, "Spenser's Garden of Adonis," *PMLA* 47 (1932):46–80; Brents Stirling, "The Philosophy of Spenser's 'Garden of Adonis' " *PMLA* 49 (1934):501–38; Robert Ellrodt, *Neoplatonism in the Poetry of Edmund Spenser* (Geneva: Librairie Droz, 1960), pp. 70–90; Nelson, *Poetry of Edmund Spenser*, pp. 210–22; and J. E. Hankins, *Source and Meaning in Spenser's Allegory* (Oxford: Clarendon Press, 1971), pp. 234–86.

souls of their unborn descendants, knitting his prophecy back into the narrative line of the poem and justifying the journey of Aeneas to Italy. While retaining the unity and continuity of his narrative, Vergil's reincarnation cycle gestures in several ways beyond its limits, toward the Roman present in which he writes the poem, and toward the Elysian eternity where a few blessed souls, Anchises among them, escape from the cycle of history.

In the "Sermon of Pythagoras" at the conclusion of the *Metamorphoses*, Ovid turns a vision of reincarnation to an opposite narrative purpose. He too places his vision exactly in the middle of Roman history, for Pythagoras is introduced as the teacher of Numa, who has succeeded Romulus as king of Rome. Livy had depicted Numa's religiosity as an important factor in the formation of the Roman character; as Romulus embodied Roman military valor, so Numa embodied *pietas*. Together they represent the two sides of the character of Vergil's Aeneas, and of Augustus, whom Ovid will praise at the end of the book. But when Pythagoras contemplates Rome's future, he sees it as one more empire in an endless succession:

> . . . sic magna fuit censuque virisque [Troia;] . . .
> clara fuit Sparte, magnae viguere Mycenae,
> nec non et Cecropis, nec non Amphionis arces. . . .
> nunc quoque Dardaniam fama est consurgere Romam,
> Appenninigenae quae proxima Thybridis undis
> mole sub ingenti rerum fundamina ponit:
> haec igitur formam crescendo mutat et olim
> immensi caput orbis erit!

> (. . . so was Troy great in wealth and men . . . Sparta was at one time a famous city; great Mycenae flourished, and Cecrops' and Amphion's citadels. . . . And now fame has it that Dardanian Rome is rising, and laying deep and strong foundations by the stream of Tiber

sprung from the Apennines: she therefore is changing
her form by growth, and some day shall be the capital
of the boundless world!)

[*Metamorphoses*, 15. 422-35]

At this moment, Pythagoras subverts the meager narrative
order that Ovid has given to his poem, for Rome too must
join the dance. Even as it denies to history its Vergilian or-
der, the "Sermon of Pythagoras" denies the Vergilian vision
of an escape from history to a place set apart. To Pythagoras,
the underworld is a tale to frighten a child. The reincarnation
of souls is an endless cycle in *this* world from which no An-
chises escapes. What is more, the "Sermon of Pythagoras"
is haunted, as I have said earlier, by its obsession with ve-
getarianism. Repeatedly it seems ready to follow the Vergi-
lian progression to increasingly abstract forms of under-
standing, only to break down to its most physical level. In
every fashion the sermon destroys the search for any coher-
ence in the *Metamorphoses* except change itself. Brooks Otis
concludes:

> Change is the only constant and the change is down as
> well as up, pejorative as well as ameliorative, a thor-
> oughly and everlastingly cyclical phenomenon . . . [in
> which] the only stable reality is that of nature itself, a
> better nature (*melior natura*), that is always overcoming
> chaos, always concerned to protect what is fundamen-
> tally good, to withstand and punish what is fundamen-
> tally bad.[32]

I can think of no more apt description of Spenser's Garden
of Adonis or of the *Faerie Queene* as a whole. Like Vergil,
Spenser portrays his garden as a space set apart, with "con-
tinuall spring, and harvest there." But the Garden of Adonis
does not lead us out of nature, for Time is in it, flinging

[32] Otis, *Ovid as Epic Poet*, pp. 373-74.

down its herbs and flowers.[33] Nor is it the ethereal soul that Spenser contemplates, but those "Infinite shapes . . . And uncouth formes" that give order to matter. In the vision of the garden, bound as it is to nature, matter is what lasts forever, for "substance is eterne . . . not chaunged, nor altered." Form, on the other hand, expresses the nature of mutability, since "forms are variable and decay / By course of kind, and by occasion."

In this triumph of form as the element of metamorphosis, Spenser destroys any lingering pretense that the form of Book 3 will be a unified or chronological narrative. No quest leads to the garden. Its ostensible link with the surrounding narrative is to explain the upbringing of Amoret, but given her role in Book 3, this is the flimsiest of pretexts, the most "ingenious" of Ovidian transitions to so exalted a vision. At the same time, the garden establishes a poetic as well as a philosophical order for the poem as Spenser acknowledges its epic form to be "variable and decayed." Amoret herself links the free lovers in the garden to the bondage exhibited in the Petrarchan episodes throughout the poem. The subversion of chronological sequence implicit in the philosophy of the garden looks backward and forward to the other uses of chronology in the book, that is, to the use of history by Britomart and its abuse by Paridell. The revelation of Cupid sporting freely with Psyche corrects in advance his tyrannical appearance in Busyrane's castle. And in his description of Venus and Adonis "Sporting . . . in safe felicity," Spenser glances ironically at the first sight of decadence in the book, the exhaustive eroticism of the tapestries in Castle Joyeous. Reversing the proverbial association of the myth of Adonis with the transience of nature, Spenser makes that very transience the source of immortality in nature, for as the father of forms Adonis is "eterne in mutabilitie."

In his revision of the myth of Venus and Adonis, Spenser

---

[33] This point is made with particular vividness by Paul Alpers, *The Poetry of the Faerie Queene* (Princeton: Princeton University Press, 1967), pp. 5-8.

makes them the embodiments of that "better nature" that protects and purifies the varied forms of the poem as they are gathered together in its center. Like half of the *Metamorphoses*, the Vergilian half, Spenser's poem aspires toward an ordered vision of nature and history that transcends the limits of poetry. Like the other half of the *Metamorphoses*, it accepts in place of that transcendence the poetic web spun out of its own echoing variety. Perhaps more than any poem, it shares the two conflicting principles of the *Metamorphoses*, its rage for chaos and its rage for order.

# *Metamorphosis as Literary System*

In a unique way the minor epic took up and combined all the elements of Elizabethan literature. For its sources and models, it looked to Ovid, Vergil, Lucan, Livy, Musaeus, and Petrarch. It drew on sonnet and satire to shape its audience, on primeval verse for an idea of the poet. It shared its imagery with painting; its narrative structures with Renaissance historiography. And in the epic it found the unified and systematized form toward which the poet constantly aspired. The significance of such a literary genre cannot be overestimated. It was a major vehicle for the assimilation of Continental Renaissance culture, an arena for poetic experimentation, the form that linked public and private experience and the apprentice poet to the master. It is, I hope, no exaggeration to claim for it the middle place in the Elizabethan hierarchy of genres, and a central place in an Elizabethan literary system.

From the vantage point of the minor epic, Elizabethan literature appears as an interlocking network of genres, ranging from the low style to the high, from the private to the public, and from the immoral to the moral. This system offers to the poet a series of choices as he writes and to his audience an initial set of assumptions as they read. It specifies the social functions of poetry, the dynamics of stylistic change, the behavioral patterns of the poet, and the modes of critical interpretation and audience response. But "system" is finally a misleading word, since it implies a static structure. Just as Spenser's epic is finally metamorphic, so this Elizabethan literary system is an unstable structure which aspires toward definition but remains fluid in reality.

The capacity of literature for system lies in the union of literary theory and literary practice within a culture. Individual works in their nature are unique, isolated in time and space from one another. Theory in its nature is coherent and comprehensive. The gap between theory and practice can be great, and nowhere does it seem greater than in the sixteenth century. Renaissance literary theory is based not only on the literary theory of classical civilization but on classical practice as well, and often seems to have no relevance at all to Renaissance poems. Bridging the gap between theory and practice are a series of intermediate levels, varying in the degree of their generality. They are the levels of critical practice, as it appears in Renaissance commentaries, commonplaces, and epithets. It is these levels on which the Elizabethan literary system is built, and which determine its nature.

Primary among these intermediate levels is the notion of genre. The word itself defines it as that which is general, not specific, about a work. Now a work may define a new genre, but genre is still not limited to that work alone. It is the "formality" of the work, the sense that from the work can be distilled certain qualities capable of imitation. Hence Renaissance notions of genre are usually based on classical exemplars but presume that the classical models will be analyzed, transformed, and made modern in the process.

If genre leads to imitation, it also leads to differentiation, to the awareness that a poem is like some works but radically different in form from others. Genre frees the poet by giving him choices, arranging the varieties of subject matter, the modes of presentation, the realms of experience, and the range of values on which he may draw. Insofar as those choices are weighted with different values, though, the system of genres becomes a hierarchy of genres. Here the epithetic evaluations of poets and genres employed in the sixteenth century become particularly important. To call Marlowe "mad" is simultaneously to define him as an inspired poet, a follower of Musaeus, and a creator of elegant erotic trifles. It suggests that the reader might himself be carried away by the words before him, and so it confesses that the writing of *Hero and Leander* may, morally speaking, be a dubious achievement. Alternatively, to call Daniel a "historian" labels him as one who tells the truth even at the cost of his personal safety and of the felicities of style. Consequently, the *Complaint of Rosamond* may be read as a poem dealing both with private amorous conduct and with public affairs, and marks a correct preparation of the sonneteer for the demands of historical epic. The poetic commonplaces serve the same function as do the epithets. The aspiration of *Lucrece* to be a "speaking picture" establishes Shakespeare as a modern Vergil whose poetry is both elevated and pathetic, able to move his audience to a profound sympathy with his heroine. The invocation of genre, epithet, and commonplace simultaneously shapes the individual work and places it within a network of ideas about the character of the poet, the nature of his verse, the mode of reading, and the value of his achievement.

The organization of these epithets, commonplaces, and genres into a coherent network was a historical process, for they began as isolated phrases or concepts and became the components of poetic theory as it developed into an autonomous and systematic branch of learning in the course of the sixteenth century. Hence even at its most coherent, Renaissance literary theory has something of the quality of a pastiche. At the same time, there is a genuine achievement at the theoretical level, an achievement especially visible at the moments when literary theory becomes capable of engaging with the other ideologies of Renaissance culture. Occasionally this takes the form of conflict, as when Giordano Bruno advances radical notions about poetic *furor*. More often it is a way of bringing poetry into harmony with political and theological orthodoxy. The theorist is inevitably eager to show that poetry increases its reader's devotion to the church and loyalty to the state.

So far I have described the Elizabethan literary system as it aspires toward order, coherence, and abstraction. But this portrait of the system is false unless we realize that this system contains its own contradiction, a series of antisystematic elements that prevent it from ever reaching total clarity. Foremost is the idea of form itself. If I have shown nothing else, I hope to have demonstrated that the form of any poem is metamorphic, that it depends in each case upon a vantage point and a provisional set of assumptions. I have had to resort to five different definitions of form—the lyric, prophetic, iconic, historical, and epic—for the minor epic, and I am certain this does not exhaust the possibilities. As the forms included within a genre may be multiple, so may be the forms of an individual poem. I might as easily have discussed iconic form in *Hero and Leander* or lyric form in *Venus and Adonis*. When one then multiplies the possible interrelations of the various forms within each poem by those among poems, the entire question of form becomes so vast as to be beyond systematization.

Contradictions also appear at the next level of generality, that of the system of genres. Insofar as the generic system includes the full range of human experience, it attempts to contain within its limits elements too diverse to arrange themselves neatly into a hierarchy of values. We have seen how the tensions between public and private experience, and between eros and heroism, have made rival claims on more than one artist. Such claims may prove too strong to be held down with Platonic ladders or different levels of style. Similarly ephemeral are the poetic epithets and commonplaces, which by their very nature shift constantly in their meaning and application. What one man means when he says that poetry is an art of imitation is not what the next means.

We return to where we began, to the breach between a classical theory and a modern practice. For all the work of commentators and exegetes, the redefinition of genres and the reapplication of epithets, there is a hole in the center of the system, a hole made by time and the change in culture, changes in geography, in language, in economic and social structures, in the production and dissemination of poetry, in the burden of the past. And the hole made by time is doubly wide, for modern literature will not stand still. No sooner has the theorist reconciled today's poetic fashion with Aristotle or Cicero than it is supplanted by newfangledness.

Such a view of the Elizabethan literary system, aspiring toward order but forever falling back into confusion and multiplicity, is, I think, far more likely to account for the variety of Elizabethan poetic practice than a system which is static in nature and ideological in its basis. Only such a system is capable of describing a genre like the minor epic and accounting for its importance in Elizabethan culture. The minor epic would stand at the center of such a system, for it is by its nature metamorphic verse.

# Index

(Titles of minor epic poems are in small capitals. Page numbers in italics refer to figures.)

Aconcio, Jacopo, 198
Adonis, 148, 166n, 270, 271; iconography of, 151-53, 168
Aertsen, Pieter, 182
Aeschylus, 101, 207
Aesop, 130
Ahl, Frederick M., 202n
Akrigg, G.P.V., 146n
Alban, St., 228-29, 231-32, 235
Alberti, Leon Battista, 188-89, 194
Alcaeus, 101
Alciati, Andraea, 79, 151n
Alcman, 101
Aldus Manutius, 130
allegory, 5-6, 25, 27, 30, 32, 37-39, 48n, 94n, 117-18, 119, 148, 248, 249, 250, 262
Allen, Don Cameron, 80n, 166n, 179, 258n
Allen, Walter, Jr., 22n
Alpers, Paul, 10n, 35n, 49, 159n, 277n
Alpers, Svetlana Leontief, 159n, 182n, 188n
Anderson, Judith H., 258n
*Annales Londoniensis*, 224
*Annales Paulini*, 224
Apelles, 182, 186
Apollo, 97, 125
Apuleius, 5, 85, 87, 88, 256
Arianism, 103
Ariosto, Ludovico, 12, 18, 22-23, 49, 166n, 175, 186, 200, 226, 248, 249, 250
Aristophanes, 101
Aristotle, 14, 18, 138, 176, 198,

283; *Poetics*, 6, 20-21, 98-99, 200, 225, 248, 249
art theory. *See* painting, Renaissance: theory of
Athenaeus, 22n
Augustine, St., 157n, 179
Augustus, 201, 204, 213, 244, 246-47, 250, 262, 275
Austin, Henry: THE SCOURGE OF VENUS, 75n
Averroes, 99n

Bacchus, 74, 97; Bacchantes, 110
Baines, Richard, 96n, 100n, 102
Baldwin, C. S., 185n
Baldwin, T. W., 104n, 146n, 157n
Baldwin, William, 25
Bale, John, 235
Barksted, William: MIRRHA, THE MOTHER OF ADONIS, 75n
Barnes, Barnabe, 58
Barnfield, Richard: CYNTHIA, 72, 76
Baron, Hans, 196n, 213n
Bartas, Guillaume de Salluste, Sieur du, 38n
Battenhouse, Roy, 179
Baudouin, François, 196-97, 198, 213, 217, 218-19
Baumann, A. Robin, 147-48n
Baxandall, Michael, 97n, 165n, 188n
Beaumont, Francis: SALMACIS AND HERMAPHRODITUS, 36, 70-75, 88, 92, 242
Beauregard, David N., 148n

Bede, 231
Bender, John B., 256n
Bennett, Josephine Waters, 274n
Beroaldus, Philippus, 85n, 86
Bible, 244; Gospels, 103, 116;
    Psalms, 223, 232-33; Romans,
    101
Bion, 143n, 148n, 151n
Blunt, Anthony, 186n
Blunt, Edward, 122-23
Boas, F. S., 96n
Boccaccio, Giovanni, 32, 116,
    148n, 151-52, 206
Bocchi, Achilles, 166n
Bodin, Jean, 13, 18, 196-97, 198,
    218-19, 223
Boiardo, Matteo, 248
Booth, Stephen, 173-74
Borghini, Raffaelo, 144
Borgia, Roderigo, 208
Boscán, Juan, 35-36n
Botticelli, Sandro, 154
Bracciolini, Poggio, 196
Bradbrook, M. C., 17n, 175, 177,
    242n
Braden, Gordon, 104, 106n
Brathwait, Richard: LOVES LABY-
    RINTH, 75n
Briggs, William Dinsmore, 103n
Brooke, C. F. Tucker, 7
Bruegel, Peter the Elder, 186
Bruni, Leonardo, 196
Bruno, Giordano, 281
Budé, Guillaume, 219
Bullough, Geoffrey, 146n, 184n
Burbage, Richard, 181
Burleigh, Lord, 99
Bush, Douglas, 25, 35n, 146n,
    157n

Caesar, Julius, 210, 244, 245, 246-
    47, 266
Callimachus, 22
Camden, William, 18, 197n, 198,
    217

Cano, Melchior, 230
Carew, Thomas, 82-83
Carr, Robert, Viscount Rochester,
    216
Cartari, Vincenzo, 32, 148, 151n,
    154, 157n, 158, *160-61*
Castelvetro, Lodovico, 99n, 186,
    199
Castor, Grahame, 108-109
Caxton, William, 198, 205-206
Chapman, George, 223; as inspired
    poet, 124-26, 140; OVID'S BAN-
    QUET OF SENSE, 32, 124; *The
    Shadow of Night*, 124; translation
    of Musaeus, 131n
    HERO AND LEANDER, 15, 20,
    32, 123n, 124-40; division into
    sestiads, 129-32; erotic fury in,
    133-40; form of, 135-40; imagery
    in, 132-33; language of, 127-28;
    opacity of, 126, 134-36; relation
    to Marlowe's *Hero and Leander*,
    96, 124-27, 129, 131-33, 138-40;
    relation to Musaeus's *Hero and
    Leander*, 126, 129, 131
Charles I, king of England, 82-83,
    84
Charles V, Holy Roman emperor,
    207, 250
Charles Louis, prince elector of the
    Palatine, 84
Charlton, H. B., 186n
Chaucer, Geoffrey, 12, 19, 24-25,
    32, 37, 38, 43, 82, 179
Cheney, Donald, 263n
Christ, 102, 103, 116-17, 247
*Chronicle of Dunmow*, 233-35
chronicles, English, 3, 5, 10, 13,
    16, 18, 88, 195, 205-206, 207,
    209, 214-15, 216, 224, 226, 263
Churchyard, Thomas, 60, 209n
Cicero, 38, 99, 100, 143n, 189n,
    196, 198, 200, 201, 283
Ciceronianism, 47-48, 50, 89, 204,
    213

Clement of Alexandria, 103, 116, 117
Cleon, 207
Cochrane, Eric, 197n
Colie, Rosalie, 34, 140
Colvin, Sidney, 180
comedy, 21, 173, 175
Comes, Natalis. *See* Conti, Natali
complaint d'amour, 42-43, 47
complaint, historical, 16-17, 19, 20, 33-34, 254
Constantine, 230
Conti, Natali, 32, 79, 148n, 151n, 157n, 168-69
Cornford, F. M., 207
Court, Franklin E., 254n, 261n
Covell, William, 209n
Cowley, Abraham: PYRAMUS AND THISBE, 33, 83
Crane, R. S., 95n
Croll, Morris W., 213n
Cromwell, Thomas, 232-33
Cujas, Jacques, 219
Culler, Jonathan, 34n
Cupid: and Psyche, 84; blindness of, 86

Daniel, Samuel, 15, 57-59, 63-64, 66, 90, 195, 210-11, 221; and historiography, 15, 18, 213-16, 221, 241; and Lucan, 199, 205, 210-14; *The Civil Wars*, 12, 18, 199, 210, 211-14, 220; *Cleopatra*, 12; *The Collection of the History of England*, 214-20; *A Defence of Ryme*, 219n; *Delia*, 12, 27, 51-57, 59-60, 61-62, 69; *Philotas*, 12, 210, 211; THE COMPLAINT OF ROSAMOND, 3, 12, 19, 20, 26-27, 32, 36, 51-52, 59-65, 70, 88, 91, 199, 205-209, 220, 222, 223, 240, 281; and historiography, 205-209, 227-28; and Petrarchism, 52, 60-63, 65, 205, 227-28

Dante Alighieri, 52-53, 57, 158
David, 100, 223
Dean, Leonard F., 197n
Desportes, Philippe, 55
Digges, Leonard: THE RAPE OF PROSERPINE, 75n
Diodorus Siculus, 116
Diogenes Laertius, 102
Dionysius of Halicarnassus, 198, 200-201, 202, 207
Donatus, 253n
Donne, John, 7, 10, 35, 66, 82
Donno, Elizabeth Story, 17, 76n
Dorsten, J. A. van, 72n
Drayton, Michael, 20n, 32, 195, 199, 214; and historiography, 15, 18, 221-22, 224, 225-26, 241; *The Barons Warres*, 199, 220; ENDIMION AND PHOEBE, 20, 31, 223; *Idea the Shepheards Garland*, 223; *Ideas Mirror*, 223; MATILDA, 18, 209n, 221, 227-28, 233-36, 237; *Mortimeriados*, 220; "Of Poets and Poesie," 96, 117, 199n; PEIRS GAVESTON, 3, 5, 18, 19, 20, 33, 221, 222-26, 230, 233, 236, 237, 240; *Poly-Olbion*, 221; ROBERT DUKE OF NORMANDY, 221, 236-41
Drummond, William, 200
Dundas, Judith, 255-56n
Dürer, Albrecht, 186

ekphrasis, 25, 28-29, 85, 106n, 112, 115, 132, 143, 176-77, 182-85, 186, 263, 270-72. *See also* painting, Renaissance: compared to poetry
Eleanor of Aquitaine, 205
elegy, 242
Elizabeth I, queen of England, 10, 37, 71-72, 74-77, 82, 186, 210, 211, 212-13, 228, 253, 271-72
Elizabeth, queen of Bohemia ("The Winter Queen"), 84

Ellrodt, Robert, 274n
emblem, 13, 30-31, 142, 190, 206
Empedocles, 122-24
epic, 17n, 19, 20, 59, 87, 175, 178,
   201, 202, 254, 267, 270, 274,
   277; historical, 195, 225, 269,
   281; and minor epic, 6, 10-11,
   12, 16, 22-23, 210, 214, 220, 242,
   243, 262, 263, 279; Ovidian, 5,
   15, 23-24, 87, 242-44, 250-51,
   262, 263-64, 266n; theory of, 12,
   14, 21, 22-24, 130, 131, 248
epigram, 11
epyllion, 16, 17, 19, 20, 22, 33-34,
   266, 267. *See also* minor epic
Erasmus, 94n, 98, 152n, 176, 184-
   85, 186
Essex, Earl of, 210-11
Euripides, 169
Eusebius, 116, 157n, 207, 216
Eworth, Hans, 72n, *73*

Fairbanks, Arthur, 182-83n
Fairchild, A.H.R., 180, 181n
Ferdinand II, Holy Roman em-
   peror, 84
Feyld, Thomas, 43
Ficino, Marsilio, 86, 98, 108, 138
fictionality, 15, 38-39, 46, 50, 209,
   221, 241, 250
Finkelpearl, Philip, 68
Fletcher, Angus, 263n
Fletcher, Giles the Elder: *Licia*,
   209n; RICHARD III, 31, 33, 209n
Fletcher, Phineas: VENUS AND
   ANCHISES, or BRITTAIN'S IDA, 33,
   36, 76-81, 85, 88, 108
Foucault, Michel, 95n
Foxe, John, 221, 230-33, 236
Franco, Giacomo, 45n
Franklin, Julian H., 197n
Fraunce, Abraham, 41n, 151n,
   152n, 154
Froissart, Jean, 214

Frye, Northrop, 20, 173
Fulgentius, 85, 143n, 148n, 154n
Fumaroli, Marc, 213n
*furor poeticus*, 15, 94, 96-103, 108-
   110, 113, 117, 120, 125, 136,
   140, 196, 244, 249, 280, 281. *See
   also* primeval poetry
Fussner, F. Smith, 197n

Galinsky, G. Karl, 244n, 261n
Ganymede, 5, 79, 106
Gardiner, Samuel R., 84n
Gascoigne, George, 47n, 48, 58,
   89; *The Complaint of Philomene*,
   43, 47-48, 50-51, 64, 90
genre, 11, 14, 15, 17n, 20-23, 34n,
   91, 93, 140, 223, 242, 280-82.
   *See also individual genres*
Geoffrey of Monmouth, 214-15
Gilbert, Allan H., 99n
Gilbert, Felix, 196n, 208
Giraldi Cinthio, Giambattista, 248-
   50, 257n, 263
Giraldi, Lilio Gregorio, 151n, 157n,
   158n, 169n
Giulio Romano, 141, 181
Glaucus, 45n
*Golden Legend, The*, 228-30, 232,
   235
Golding, Arthur. *See* Ovid, *Meta-
   morphoses*, trans. Arthur Golding
Goldman, Michael, 94-95n
Gombrich, E. H., 149n, 166n, 172,
   182, 183n
Gonzaga, Francesco, 246
Gordon, D. J., 125n, 137-38
Gorges, Sir Arthur, 202, 204
Gosson, Stephen, 38n
Goulart, Simon, 38
Gower, John, 82
Grafton, Richard, 214, 216
Greenblatt, Stephen J., 103n
Greene, Robert, 96, 100, 175, 199
Gresham, James: THE PICTURE OF

INCEST . . . IN THE HISTORY OF
CINYRAS AND MYRRHA, 75n
Greville, Fulke, 64
Grube, G.M.A., 100n
Guicciardini, Francesco, 196, 198,
207-209, 223, 236
Guilpin, Everard, 199n

Hagstrum, Jean, 176
Halle, Edward, 214
Hamilton, A. C., 147n
Hankins, J. E., 274n
Harington, Sir John, 166n, 200n
Hathaway, Baxter, 100n
Haydocke, Richard, 189n
Hayward, John, 210
Heckscher, W. S., 181
Heere, Lucas de, 72n
Helgerson, Richard, 57-58n
Henrietta Maria, queen of England,
82-83
Henry II, king of England, 205,
217
Henry VIII, king of England, 13
Henry, Prince of Wales, 81
Hermes Trismegistus, 116
Hermogenes, 185
Herodotus, 201n, 225
Hesiod, 124, 154n, 166n, 246
Heywood, Thomas: OENONE AND
PARIS, 19, 85
Higden, Ranulf, 205-207, 216
Hilliard, Nicholas, 142
Hirsch, E. D., Jr., 34n
historical poetry, 18-19, 20, 195,
197-98, 201, 205, 236, 237. *See
also* complaint, historical; epic,
historical; legend; minor epic;
and historiography
historiography, classical, 200-201,
208, 225
historiography, Renaissance, 15,
18, 220, 221, 222-23, 236, 241,
263; Christian, 216, 221, 228,

230, 235; English, 197-98, 205-
206, 230; French "new history,"
196-97, 198, 206, 213-14, 217-19,
220, 221, 230; humanist, 196,
198, 206, 215, 216, 217, 220,
221; political, 196, 207-209, 210,
216, 221, 235; theory of, 13, 195-
96, 198, 225-27
history, literary. *See* literary history
Hoefnagel, Joris, 72n
Holinshed, Raphael, 195, 198, 236
Holland, Hugh: PANCHARIS, 75
Homer, 18, 58, 98, 104, 106, 124,
131, 186, 200, 202, 204, 248,
249; *Iliad*, 129, 176, 185;
(pseudo-Homeric) *Batrachomy-
omachia*, 130, *139*, 140
*Homeric Hymns*, 81, 88
Horace, 94, 99-101, 124, 188, 189n
humanism, 6, 13-14, 36, 37-38, 39,
88, 89, 142, 180, 195, 196, 200,
201, 248, 251, 253
Hunter, G. K., 38n
Huntington, Henry of, 214
Huntington, John, 126n
Huppert, George, 197n
Hyginus, 143n
Hynes, Sam, 178n

iconography, 143, 147-49, 174
Inns of Court, 13, 39-40, 44, 50,
74, 90
inspiration. *See furor poeticus*
inspired poetry. *See* primeval po-
etry

James I, king of England, 75, 81
Jameson, Fredric, 34n
Javitch, Daniel, 250, 251
Jerome, St., 118
John, king of England, 234, 235
John, St. (disciple), 102
John of Trevisa, 205-206
Johnson, Samuel, 6

Jonson, Ben, 75, 81-82, 199, 200n, 214
Juno, 71-72
Justin, 102, 116, 117

Kahn, Coppélia, 190n
Keach, William, 10n, 17n, 35n, 39n, 45n, 67-69, 71n, 147n
Kelley, Donald R., 197n, 213n, 219n
Kelly, Henry Angsar, 197n
Kennedy, William J., 35-36n
Kyd, Thomas, 96n, 102, 103

La Branche, Anthony, 213n
Lactantius, 103, 116
Lactantius Placidus, 24
Landino, Christoforo, 79
Lanham, Richard, 242n
Lecoq, Anne-Marie, 180n
Lee, Rensselaer W., 164n
legend, 18-20, 221-22, 227-33, 235, 236, 237
Leicester, Earl of, 150
Le Roy, Louis, 196-97, 213, 219n
Lessing, Gotthold Ephraim, 158-59
Lever, J. W., 147, 166n
Lévi-Strauss, Claude, 172-73
Levy, F. J., 197n
Lewis, C. S., 16-17, 37
literary history, 14, 89-90, 91
literary system, 14, 15, 93, 140, 279-80; Elizabethan, 4, 13-15, 281-83
literary theory. *See* poetic theory
Livy, 18, 19, 179, 196, 215-16, 275, 279
Lodge, Thomas, 15, 66, 75; *An Alarum Against Usurers*, 37-39; "The Discontented Satyre," 67; "Glaucus Complaint," 67; "In praise of the Countrey life," 43; *Phyllis*, 37, 46-47, 67, 69; *Reply to Gosson*, 37-38, 48; *Rosalynde*,

37; *Truth's Complaint over England*, 37-38, 47, 50
SCILLAES METAMORPHOSIS, 3, 19, 20, 25, 26-27, 32, 36, 37-51, 52, 57, 60, 67, 70, 81, 88, 90, 91; allegory in, 39, 51; audience of, 39-42, 48-51, 64, 65; and book dealers, 39-42, 51; and Elizabethan theater, 39-40; Petrarchism in, 44-48, 50, 52, 65; prefatory epistle of, 39-42
Lomazzo, Giovanni Paolo, 189
Lucan, 199-205, *203*, 210-14, 279
Lucian, 151n, 198, 201n
Lucretius, 103
Luther, Martin, 230
Lydgate, John, 67, 82
Lyly, John, 186
Lyly, William, 38n

McCall, Marsh H., Jr., 176n
Machiavelli, Niccolò, 196, 208, 236
Macrobius, 151n, 168n
Malmesbury, William of, 214
Mander, Carel van, 181-82
Marc Antony, 210
Marcus, Leah Sinanoglou, 81n
Marino, Giambattista, 36n
Marlowe, Christopher, 75, 93, 101n, 199; as inspired poet, 96, 99-100, 102-103, 124, 127, 140, 280-81; *Doctor Faustus*, 117, 241; *Tamburlaine*, 117
HERO AND LEANDER, 3, 5, 6, 9-11, 17, 33, 70, 77, 104-24, 146, 282; allegory in, 116-19; audience of, 106, 108; and Chapman's *Hero and Leander*, 124-27, 130-31, 135, 137; ekphrasis in, 29-30, 112, 115; erotic fury in, 65, 105-12, 120-24; fragmentary, 122-24; as inspired poem, 15, 94-96, 105-109, 114, 117-19, 281; irony in, 10-11; language in, 113-15, 119-

20; Mercury digression in, 31, 99, 115-19, 131; and Musaeus's *Hero and Leander*, 103-104; narrator in, 105-106; and Ovid, 94, 242

Marmion, Shakerley: CUPID AND PSYCHE, 36, 83-89, 92

Mars, 157, 166, 169

Marston, John, 36; "Certayne Satyres," 66, 70; THE METAMORPHOSIS OF PIGMALION'S IMAGE, 20, 66-70, 74, 75, 88, 92

Martial, 77

Martz, Louis, 123n

marvelous, the, 22-23, 102, 226-27, 228, 230-33, 235, 236, 241, 260

Mary Tudor, 230

Maskell, David, 214n

masque, 81-83, 270

May, Thomas, 200, 202, 212n

Mazzoni, Jacopo, 199

Medici, Lorenzo de (the Magnificent), 207

Merchant, W. Moelwyn, 181n, 186n

Mercury, 116, 149

Meres, Francis, 156, 209n

Merula, Bartholomew, 151n

metamorphosis, 4, 98, 242n, 243, 260, 266, 277, 279, 282-83

metaphysical imagery, 6-7, 11

Metaphysical poets, 7, 88

Michelangelo, 123-24, 141

Mignault, Claude, 151n

Millar, Oliver, 73n

Miller, E. H., 56n

Miller, Paul W., 17n

Milton, John, 98, 118-19

Minerva, 71-72

minor epic, 3-4, 12-15, 16-23, 33-34, 109, 242, 283; allegory in, 5-7; audience of, 15, 26, 36-37, 65, 67, 74, 89-92, 93, 108-109, 279; form of, 5, 6, 11, 16, 25-26, 279;

history of, 32-33, 36-37, 65-67, 75-76, 81-83, 88-92; imagery in, 6-11, 15, 23, 30, 32, 35, 46-47, 177, 279; metamorphosis in, 4-12, 283; as mixed genre, 12, 14, 93, 242, 279; mode of, 28, 31-33; narrative technique in, 2, 4, 11, 13, 30-32, 241; sources of, 4-5, 12, 17, 19, 279; subject matter of, 3, 6, 11, 17-18, 33

and career of poet, 11-12, 57-60, 195, 220, 279, 281; and image of poet, 15, 95-96, 279; and historiography, 5, 13, 15, 18-20, 195, 198-99, 220-21, 241, 279, 282; and Ovid's *Metamorphoses*, 4-5, 19, 242; and painting, 13, 15, 279, 282

and epic, 6, 10-11, 12, 16, 22-23, 210, 214, 220, 242, 243, 262, 263, 279; and masque, 83; and Petrarchan sonnet, 6, 12, 13, 15, 16, 35-37, 64-65, 66, 69-70, 89, 90-91, 93, 228, 279, 282; and pastoral, 6, 12, 15, 65, 83; and primeval poetry, 15, 279, 282; and satire, 15, 66-67, 75, 89, 279. *See also* complaint, historical; epyllion

Minturno, Antonio, 158n, 199

mirror. *See* complaint, historical

*Mirror for Magistrates*, 17, 19, 24-25, 42, 43, 60, 206

Momigliano, Arnaldo, 208n

Mor, Antonis, 142

Moses, 100, 116, 245, 248

Mountjoy, Lord, 210

Muir, Kenneth, 147n

Murrin, Michael, 6n, 227n, 262n

Musaeus, 5, 97, 101-102, 105, 116, 117, 130, 136, 279, 280; *Hero and Leander*, 18, 94, 103-104, 110, 124-25, 126n, 129-32, 140

Muses, 95, 97, 104-105, 125

Musurus, Marcus, 104n
myth, 3, 13, 16, 18, 35, 102, 172–
73, 223, 236, 242-43. *See also in-
dividual myths*

Narcissus, 38n, 146
Nashe, Thomas, 200
Nelson, William, 209n, 258n, 274n
Neoplatonism, 20, 32, 69, 74, 83,
85, 109, 116, 122, 165n, 166,
223, 282
Nero, 199, 201-204, 211, 212-13
Newdigate, Bernard H., 224n,
233n, 236n
Newman, Thomas, 51, 57, 66
Nohrnberg, James, 263n

*Oberon* (masque), 81
Oliver, Isaac, 142
Omnibono, Vicentino, 202n
Orgel, Stephen, 81n
Orpheus, 94, 97, 98, 101-102, 105,
110, 116, 117
*Orphic Hymns*, 86, 143n, 151n
Ortelius, Abraham, 186
Otis, Brooks, 22n, 23, 244n, 261n,
266n, 276
Ovid, 10n, 12, 35, 85, 88, 117,
126n, 279; *Amores*, 264; *De Arte
Amandi*, 151n; *Fasti*, 19, 179;
*Heroides*, 130
  *Metamorphoses*, 25, 45n, 47, 82,
  102, 129-30, 256, 266-67, 269,
  278; Creation epic (Book 1), 85,
  168, 243-46, 248; tapestry of
  Arachne (Book 6), 85, 256, 260-
  61, 270; Venus and Adonis
  (Book 10), 5, 24, 29, 143n, 144,
  151-52, 157n, 159-60, 165, 267;
  Sermon of Pythagoras (Book
  15), 5, 244, 245, 247, 249, 259-
  60, 261, 263-64, 274, 275-76
  *Metamorphoses*: as epic, 5, 15,
  23-24, 87, 242-44, 250-51, 262,

263-64, 266n; and minor epic, 4–
5, 19, 242
  *Metamorphoses*, commentaries:
  medieval, 244-50, 260; Renais-
  sance, 14, 24, 32, 38n, 242, 245-
  51, 260; of Arnulf of Orleans,
  246-47; of Giovanni del Virgilio,
  244-45, 260n; of Giraldi Cinthio,
  248-50, 257-58, 261
  *Metamorphoses*, editions: of Al-
  dus Manutius, 247, 250; of Pierre
  Bersuire, 244-45, 260n; of Johan-
  nes Raenerius, 260n; of Raphael
  Regius, 245-47, 250, *251*, 257-58,
  260n, 261; of Raphael Regius and
  Jacobus Micyllus, 22, 32, 148n,
  151, 152n, 157n, 166n, 247; of
  Georgius Sabinus, 32, 151n,
  152n, 166n, 169n; of Johannes
  Sprengius, *162*
  *Metamorphoses*, translations: by
  Giovanni dell'Anguillara, 45n,
  152n; by William Caxton, 245,
  *246*; by Lodovico Dolce, 250,
  *252*, 258; by Arthur Golding, 5,
  150-51, 247-48, 258, 260n; by
  (anon.) *Ovide moralisé*, 244-45; by
  George Sandys, 32, 85
Ovidianism, 10, 16-17, 24, 27, 32,
66, 126, 206, 222, 223. *See also
Marlowe, Christopher: Hero and
Leander*, and Ovid; Shakespeare,
William: *Venus and Adonis*, and
Ovid; Spenser, Edmund: *The Fa-
erie Queene*, as Ovidian epic;
Spenser, Edmund: *Muiopotmos*,
and Ovid

painting, Renaissance, 15, 141;
compared with poetry, 141-43,
158-59, 163-64, 176, 185-86, 196.
281; Elizabethan, 141-42, 180;
theory of, 13, 97n, 142, 176,
188-89, 197-98
Palmer, D. J., 122n

Panofsky, Erwin, 79n, 143, 144n, 159, 166n
Paradise, N. Burton, 39n
Paris, Matthew, 214
Paris, judgment of, 71-74
Parker, Martin: PHILOMELA, 75n
Parker, Matthew, 230
Parrhasios, 182
pastoral, 15, 17n, 23, 65, 73n, 242; and Daniel, 60; and Drayton, 223; and Phineas Fletcher, 77, 78, 81, 85; and Lodge, 49; and minor epic, 6, 12, 15, 65, 83; and Shakespeare, 175; and Spenser, 76, 243, 263
Patrizi, Francesco, 13, 100, 196, 198
Paul, St., 101-102, 107
Pausanias, 102, 151n
Peele, George, 72
Pericles, 207
Peruzzi, Baldassare: *The Death of Adonis*, 162, *163*
Peterson, Douglas, 47n
Peterson, Richard S., 81n
Petrarch, 206, 279; *Africa*, 57, 58; *Canzoniere*, 11, 35, 53, 57, 58, 60n, 62, 65, 67, 69, 89, 195, 264-65; *Trionfi*, 58. *See also* Petrarchism
Petrarchism, 13, 15, 68, 76, 85, 88, 263; and audience, 37, 65, 90-91, 93; imagery of, 9, 10, 46, 71-72, 77, 167; and minor epic, 15, 35-36, 65-67, 89, 90-91, 93, 228; and Neoplatonism, 69, 83; paradox and ambivalence in, 45, 60, 66, 70, 78
Philip II, king of Spain, 145-46
Philostratus, 182-83, 185, 188
Pico della Mirandola, Gianfrancesco, 101-102n
Pico della Mirandola, Giovanni, 86, 170
Pindar, 100n

Piso, Gaius Calpurnius, 201
Plato, 86, 166, 183, 246; *Ion*, 94, 97, 98, 99n, 104-105, 123n; *The Laws*, 79-80; *Phaedrus*, 74, 79-80, 94, 97, 98, 100, 105, 106-107, 113, 119-20, 130; *The Republic*, 98, 112, 116, 209; *The Symposium*, 130; *Timaeus*, 168n. *See also* Neoplatonism
Pléiade, 13, 66
Pliny the Elder, 182, 186, 188
Plomer, Henry R., 40n
Plotinus, 274
Plutarch, 166n, 185
Pocock, J.G.A., 197n, 219n
poetic theory, Renaissance, 13-14, 17-18, 42, 57, 93, 142, 247, 280-81, 282-83; and epic, 12, 14, 21, 22-24, 130, 131, 248; epithets and commonplaces in, 96-97, 109, 142, 195-96, 280-81, 282; and historiography, 195, 199-200, 201; and minor epic, 4, 12
Polybius, 209
Polydore Vergil, 198, 214, 216
Pontano, Giovanni, 151n
Praxiteles, 272
primeval poetry, 93, 114, 117, 119-20, 123, 124, 140, 263; and minor epic, 15, 279, 282. *See also* *furor poeticus*
Prince, F. T., 25
*Prince Henry's Barriers* (masque), 81
Prometheus, 38n
prophetic poetry. *See* primeval poetry
Puttenham, George, 18-19
Pythagoras, 85, 259, 275-76

Quintilian, 38n, 177n, 184-85, 200, 201

Rabkin, Norman, 147n, 173-74
Raphael (archangel), 149
Raphael Sanzio, 98

Rees, Joan, 56n
Reilly, J. F., 22n
Reynolds, Henry: NARCISSUS (in *Mythomyestes*), 85
*Rhetorica ad Herennium*, 38n, 176, 177n
Richard II, king of England, 210
Richards, I. A., 27-28, 29n
Regoli, Sebastiano, 80
Robortello, Francesco, 198
Roche, Thomas P., Jr., 271
Rollins, Hyder, 146n, 184n
romance, 16, 19, 20, 23, 32, 248-49, 250, 253
Ronsard, Pierre de, 67, 157n, 158n, 214
Rosand, David, 143-44, 162n, 165n, 186n, 214n
Rossiter, A. P., 173n
Rota, Martino, 145
Rowse, A. L., 146n

Sackville, Thomas, Earl of Dorset, 42
Saintsbury, George, 88
Sale, Roger, 10-11
Sallust, 18
Salmacis and Hermaphroditus, 146
Salutati, Coluccio, 118, 196
Sanuto, Giulio, 145, *145*
satire, 11, 17n, 21, 66-67, 88, 242; and Francis Beaumont, 71-75; and Lodge, 49, 50; and Marston, 68, 70, 75; and minor epic, 15, 66-67, 75, 89, 279; and Spenser, 243, 263
Saunders, J. W., 56-57n
Scaliger, Julius Caesar, 100-101n, 129-31, 199
Schoenbaum, Samuel, 70n
Seaton, Ethel, 76n
Sebastiano del Piombo, *The Death of Adonis*, 148, *149*, 162
Segal, Charles, 261n

Selden, John, 195, 221
Seneca, Lucius Annaeus, 201, 202, 205
Seronsy, Cecil C., 213n
Servius, 79, 143n
Shakespeare, William, 9, 36, 65, 75, 90; knowledge of painting, 141-43, 180-81; misogyny of, 179, 189-92; *As You Like It*, 173; *Hamlet*, 158, 174; *Henry VI*, 192; *King Lear*, 192; *Macbeth*, 158; *Measure for Measure*, 173, 191; *Much Ado About Nothing*, 192; *Pericles*, 181; *Sonnets*, 63-65, 155, 156, 170, 173-74, 186; *Timon of Athens*, 181, 186; *The Winter's Tale*, 181
LUCRECE, 3, 6, 15, 25, 33, 175-94, 281; *ekphrasis* in, 28-31, 143, 175-76, 177, 179-82, 186-89, 190-91, 192-93; Lucrece as heroine in, 178-80, 189-94; as minor epic, 175, 178-80; relation of to *Venus and Adonis*, 12, 29, 31, 58, 64, 142, 175; role of Brutus in, 193-94; sources of, 19, 184n
VENUS AND ADONIS, 3, 6, 15, 17, 19, 36n, 75n, 77, 108, 143-75, 181, 282; iconographic form of, 143, 159, 174, 176; iconography of Adonis in, 148-54; iconography of Venus in, 154-58; and Ovid, 5, 24, 29, 242; paradox in, 31, 172-75; relation of to *Lucrece*, 12, 29, 31, 58, 64, 142, 175; sources of, 143-46; structure of, 164-72
Sidney, Sir Philip, 3, 11, 27, 35, 36, 57, 59, 64, 141; *Arcadia*, 23; *Astrophel and Stella*, 12, 51, 53-54, 57, 66, 69; *The Defence of Poetry*, 16, 90, 100, 199
Sidney, Sir Robert, 99, 100n
Simonides, 185

Simplicius, 122
Smith, Hallett, 16-17, 20, 35n, 73n
Smith, William, 71-72
Snuggs, Henry L., 249n
Socrates, 98
sonnet, Petrarchan, 5, 9, 49, 175, 242, 243, 281; Elizabethan, 11, 16, 17n, 35-57, 39n, 65-66, 89; and minor epic, 6, 12, 13, 15, 16, 35-37, 64-65, 66, 69-70, 89, 279, 282
Sophocles, 101
Southampton, Earl of, 146, 175, 194
Spencer, John R., 164n
Spenser, Edmund, 19, 36, 58-59, 65, 71, 76n, 82, 141; influence of, 75-77, 81-82; *Amoretti*, 76; *Colin Clouts Come Home Again*, 12n, 58-59; *Complaints*, 12, 243, 254; *Daphnaida*, 58n; *The Shepheards Calendar*, 76, 243

   *The Faerie Queene*, 10n, 22-23, 49, 76-77, 175, 221; Book 1, 98, 253; Book 2, 87; Book 3, 7-11, 165, 176, 228, 243, 262-78; Garden of Adonis, 80, 259, 273-74, 276-78; Book IV, 239-40; "Mutabilitie Cantos," 243; allegory in, 117, 233; and historiography, 18, 243, 263, 267-70, 277; and minor epic, 11, 12, 175, 243, 253-54, 270; as Ovidian epic, 15, 243, 251, 253-54, 262-64, 265-67, 270, 277-78, 279; Petrarchism in, 243, 263, 264-65, 271, 277; and Vergil, 253-54, 262, 266-67, 268-69, 277, 278; and visual arts, 263, 264, 270-73, 277

   MUIOPOTMOS, 3, 33, 254-62, 273-74; allegory in, 32, 258-59, 261; *ekphrasis* in, 258, 260-61; and *Faerie Queene*, 11-12, 262; and Ovid, 12, 15, 243, 251, 253-

54, 256-59, 260-62; and Vergil, 243, 253-55, 259, 260-62
Spini, Giorgio, 196n, 198n
Statius, 200n
Steadman, John, 22n
Stephen, king of England, 217
Stirling, Brents, 274n
Stow, John, 18, 197n, 224, 234-35, 236
Strong, Roy C., 73n, 141
Struever, Nancy S., 196n
Suetonius, 253n
Sulpizio, Giovanni, 202n, 204
Surrey, Earl of, 60n

Tacitus, 196, 201, 204, 217
Tasso, Torquato, 12, 18, 22, 60, 199; *Amyntas*, 80; *Discourses on the Heroic Poem*, 18, 130, 199-200n, 225-27; *Gerusalemme Liberata*, 227, 250
Tatian, 116n
Tenney, E. A., 39n
Tervarent, Guy de, 166n
Theocritus, 143n, 151, 157n
Theophilus, 116n
theory, poetic. *See* poetic theory
Thorp, Margaret, 180
Thucydides, 196, 201, 207, 208-209, 225
Tillet, Jean du, 213
Tillotson, Kathleen, 224n, 233n, 236n
Titian, 186; *Sacred and Profane Love*, 166n; *Venus and Adonis*, 143-46, *144*, 159-64, 166, 172
Tobias, 149
Todorov, Tzvetan, 34n, 225
tragedy, 21, 175, 236
Tuckyr, Francis, 85
Turner, Myron, 122n
Tuve, Rosemond, 10n, 11n, 26n, 32n, 114n
Tyard, Pontus de, 108

*ut pictura poesis. See* painting, Ren-
aissance: compared with poetry

Van Dyck, Anthony, 84n
Varius, 253
Vasari, Giorgio, 181
Velz, John W., 184n
Venus, 71-72, 97, 270; iconography
of, 148, 149, 154, 158, 165n,
166, 169
Vergil, 5, 18, 58, 250, 259, 260,
261-62, 278, 279, 281; and Au-
gustus, 202, 204, 213; *gradus Ver-
gilianus,* 12, 57, 175, 195;
(pseudo-Vergilian) *Ciris,* 266-67,
(pseudo-Vergilian) *Culex,* 77,
130; *Eclogues,* 79n
    *Aeneid,* 143n, 204, 243, 244;
    Book 1, 165, 176, 183-85, 187,
    264-65; Book 2, 183, 268-69;
    Book 6, 79-80, 116, 269, 274-75,
    276; as epic, 131, 242, 248, 253-
    55; Renaissance commentaries
    on, 38n, 248
verisimilitude, 18, 221, 225-26,
232-36, 241
Veronese, Paolo, 141
Verrocchio, Andrea del: *Tobias and
the Archangel,* 149, *150*
Vessey, D.W.T.C., 22n
Vigenère, Blaise de, 183
Villiers, Mary, 76-77
Voragine, Jacobus da, 228
voyeurism, 51, 105-107, 122-23

Waddington, Raymond B., 125-
26n, 223

Walker, D. P., 102n, 116n
Walkley, Thomas, 76
Walsingham, Lady (Thomas), 129
Warren, Austin, 95n
Waterhouse, Ellis, 73n
Watson, Donald G., 147n
Watson, Thomas, 53, 56, 58
Webbe, William, 199
Weil, Judith, 94n
Weinberg, Bernard, 18n, 22n, 96,
109n, 128n
Weiner, Andrew D., 261-62n
Wellek, René, 95n, 158n
Wernham, R. B., 99n
White, Helen, 228n
Wilbur, Richard, 147
Wilkinson, L. P., 22n, 261n
William the Conqueror, 217, 236
Williams, Kathleen, 263n
Wilson, Thomas, 26, 38n
Wind, Edgar, 79n, 86n, 123n,
165n, 166n
Winters, Yvor, 35n
Witt, Ronald, 100n, 118n
Wolf, Johann, 198, 217n
Wyatt, Sir Thomas, 60n
Wyndham, George, 154

Xenophon, 79

Yates, Frances, 108n

Zeuxis, 182, 272
Zocca, Louis R., 17n, 35n
Zuccaro, Federico, 142

*Library of Congress Cataloging in Publication Data*

Hulse, Clark, 1947-
  Metamorphic verse.

  Bibliography: p.
  Includes index.
  1.  English poetry—Early modern, 1500-1700—History and
criticism.    2.  Epic poetry, English—History and
criticism.    3.  Metamorphosis in literature.    I.  Title.
PR539.E64H8        821'.03'09        81-47135
ISBN 0-691-06483-0                        AACR2

*Clark Hulse is Associate Professor of English, University of Illinois at Chicago Circle.*